ORACLE®

Oracle Press™

Raspberry Pi with Java

About the Authors

Stephen Chin is the Lead Java Community Manager at Oracle and JavaOne Content Co-Chair. He has keynoted numerous Java conferences around the world, including JavaOne, where he is a four-time Rock Star Award recipient. Stephen is an avid motorcyclist who has done several pan-European evangelism tours, interviewing hackers in their natural habitat and posting the videos on http://nighthacking.com/. When he is not traveling, Stephen enjoys teaching kids how to do embedded and robot programming together with his 12-year-old daughter.

James Weaver is a Java developer, author, and speaker with a passion for helping Java to be increasingly leveraged in rich-client applications and the Internet of Things. James has authored and co-authored several books, including *Inside Java*, the Beginning J2EE series, and the Pro JavaFX series. He also speaks internationally at software technology conferences about Java, JavaFX, IoT, and cloud computing. James tweets as @JavaFXpert, and blogs at both http://JavaFXpert.com and http://CulturedEar.com.

About the Technical Editor

Mark Heckler is a Pivotal Developer Advocate, conference speaker, and published author focusing upon software development for the Internet of Things and the Cloud. He has worked with key players in the manufacturing, retail, medical, scientific, telecom, and financial industries and various public sector organizations to develop and deliver critical capabilities on time and on budget. Mark is an open source contributor, author/curator of a developer-focused blog (HYPERLINK "http://www.thehecklers.org/" http://www.thehecklers.org), and possessor of an occasionally interesting Twitter account (@MkHeck). Mark lives with his very understanding wife in St. Louis, MO USA.

ORACLE®   *Oracle Press*™

Raspberry Pi with Java

Programming the
Internet of Things (IoT)

Stephen Chin
James L. Weaver

New York   Chicago   San Francisco
Athens   London   Madrid   Mexico City
Milan   New Delhi   Singapore   Sydney   Toronto

Cataloging-in-Publication Data is on file with the Library of Congress

Raspberry Pi with Java: Programming the Internet of Things (IoT)

1 2 3 4 5 6 7 8 9 0   DOC DOC   1 0 9 8 7 6 5

ISBN   978-0-07-184201-3
MHID   0-07-184201-2

Sponsoring Editor	**Copy Editor**	**Composition**
Brandi Shailer	William McManus	Cenveo Publisher Services
Editorial Supervisor	**Proofreader**	**Illustration**
Janet Walden	Claire Splan	Cenveo Publisher Services
Project Manager	**Indexer**	**Art Director, Cover**
Tanya Punj,	Jack Lewis	Jeff Weeks
Cenveo® Publisher Services	**Production Supervisor**	
Technical Editor	James Kussow	
Mark Heckler		

Contents at a Glance

Contents

Acknowledgments

I want to thank my wife, Justine, and two daughters, Cassandra and Priscilla, for their support, encouragement, and sacrifice to make this book happen.

—*Stephen Chin*

I'd like to thank Stephen Chin for envisioning this book and inviting me to help write it, Mark Heckler for agreeing to review the book for technical accuracy, and Brandi Shailer for shepherding the process. Of course, I'd like to thank my wife Julie, daughters Lori and Kelli, and grandchildren Kaleb and Jillian for their unbounded love and support. Psalm 28:7.

—*James L. Weaver*

Introduction

The Raspberry Pi has started a revolution in embedded development, reducing the barriers of entry for computer programmers to build devices that interact with the physical world. Java SE and Java ME Embedded use the Raspberry Pi as their reference platform, making it the platform of choice for Java developers who are getting started in embedded development. Java also comes preinstalled on the official Raspbian image, making it the highest-performing high-level language available for the Raspberry Pi. We, the authors, took advantage of the sweet spot of programming the Raspberry Pi with Java to help you get up to speed on developing for the Internet of Things, and joining the IoT revolution.

Who Is This Book For?

Whether you are an experimenting hobbyist or a seasoned professional, you'll find this book to be of value for increasing your skill in creating applications that run on embedded devices. We purposely chose relatively low-cost projects and associated hardware to reduce the barrier to entry. We also employed a project-based learning approach with a gradual learning curve to make this book approachable.

What Does This Book Cover?

The pages of this book contain several projects designed to increase your skill in embedded application development applicable to various home and industry scenarios. Here's a rundown of what you can expect to see as you work through this book.

Chapter 1: Baking Pi   This chapter walks you through the process of setting up your Raspberry Pi, networking it to your computer, and testing it with a simple Java application.

Chapter 2: Your First Java Project   In this chapter, you'll set up a Java Integrated Development Environment (IDE), specifically NetBeans, on your computer. You'll use this IDE for developing and remotely deploying Java applications on the Raspberry Pi. You'll also build a tasty project in which Java and a Pi will be leveraged to brew a perfect cup of coffee.

Chapter 3: Binary Timer   You'll utilize the GPIO (general purpose I/O) capabilities of the Raspberry Pi to create a binary timer. In the process you'll discover how to use the Pi4J library, written by Robert Savage, to make quick work of a discrete-device I/O project.

Chapter 4: IoT Hat   This chapter guides you through the steps of creating a magic hat that demonstrates various forms of device I/O. This project is certainly a fun example of wearable computing, and one that will amaze your friends!

Chapter 5: Line Runner   In this chapter, you'll create an autonomous robot by utilizing the Makeblock robotics platform and, of course, a Raspberry Pi with Java.

Chapter 6: Tea Station   Revisiting the coffee-brewing example from Chapter 2, you'll leverage higher-precision equipment, and employ a touchscreen, to make a perfect cup of tea.

Chapter 7: Autonomous Drone   You'll turn a quadcopter into an autonomous drone by outfitting it with a Raspberry Pi for its brain.

Chapter 8: Retro Video Game Emulator   In this chapter, you will build a Java-powered emulator that lets you play classic Nintendo Entertainment System (NES) games on the Raspberry Pi.

Chapter 9: NightHacking RetroPi   This chapter shows you how to turn the NES emulator from Chapter 8 into a portable gaming system with a retro-style case produced by a 3D printer, enabling you to revive the classic video gaming experience on modern hardware.

Code Downloads

You can download the code samples shown in this book from the McGraw-Hill Professional website at **www.mhprofessional.com**. Simply search for the book by ISBN to access available downloads.

In addition, you can access code for projects in this book on GitHub at **https://github.com/RaspberryPiWithJava**.

It is our hope that you'll find this book to be a valuable resource in creating embedded projects for your hobbies as well as your professional IoT applications. Turn the page and let's get started!

CHAPTER
1
Baking Pi

I n this chapter I'll walk you through the process of setting up (or baking, if you will) your Raspberry Pi.

This chapter will take you through a first-time installation of Raspbian on a Raspberry Pi with the latest Java version. I will also detail some additional configuration that you may want to change to optimize Java and other visual applications. Finally, I will show you how to create a network between your Raspberry Pi and another machine and run a simple Java application.

Powering Your Raspberry Pi

The Raspberry Pi is a great platform for getting started with embedded computing. It has a great community supporting it with lots of options for hardware. If this is your first time setting up a Raspberry Pi, you will need the following hardware to get started:

- **Raspberry Pi**   The same instructions apply to Models B+, A+, B, A, and 2, but in this guide I will be using a B+.

- **SD card**   A good quality 8GB or larger SD card is recommended. If you purchase one with the New Out Of Box Software (NOOBS) preinstalled, you can save some time in setup.

- **Power supply**   The Raspberry Pi is powered by a micro-USB cable, the recommended specifications for which are 2A at 5V. You can often get away with a smaller power supply (as small as 700mA) depending on what USB devices are connected.

- **Keyboard and mouse**   Pretty much any USB keyboard will do. The mouse is optional if you don't mind navigating the GUI via the keyboard.

- **Monitor or TV**   The Raspberry Pi supports composite or HDMI displays. HDMI is readily convertible to DVI or VGA if that is what your monitor supports.

The first step is to set up your SD card. If you have a Model 2, B+, or A+ Raspberry Pi, then this will be in the form of a microSD card. If you have the older Model B or A, then this will be a full-size SD card. Both types of cards

FIGURE 1-1. *NOOBS microSD card with full-size adapter*

operate the same, and microSD cards usually come with adapters to fit in full-size slots, so that is the obvious choice. The difference in size between a microSD card and a full-size SD card can be seen in Figure 1-1.

The Raspberry Pi foundation ships SD cards with NOOBS preinstalled, as photographed in Figure 1-1. This is a good trade-off between cost, convenience, and performance, and is recommended for anyone who is just getting started. Most online retailers offer a Raspberry Pi bundle that includes the NOOBS SD card for a small incremental cost.

If you have purchased an SD card with NOOBS preinstalled, skip to the section entitled "Installing Raspbian."

Purchasing Compatible SD Cards

If you need a higher-performance or larger-capacity card, you can buy SD cards and format them yourself. This is also typically less expensive, especially if you are purchasing in bulk. The key criteria to use when selecting an SD card are size, write performance, and quality.

The minimum size card you can use with the Raspbian distribution is 4GB, although this is not large enough to support NOOBS and will leave very little room for your software. At least 8GB is recommended, and for a small incremental cost you can get a 16GB card. The largest-capacity card that is supported in the Raspberry Pi is 64GB, although this will only be helpful if you are doing data-intensive tasks, such as storing sensor data or video over a long period of time.

When shopping for SD cards, you can find a class identifier written on them. A higher number indicates better write performance, with the minimum sustained write speed equal to the number. For example, a class 4 card is tested to support a sustained write speed of 4 megabytes per second (MBps). Similarly, a class 10 card is tested to support a sustained write speed of 10MBps. This matters most if you are developing an application that will write a large amount of sequential data. It also can significantly speed the initial setup time of your card. However, this is an indication of neither read performance nor nonsequential write performance, so the real-world performance of your SD card may vary.

Perhaps the most important factor is the quality of the card. Buying from a well-known manufacturer and reputable vendor greatly increases the chances you will get the size and performance you are paying for. Unknown manufacturers and ill-reputed vendors may sell you low-quality or counterfeit cards that perform well below their advertised specs. A good community resource for researching SD card compatibility and performance is the Raspberry Pi SD cards page on the Embedded Linux (eLinux) wiki: http://elinux.org/RPi_SD_cards.

Formatting SD Cards

The NOOBS installer requires that your SD card be formatted with a File Allocation Table (FAT) filesystem. Both FAT16 (more commonly referred to as FAT) and FAT32 are supported, but not ExFAT. If you have purchased a large SD card, it often comes formatted with ExFAT, so you will need to reformat it with FAT32 in order to proceed with the NOOBS install. The easiest way to make sure your SD card is formatted correctly is to use the SD Association's SDFormatter utility on OS X or Windows: https://www.sdcard.org/downloads/formatter_4/.

Figure 1-2 shows a screenshot of what the SDFormatter utility looks like on OS X. Make sure that the correct SD card is selected so that you don't accidentally delete the wrong drive, and then choose the Overwrite Format option. Specify the name of the card and click the Format button. This process will take a while depending upon the speed and size of your SD card, so this may be a good time to take a coffee break.

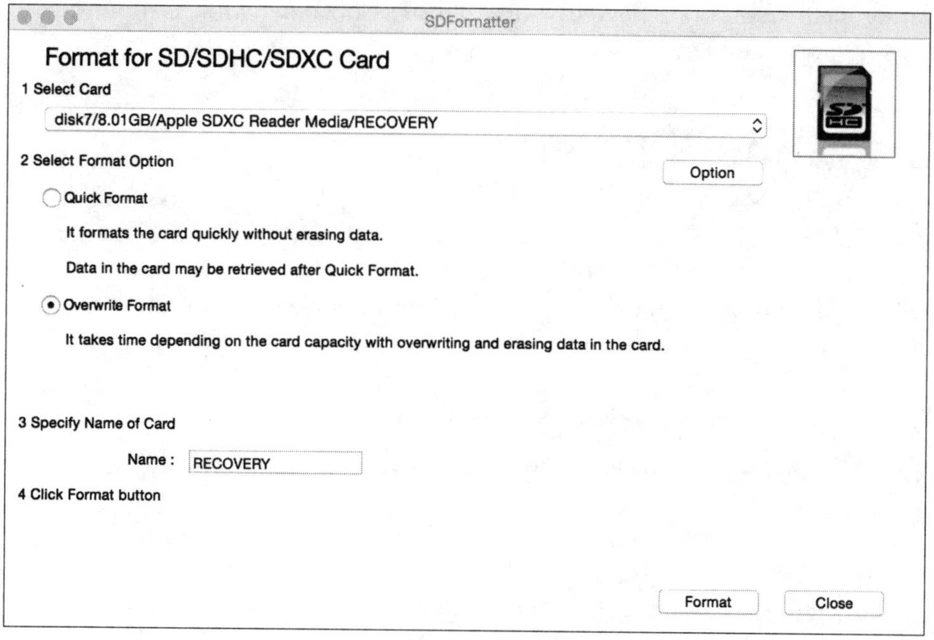

FIGURE 1-2.   *SDFormatter utility*

If you are on Linux, you can accomplish the same thing with the GParted tool, which is a visual disk manager. Make sure that you select the correct partition and format as FAT or FAT32.

Once you have a properly formatted card, the rest of the installation is as simple as following these steps:

1. Download the latest version of NOOBS from the Raspberry Pi website: www.raspberrypi.org/downloads/.

2. Unzip the downloaded NOOBS archive. Most operating systems come with built-in unzipping functionality.

3. Copy the contents of the extracted folder to your SD card. Make sure that you do not have an enclosing folder.

Either NOOBS or NOOBS LITE will work, although I recommend the former so that you don't have to worry about networking your Raspberry Pi to get it up and running.

Installing Raspbian

Once you have an SD card with NOOBS on it, you are ready to install the Raspbian operating system and set up your Raspberry Pi. This process has been streamlined with the latest installers, so you should have no trouble getting set up quickly. Along the way I will point out common pitfalls that you may encounter, especially with the older Raspberry Pi models.

Connecting Your Raspberry Pi

Here are the connections you will need to make the first time you turn on your Raspberry Pi:

CAUTION
Never insert or remove the SD card while your Raspberry Pi is plugged in. This can result in corruption of the filesystem and lose important data that you have stored on your Raspberry Pi.

1. Insert the SD card into the slot on the bottom.

   On Models A and B this slot is a full-size friction fit socket, so be careful that you don't use too much force (it goes in upside down). On Models A+, B+, and 2 this slot is a spring-loaded microSD socket that clicks upon insertion (also upside down). When removing the SD card, you can simply pull out the card on Models A and B, but for Models A+, B+, and 2, press it in and allow the spring to eject it.

TIP
The SD slots on Models A and B are easy to damage if you use too much force (for example, if you force the SD card in incorrectly). Fortunately, this can often be remedied by simply bending the pins back in shape.

2. Connect the HDMI or composite cable to your monitor or TV.

   HDMI will give you better resolution and is preferred if you have a supported monitor. If you're using HDMI, plug in your monitor and turn on the power before booting. Using composite on Models A and B is fairly straightforward via the yellow RCA jack. However, on Models A+, B+, and 2 you will need to use an adapter to get the video signal out of the 3.5mm TRRS jack that is shared with audio. For more details on this, see the example project in Chapter 8 that talks about tip ordering and compatible cables.

NOTE
The reason why you should always plug in HDMI and turn on your monitor before booting is because the Raspberry Pi defaults to composite input, which will give you a black screen if you later hook up an HDMI device. However, this is not the case when running NOOBS, so you can get by the first boot without doing this in a specific order.

3. Plug in your keyboard and mouse.

   These devices plug into the full-size USB host ports on the Raspberry Pi. If you are using a Model A or A+, you will be limited to one USB port, so you can either navigate via keyboard shortcuts and skip the mouse altogether, or plug in a powered USB hub to connect more devices.

CAUTION
On Models A and B the USB ports are not hot swappable, so inserting or removing devices can reset the Raspberry Pi, resulting in lost work or filesystem corruption. This was fixed on Models A+, B+, and 2.

4. Connect the micro-USB power.

As mentioned earlier, make sure you have a power supply that can provide 5V and ideally 2A of power. Higher current is fine since the Raspberry Pi will only consume the power it needs, but with only a keyboard and mouse hooked up, you can get away with a 700mA power supply. Your typical computer USB slot will only provide 500mA and thus is not safe to use with the Pi. On Models A and B, insufficient voltage from a poor USB cable or insufficient current from a bad power supply can result in crashes and filesystem corruption. Fortunately, the Raspberry Pi B+, A+, and 2 come with power circuitry that ensures the voltage and current are sufficient before turning on. They also draw less power than the older models, saving precious battery life for embedded projects.

How to Tell Your Raspberry Pi Is Working

Once powered on, you will notice that the LED status lights on the Raspberry Pi will light up. The red PWR LED indicates power and will stay solid as long as the Raspberry Pi is plugged in. The green ACT LED indicates activity and will start blinking irregularly shortly after you plug in the Pi. If the PWR LED comes on but the ACT LED does not blink irregularly for a few seconds, this is most likely a sign that the SD card is not working. This could be a bad connection or an improperly formatted or installed card. Here are some troubleshooting steps to try out:

- If the red PWR LED is flickering, you likely have a Model A+, B+, or 2 and have tripped the brownout circuitry. Try a different power supply (higher current) or replace your micro-USB cable (which may be too long, thin, or damaged).

- If the green ACT LED doesn't flash irregularly for a few seconds:

  - Try reseating your SD card. Turn off the power, unplug the SD card, and then plug it in again, making sure it is fully inserted. Remember that the SD card goes in upside down and should not require a lot of force to insert or remove.

  - Check your SD card formatting and installation. Your SD card should be formatted as FAT or FAT32 and have the NOOBS files in the root of the filesystem (not in a folder). You can always buy a preinstalled copy of NOOBS if you want to simplify this.

Once you know the Raspberry Pi is working from seeing a few seconds of activity on the ACT LED, the next thing to check is your display. Upon boot the Raspberry Pi shows a rainbow test pattern for a second and then displays a recovery screen for a few more seconds. After this it automatically boots into the NOOBS installer, and you should see the installation screen shown in Figure 1-3.

If your Raspberry Pi is booting according to the LEDs, but you don't see the NOOBS installation screen, try these troubleshooting tips:

■ Make sure your monitor power is on and the monitor is set to the correct input (for example, it is easy to forget to switch the input from VGA to HDMI).

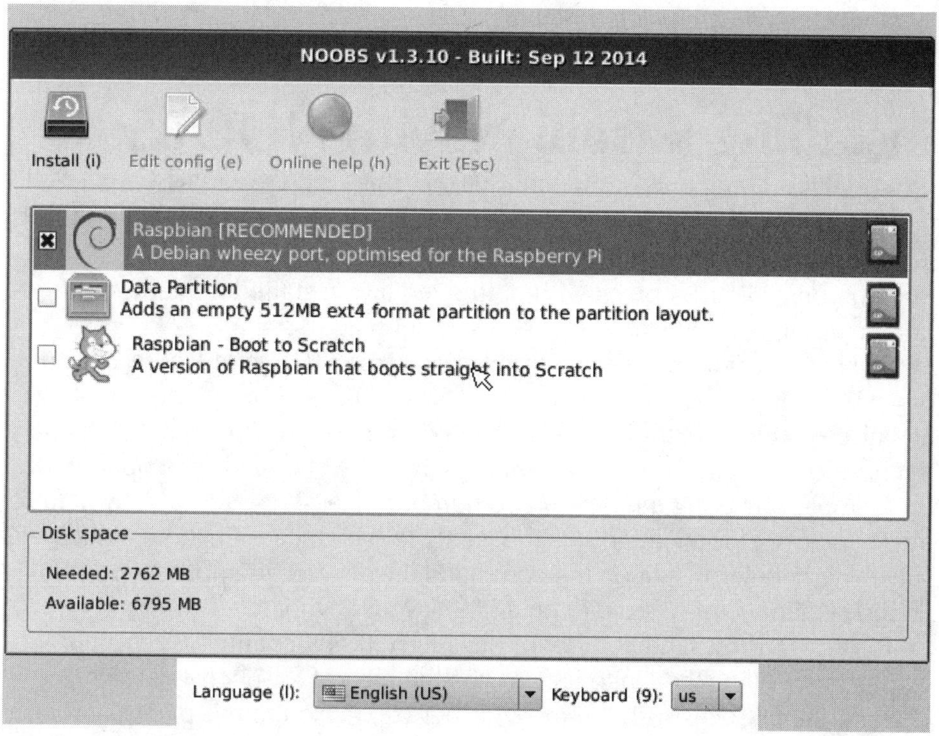

FIGURE 1-3. *NOOBS installer screen*

- If using HDMI, try safe mode. This is accomplished by pressing the number 2 on your keyboard in NOOBS. Safe mode forces a 640 × 480, 60-Hz resolution that most monitors can support. It also boosts the HDMI signal, which may help with long cables or high interference.

- If using composite, switch to PAL or NTSC. This is accomplished by pressing the number 3 (for PAL) or 4 (for NTSC) to switch to composite input and is only required when booting from NOOBS, which defaults to HDMI.

NOTE
When switching NOOBS video modes with your keyboard, make sure it is fully loaded (ACT LED should have stopped blinking). Also, enable NUMLOCK if you are using the numeric keypad.

Installing Raspbian with NOOBS

Raspbian is a Linux-based operating system that is a port of Debian and optimized for the Raspberry Pi. It was created by Mark Thompson and Peter Green and has been helped along by enthusiastic members of the Raspberry Pi community. It also comes with optimized Java installed right out of the box thanks to support from Oracle.

Picking up from the NOOBS installation screen shown in Figure 1-3 in the previous section, you will want to select Raspbian as your operating system and also set the correct locale and keyboard for your region. If you don't have a mouse connected, you can access the Language and Keyboard options via the keyboard by using the letter l and number 9 keys, respectively. By default the Raspberry Pi foundation sets the locale to the United Kingdom, which will leave you hopelessly lost on the command line as you attempt to type the pound symbol (#) or at sign (@) on a U.S. layout keyboard.

Figure 1-4 shows the number of Raspberry Pis by country as reported by Rastrack. While the United States has the highest Raspberry Pi sales by country, the UK wins with the most Pis per capita, so there is plenty of room for growth in the rest of the world!

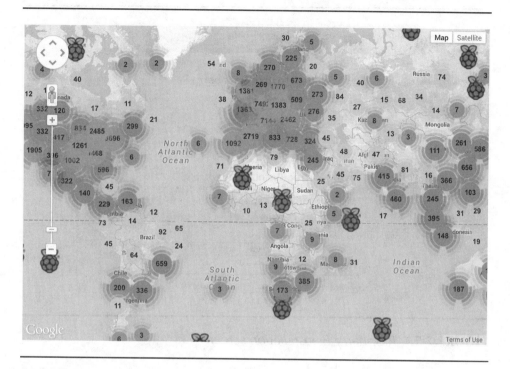

FIGURE 1-4. *Distribution of Raspberry Pis across the world*

After selecting the options, click the Install button or type the letter i to begin the installation process. Installation takes about 20 minutes, give or take a few minutes depending on the speed of your SD card. The installation screen has a pretty accurate progress bar at the bottom, as shown in Figure 1-5, and provides some helpful hints on the top for new Raspberry Pi owners. This is a good time to grab a cup of joe as you wait for the success screen to pop up.

Once you click the OK button or press ENTER, the Raspberry Pi will reboot and start up Raspbian for the first time. Raspbian has a typical Linux boot screen with lots of scrolling text, and a cute Raspberry Pi logo in the top-left corner.

Raspbian is set to automatically log in on your first boot and run the Raspberry Pi Software Configuration Tool (`raspi-config`), as shown in Figure 1-6. It is highly recommended to change the default password (as discussed in the following list), but if you need to log in before you get a chance to set it for some reason, the default username is pi and the default password is raspberry.

Welcome to your Raspberry Pi
We're currently setting up your SD card but don't worry, you'll be able to start programming very soon.
Raspbian: Creating filesystem (ext4)
0%
9 MB of 2309 MB written (1.2 MB/sec)
Language (l): English (US)
Keyboard (9): us

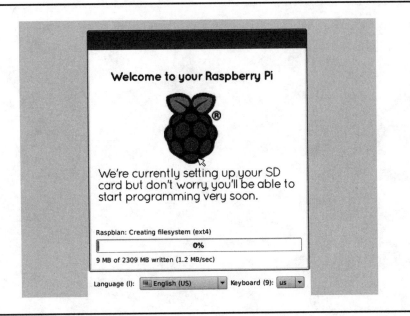

FIGURE 1-5. *Raspberry Pi installation screen*

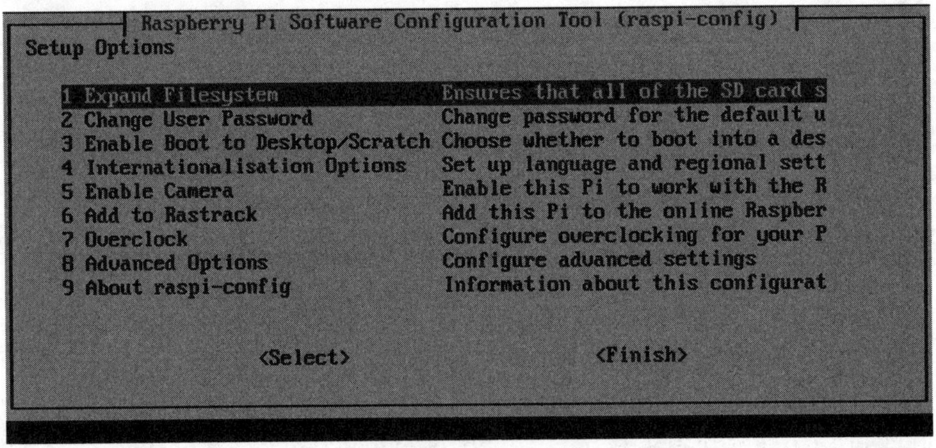

Raspberry Pi Software Configuration Tool (raspi-config)
Setup Options
1 Expand Filesystem Ensures that all of the SD card s
2 Change User Password Change password for the default u
3 Enable Boot to Desktop/Scratch Choose whether to boot into a des
4 Internationalisation Options Set up language and regional sett
5 Enable Camera Enable this Pi to work with the R
6 Add to Rastrack Add this Pi to the online Raspber
7 Overclock Configure overclocking for your P
8 Advanced Options Configure advanced settings
9 About raspi-config Information about this configurat
<Select>
<Finish>

FIGURE 1-6. *Raspberry Pi Software Configuration Tool*

Here is a quick rundown of what the different options do (recommended changes are noted):

- **Expand Filesystem**   This lets you expand the root filesystem to fit the size of the SD card. If you used NOOBS to install, this has already been taken care of during the install.

- **Change User Password**   Changing the password is highly recommended for security purposes. Anyone who can access the Raspberry Pi over the network will have root access if you don't change this.

- **Enable Boot to Desktop/Scratch**   This lets you boot to a graphical user interface (GUI) with X Window System and optionally open Scratch for visual programming. This book steers you to using the command line, but anytime you want to open X Window System, you can type **startx**.

- **Internationalisation Options**   If you forgot to change this during the NOOBS install, you have another chance to rescue your keyboard layout.

- **Enable Camera**   This enables support for the Pi Camera and is a recommended setting.

- **Add to Rastrack**   This adds your Pi to a worldwide list of Raspberry Pi locations on a map. It is fun to join in and provides valuable statistics on the Raspberry Pi community as you discovered earlier. Since this requires an Internet connection, you may want to revisit this option after completing the upcoming "Networking Your Raspberry Pi" section.

- **Overclock**   The default speed of the Raspberry Pi's processor is 700 MHz for the A, B, A+, and B+, and 900 MHz for the Raspberry Pi 2. You can optionally raise this; however, it is recommend to start with the default speed. Overclocking the Pi may result in it running hotter and shortening the life of its components.

- **Advanced Options**   Discussed in more detail in the next list.

- **About raspi-config**   This displays an information screen about the Raspberry Pi.

Selecting Advanced Options brings up a submenu with the following additional options:

- **Overscan** This allows you to enable or disable overscan. If you have a modern LCD, you can safely disable this and get a little more screen real estate at the edges of your monitor.

- **Hostname** Feel free to change your hostname to be unique.

- **Memory Split** The memory on the Raspberry Pi is shared between the CPU and the GPU. To improve performance of graphics-intensive applications, I recommend setting GPU memory to at least 128MB.

- **SSH** This option is for Secure Shell, which is enabled by default, and is required for deployment of Java apps.

- **SPI** This is general purpose input/output (GPIO) functionality that needs to be enabled for some of the example projects in later chapters.

- **I2C** Another GPIO feature for managing a connected bus of devices, this option also needs to be enabled to support projects in later chapters.

- **Serial** This enables shell access over serial, although you will need to disable it to free up the serial ports for a later project.

- **Audio** This lets you force audio to go out over the HDMI or 3.5mm headphone jacks.

- **Update** This updates the `raspi-config` tool to the latest version.

On the list of options, the recommended changes are to change your password, enable the Pi Camera, set/confirm the memory split to 128MB, enable SPI, enable I2C, and disable serial. If you forget to do any of these steps, don't worry; I will remind you in future sections when the required functionality is needed and instruct you to enable it if you haven't already.

Once you are done making configuration changes, press the TAB key and select Finish. This will reboot your Raspberry Pi and give you your first login prompt as shown in Figure 1-7. To log in, type the username **pi** and the new password you chose.

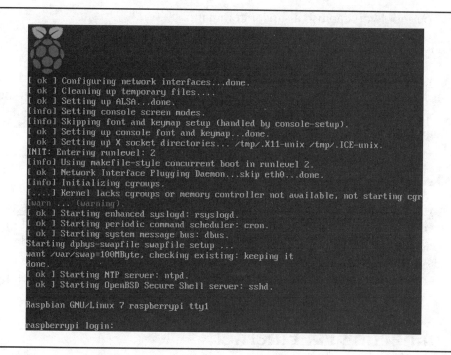

```
[ ok ] Configuring network interfaces...done.
[ ok ] Cleaning up temporary files....
[ ok ] Setting up ALSA...done.
[info] Setting console screen modes.
[info] Skipping font and keymap setup (handled by console-setup).
[ ok ] Setting up console font and keymap...done.
[ ok ] Setting up X socket directories... /tmp/.X11-unix /tmp/.ICE-unix.
INIT: Entering runlevel: 2
[info] Using makefile-style concurrent boot in runlevel 2.
[ ok ] Network Interface Plugging Daemon...skip eth0...done.
[info] Initializing cgroups.
[....] Kernel lacks cgroups or memory controller not available, not starting cgr
[warn ... (warning).
[ ok ] Starting enhanced syslogd: rsyslogd.
[ ok ] Starting periodic command scheduler: cron.
[ ok ] Starting system message bus: dbus.
Starting dphys-swapfile swapfile setup ...
want /var/swap=100MByte, checking existing: keeping it
done.
[ ok ] Starting NTP server: ntpd.
[ ok ] Starting OpenBSD Secure Shell server: sshd.

Raspbian GNU/Linux 7 raspberrypi tty1

raspberrypi login:
```

FIGURE 1-7. *Raspberry Pi login prompt*

If you need to bring up the raspi-config utility again, you can always do this from the command line by typing

```
sudo raspi-config
```

This is probably also a good time to mention the correct way to shut down your Raspberry Pi. If you disconnect power from the Raspberry Pi while it is running, you may damage the filesystem and cause corruption and data loss. To prevent this, make sure that you properly halt the Raspberry Pi before powering it off by using the following command:

```
sudo shutdown -h now
```

This command logs off all users, cleanly closes the filesystem, and terminates before you power off the Pi. You will know your Pi is ready to unplug when you see the green ACT LED flash ten times in sequence.

To reboot you can use a similar command:

```
sudo shutdown -r now
```

As a shortcut you may see some Raspberry Pi users use the `halt` and `reboot` commands. These behave as expected and are perfectly safe on the Raspberry Pi, but they are not best practices when you are administering a variety of Unix operating systems, because the behavior varies.

Networking Your Raspberry Pi

To communicate from your computer to the Raspberry Pi, you will have to put your Raspberry Pi and computer on the same network so that your Pi is accessible via TCP/IP. This is also the easiest networking option for Models A and A+ that lack an Ethernet port. There are several different ways to do this depending on the physical location of your computer, the network topology, and your available hardware.

Connecting via Ethernet

If you have a router that acts as a Dynamic Host Configuration Protocol (DHCP) server, you can simply plug the Raspberry Pi into your network using an Ethernet cable. This only works for Raspberry Pi Models B, B+, and 2, because Models A and A+ lack an Ethernet port.

Once connected, the Raspberry Pi will automatically try to get a network address from the DHCP server. You can check for the IP address that the Raspberry Pi acquired by typing the following command:

```
ip addr show eth0
```

Connecting via a Local Computer Network

You can also connect your Raspberry Pi directly to your PC using an Ethernet cable. Again, this option is only available for Raspberry Pi Models B, B+, and 2, but can be a great alternative if you are traveling or in a setting where the network topology doesn't allow your computer and Raspberry Pi to talk.

TIP
The Raspberry Pi Ethernet adapter includes auto-MDIX to detect and fix cable types, so you can use either a crossover cable or a more common straight Ethernet cable to connect devices.

The easiest way to accomplish this is to assign static IP addresses to both your computer and the Raspberry Pi so they are both in the same subnet. A common local subnet to use is 192.168.x.x, which is one of the reserved subnets for local area networks. The configuration on your desktop computer will look something like Figure 1-8 for OS X or Figure 1-9 for Windows.

On the Raspberry Pi you will need to modify the cmdline.txt file in the boot folder. To do so, log in to the Raspberry Pi with the following command:

```
sudo nano /boot/cmdline.txt
```

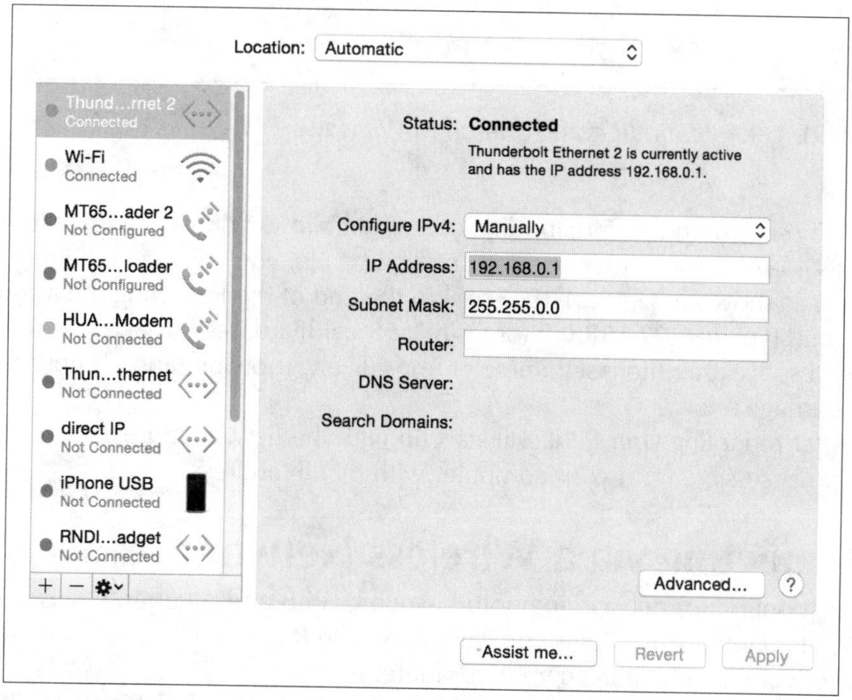

FIGURE 1-8. *Static IP configuration in OS X*

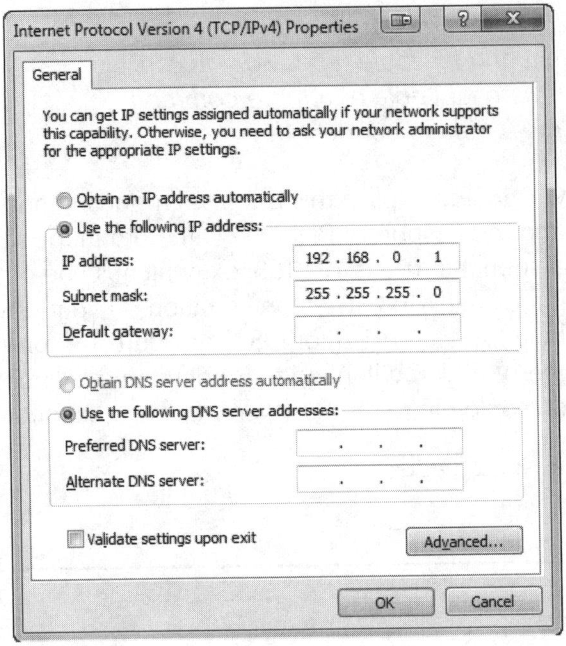

FIGURE 1-9. *Static IP configuration in Windows*

Nano is a simple command-line editor that allows you to edit text files on Unix systems. When you open the cmdline.txt file, you will get an editing screen as shown in Figure 1-10. Scroll to the end of the line using the arrow keys and type **ip=192.168.0.2** (or a similar local IP address). Make sure to leave a space after the last parameter (most likely, rootwait) and do not add any carriage returns.

After rebooting your Pi, it will start up with the new IP address fixed, and will be accessible from your computer with that IP address.

Connecting via a Wireless Network

A great option for networking both Raspberry Pi B and A variants is to use a Wi-Fi adapter. This allows you to connect the Raspberry Pi to a wireless network and access it from your computer remotely.

For this you will need a compatible Raspberry Pi Wi-Fi USB adapter. In general, Wi-Fi devices utilizing the RTL8188CUS chipset are well supported

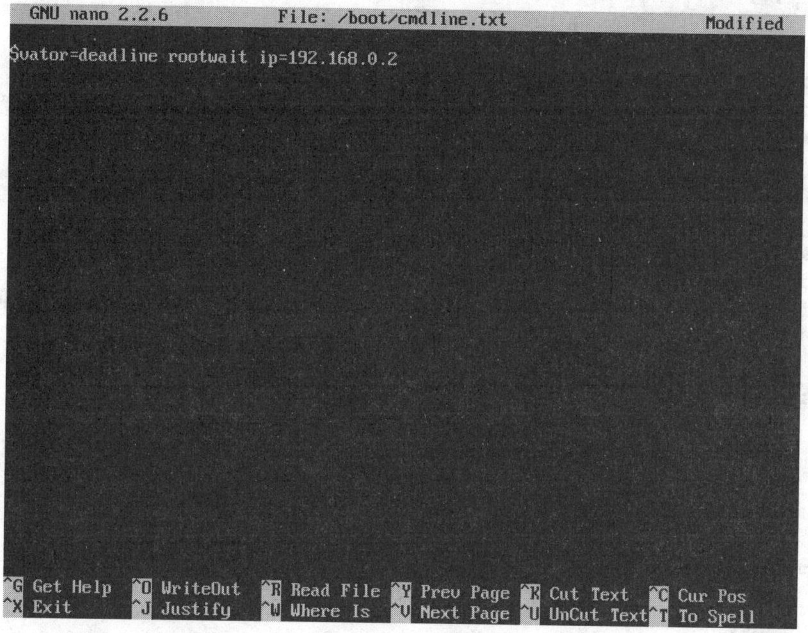

```
GNU nano 2.2.6              File: /boot/cmdline.txt                Modified

$vator=deadline rootwait ip=192.168.0.2




















^G Get Help    ^O WriteOut    ^R Read File   ^Y Prev Page   ^K Cut Text    ^C Cur Pos
^X Exit        ^J Justify     ^W Where Is    ^V Next Page   ^U UnCut Text  ^T To Spell
```

FIGURE 1-10. *Setting a static IP address on the Raspberry Pi*

on the Raspberry Pi. Often you will find certified Wi-Fi devices sold alongside Raspberry Pis at vendor websites, but you may be able to find a cheaper or faster Wi-Fi adapter with a little bit of research. For a full list of devices that are known to work by the community, check the eLinux Wi-Fi adapter listing here: http://elinux.org/RPi_USB_Wi-Fi_Adapters.

Raspbian comes with wpa_supplicant installed and set up for a wireless network, so all you have to do is add your network configuration options from the command line. To do this, I recommend using the WPA command-line tool (wpa_cli), which lets you scan your network and add new wpa_supplicant configurations. The advantage of using the command-line tool over editing the configuration file directly is that you can't make an error in your configuration by missing punctuation or formatting.

Listing 1-1 shows an example of how to use wpa_cli to configure your wireless settings. Obviously, you should replace ssid and psk with the SSID and preshared key of your local network configuration, and this assumes that you are using a network that broadcasts the SSID. Both WPA and WPA2 networks are supported by this configuration.

Listing 1-1 *WPA command-line tool for configuring Wi-Fi*

```
pi@raspberrypi ~ $ wpa_cli
Selected interface 'wlan0'
Interactive mode
> scan
OK
<3>CTRL-EVENT-SCAN-RESULTS
<3>WPS-AP-AVAILABLE
> scan_results
bssid / frequency / signal level / flags / ssid
12:0d:7f:8b:be:9e 2437 92 [WPA2-PSK-CCMP][ESS] NightHacking-Guest
> add_network
0
> set_network 0 ssid "NightHacking-Guest"
OK
> set_network 0 psk "steveonjava"
OK
> enable_network 0
OK
> save_config
OK
> reconnect
OK
> quit
```

TIP
If you are still using WEP, it is possible to connect your Raspberry Pi, but I don't recommend it. WEP has been proven insecure and can be cracked in under a minute by low-end hardware and freely available software. There are also some new cryptographic attacks against WPA involving vulnerabilities in TKIP. In short, upgrading your network to WPA2 is an important security practice.

Updating and Upgrading

Now that you are on the network, the very first thing you should do is to update your Raspbian distribution. This will ensure you have the latest package listing and current versions of all of the core files. To do this, first execute the following command to download the latest package listing:

```
sudo apt-get update
```

Then you can perform an upgrade of your Raspberry Pi distribution by using this additional command:

```
sudo apt-get upgrade
```

Depending upon how old the NOOBS distribution you originally used was, and how fast your network connection and SD card are, this could take quite a while. This might be a good opportunity to brew another cup of coffee.

Setting Up a Hostname

If your Raspberry Pi gets its IP address from DHCP, the address can change on every reboot. If you are running the Raspberry Pi headless (without a monitor or display), this can make it a chore to search for the new IP address. A good alternative is to use Bonjour/Zeroconf, which broadcasts your hostname over multicast. This way you can refer to your Raspberry Pi as raspberrypi.local (or, in general, hostname.local) from anywhere on your local network.

The first step is to set a unique hostname. This can be done from the Advanced Options in the Raspberry Pi configuration utility. To bring up the configuration utility from the command line, type the following:

```
sudo raspi-config
```

After setting the hostname, you will be asked to reboot the Pi to update the network configuration. After reboot, you can install Bonjour on the Raspberry Pi by running the following command:

```
sudo apt-get install libnss-mdns
```

After this command completes, you are ready to access the Pi on the network. From any computer on the same network where multicast packets reach, you can replace the IP address of your Pi with hostname.local. For example, Listing 1-2 shows the output of pinging my Raspberry Pi with hostname nighthackingpi.

Listing 1-2   *Pinging nighthackingpi via Bonjour*

```
NightHacking-Presenter:~ sjc$ ping nighthackingpi.local
PING nighthackingpi.local (192.168.1.10): 56 data bytes
64 bytes from 192.168.1.10: icmp_seq=0 ttl=64 time=76.379 ms
64 bytes from 192.168.1.10: icmp_seq=1 ttl=64 time=93.390 ms
```

Notice that it automatically translates from the hostname to an IP address of 192.168.1.10. However, if this address changed in the future, I could use the same command to access my Pi.

Bonjour is installed by default on OS X and Ubuntu Linux. If you are running on Windows, you already have Bonjour installed if you have previously installed iTunes. Otherwise, the easiest way to get it is to install Bonjour Print Services for Windows from Apple: http://support.apple.com/kb/DL999.

Connecting to Your Raspberry Pi with SSH

Using an SSH client from your computer is a convenient and secure way of interacting with your Raspberry Pi. Once you have networking configured on both machines, this is as simple as connecting with the hostname or IP address.

For Unix or OS X you can simply use a terminal window and the version of SSH that ships with your operating system. Figure 1-11 shows an example of an SSH login from an OS X computer.

```
⬆ sjc — pi@raspberrypi: ~ — ssh — 80×23 — ⌘1

NightHacking-Presenter:~ sjc$
NightHacking-Presenter:~ sjc$
NightHacking-Presenter:~ sjc$
NightHacking-Presenter:~ sjc$ ssh pi@192.168.1.10
The authenticity of host '192.168.1.10 (192.168.1.10)' can't be established.
RSA key fingerprint is 0c:b4:c5:3c:1c:2b:8e:ef:fe:97:26:18:a1:33:1b:bf.
Are you sure you want to continue connecting (yes/no)? yes
Warning: Permanently added '192.168.1.10' (RSA) to the list of known hosts.
pi@192.168.1.10's password:
Linux raspberrypi 3.12.35+ #730 PREEMPT Fri Dec 19 18:31:24 GMT 2014 armv6l

The programs included with the Debian GNU/Linux system are free software;
the exact distribution terms for each program are described in the
individual files in /usr/share/doc/*/copyright.

Debian GNU/Linux comes with ABSOLUTELY NO WARRANTY, to the extent
permitted by applicable law.
Last login: Tue Jan 13 02:11:13 2015 from 192.168.1.164
pi@raspberrypi ~ $ java -version
java version "1.8.0"
Java(TM) SE Runtime Environment (build 1.8.0-b132)
Java HotSpot(TM) Client VM (build 25.0-b70, mixed mode)
pi@raspberrypi ~ $ ▯
```

FIGURE 1-11. *SSH from OS X*

To connect via SSH on the command line, simply issue the following ssh command:

```
ssh user@hostname
```

where "user" is your username (most likely, pi) and "hostname" is your Pi's network name or IP address (for example, 192.168.0.2).

If this is the first time you are connecting, you may be asked to verify the RSA key fingerprint. This is a security measure to ensure that the device to which you are creating an encrypted connection is in fact the device you intended to communicate with. If your network has been compromised (or you are on a public network), then it is possible for someone to launch a man-in-the-middle attack and spoof as your device.

To verify the RSA key fingerprint, physically log on to the Raspberry Pi and type the following command:

```
ssh-keygen -l -f /etc/ssh/ssh_host_rsa_key.pub
```

This returns a fingerprint that you can verify against the one returned by the SSH tunnel, which will look something like the following:

```
2048 0c:b4:c5:3c:1c:2b:8e:ef:fe:97:26:18:a1:33:1b:bf  root@raspberrypi (RSA)
```

CAUTION

Checking the RSA key fingerprint after logging on to the Raspberry Pi is as good as not checking at all. Once someone else has established a man-in-the-middle attack, they can simply intercept the command and return a matching fingerprint.

Now that the connection has been established as secure, SSH will ask for your password. Once authenticated, you can issue commands just as if you were physically at the keyboard. This is often more convenient, and it lets you interact with a headless Raspberry Pi to do redeployment, diagnostics, or troubleshooting.

On Windows you will have to install an SSH client yourself. A well-known and free SSH client is PuTTY, which is maintained by a small team based in Cambridge, England. You can find the PuTTY downloads here: www.chiark .greenend.org.uk/~sgtatham/putty/download.html.

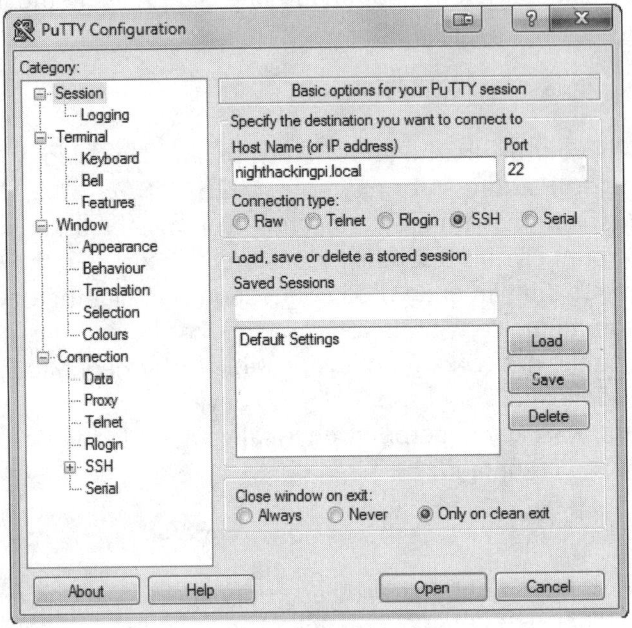

FIGURE 1-12. *PuTTY SSH client for Windows*

The initial configuration screen of PuTTY is shown in Figure 1-12. Simply enter the IP address or hostname of your Raspberry Pi, make sure SSH is selected, and click Open. This will start a secure connection that prompts you to verify the RSA key fingerprint (as just discussed) and then lets you connect with your username and password.

Creating a Simple Raspberry Pi Application

Now that you have a convenient SSH prompt to access your Raspberry Pi, you are ready to try running Java remotely. In the next chapter you will install a full-featured integrated development environment (IDE) to speed up development, but for this simple `HelloRaspberryPi` application, it is easy enough to type it in on the command line.

To create the application, you use the echo and append (>) commands to generate a simple Java class. Listing 1-3 shows the commands (in bold) you type into the SSH sessions.

Listing 1-3   *Creation of the* `HelloRaspberryPi` *class*

```
pi@nighthackingpi ~ $ echo "class HelloRaspberryPi {
>   public static void main(String[] args) {
>     System.out.println(\"Hello Raspberry Pi\");
>   }
> }" > HelloRaspberryPi.java
```

Notice that you can continue a command within quotation marks on the next line simply by pressing ENTER. The command prompt (>) on each line is automatically typed by the system, and in this example I used spaces for indentation. The only other difference from normal Java code is that the double quotes (" ") need to be escaped with a preceding backslash (\).

The last line writes this application to a file called HelloRaspberryPi.java that you can compile by using `javac` with the following command:

```
pi@nighthackingpi ~ $ javac HelloRaspberryPi.java
```

Executing the application is as simple as running `java` in the same directory with the main class name:

```
pi@nighthackingpi ~ $ java HelloRaspberryPi
```

My shell console is shown in Figure 1-13 along with the output of the program.

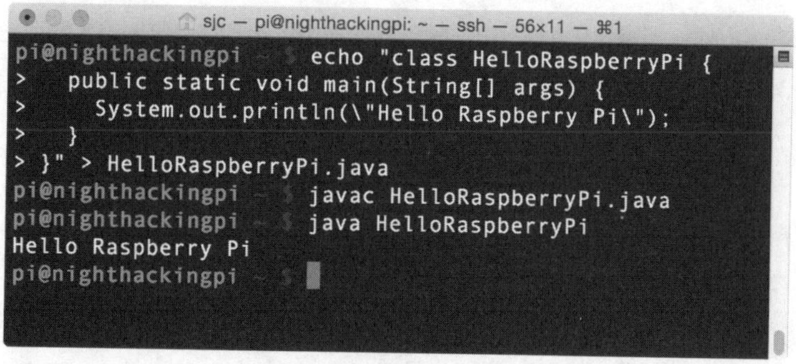

FIGURE 1-13.   *Output of the* `HelloRaspberryPi` *application*

Congratulations on setting up your first Raspberry Pi and running a simple Java application on it! The work you completed in this chapter on hardware, configuration, and networking has set the foundation for the rest of your Raspberry Pi projects. In the next chapter we will explore the visual capabilities of the Raspberry Pi and set up a full Java IDE to streamline future projects.

CHAPTER

2

Your First Java Project

The fully functioning Raspberry Pi embedded computer that you set up in Chapter 1 comes preloaded with Oracle Java 8, so getting started with Java is as simple as typing the `java` command at the prompt. However, to simplify the development workflow, this chapter is going to take you through the installation and setup of a Java IDE that gives you a full-featured programming environment.

Bill of Materials

To complete the project in this chapter you will need a Raspberry Pi of your choice and a USB scale. Since you will be connecting the Raspberry Pi to your computer for remote debugging and output, make sure that you choose a Raspberry Pi model that you can easily network. For this reason, you probably don't want to use either the Model A or A+ since they both have a single USB port and no Ethernet.

What you will need:

- **Raspberry Pi with SD card**   Model B, B+, or 2 recommended.

- **Digital scale with USB support**   The Dymo M10 or Dymo M25 is recommended. Here is a link to the M10 on Amazon: www .amazon.com/DYMO-1772057-Digital-Shipping-10-pound/dp/ B0053HCWRE.

- **Aeropress coffee maker**   Made by Aerobie, and you can find it on Amazon or at premium coffee roasters: www.amazon.com/ Aeropress-Coffee-and-Espresso-Maker/dp/B0047BIWSK.

- **Coffee grinder**   If you do not already have a high-quality electric grinder, a manual coffee grinder is a great value for the occasional cup and an essential for traveling. The Japanese made Porlex Mini Coffee Grinder is a great choice: www.amazon.com/Porlex-Mini-Stainless-Coffee-Grinder/dp/B0044ZA066.

In addition to the hardware you will need some consumables, such as filters and coffee beans. The Aeropress comes with plenty of filters to get you started. For beans you should source a local coffee roaster, or, if there are no coffee roasters in your vicinity, another option is to order coffee by mail from a high-quality roaster like Four Barrel: http://fourbarrelcoffee.com.

Getting Started with NetBeans

For coding with the Raspberry Pi you can use any Java IDE of your choice. You can even edit and compile directly on the Raspberry Pi; however, I don't recommend doing this since the Raspberry Pi takes considerably longer than a modern PC to do processor-intensive tasks. This book shows you how to use the NetBeans IDE since it has convenient integration that lets you run and deploy applications directly from your computer via SSH.

Downloading and Configuring NetBeans

You can download NetBeans directly from http://netbeans.org/ for your operating system. There are five different download bundles available, as shown in Figure 2-1, with different sets of plug-ins contained in each. The two main flavors of Java are Standard Edition (SE) and Micro Edition (ME). Java SE is what you use on the desktop and in server applications, and Java ME is an interpreted-only version designed for highly resource-constrained devices. Since we will be using Java SE Embedded, we only require the Java SE distribution, which also happens to be the smallest Java bundle. If you later decide to add additional support, such as Java ME (which I highly recommend trying on your Raspberry Pi), then you can always add the additional plug-ins later directly from within NetBeans.

	NetBeans IDE Download Bundles				
Supported technologies *	Java SE	Java EE	C/C++	HTML5 & PHP	All
NetBeans Platform SDK	•	•			•
Java SE	•	•			•
Java FX	•	•			•
Java EE		•			•
Java ME					—
HTML5		•		•	•
Java Card™ 3 Connected					—
C/C++			•		—
Groovy					•
PHP				•	•
Bundled servers					
GlassFish Server Open Source Edition 4.1		•			•
Apache Tomcat 8.0.15		•			•
	Download	Download	Download	Download	Download
	Free, 105 MB	Free, 222 MB	Free, 72 MB	Free, 72 MB	Free, 243 MB

FIGURE 2-1. *NetBeans IDE download bundles*

You also need the latest Java Development Kit (JDK) to match your Raspberry Pi Java version, so it is a good idea to update this as well. You can download the JDK separately, or you can download a JDK with NetBeans bundle from the following Oracle Technology Network site: www.oracle.com/technetwork/java/javase/downloads/index.html.

Once NetBeans is installed and running, you can set up the remote connection to your Raspberry Pi. To accomplish this, add a new Java Platform by going to Tools | Java Platforms. In the Java Platform Manager, click the Add Platform button, which opens the Add Java Platform wizard. The first screen lets you select a local or remote JDK, so choose Remote Java Standard Edition. Click Next to advance to the second screen, where you can add the host information as shown in Figure 2-2.

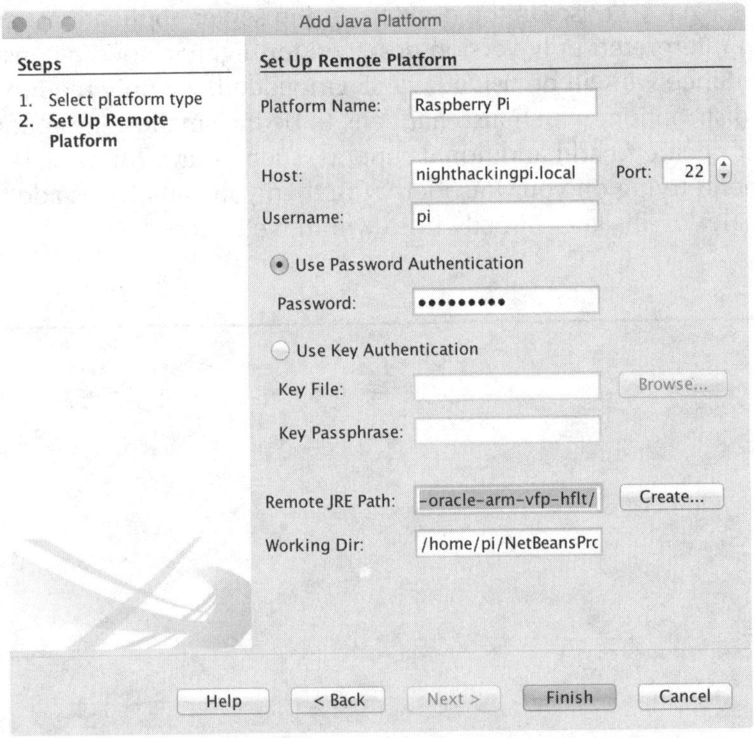

FIGURE 2-2. *Adding a remote JDK platform for your Raspberry Pi*

Here are the fields that you will need to configure:

- **Platform Name** Choose a name that distinguishes the remote platform from other local or remote JDKs
- **Host** The hostname or IP address of your Raspberry Pi
- **Username/Password** Login credentials for the Raspberry Pi
- **Remote JRE Path** Location of your Java install on the Raspberry Pi

The Remote JRE Path is slightly harder to configure. Since you want to point this to your existing Java installation on the Pi, you need to log in via SSH or console and find the path by using the following command:

```
sudo update-alternatives --display java
```

This will display the location(s) of the Java installation along with the full path, giving you output similar to the following:

```
java - auto mode
  link currently points to ↵
/usr/lib/jvm/jdk-8-oracle-arm-vfp-hflt/jre/bin/java
/usr/lib/jvm/jdk-8-oracle-arm-vfp-hflt/jre/bin/java - priority 318
  slave java.1.gz: /usr/lib/jvm/jdk-8-oracle-arm-vfp-hflt/man/man1/java.1.gz
Current 'best' version is '/usr/lib/jvm/jdk-8-oracle-arm-vfp-hflt/jre/bin/java'.
```

In this case you would enter a value of /usr/lib/jvm/jdk-8-oracle-arm-vfp-hflt/jre/ for the Remote JRE Path.

Revisiting HelloRaspberryPi

To test your embedded setup, this section shows you how to use NetBeans to re-create the `HelloRaspberryPi` application from Chapter 1. Choose File | New Project to enter the Project Wizard. On the first screen, use the default project type of Java Application and click Next. On the second screen, enter the project name as **HelloRaspberryPi**, as shown in Figure 2-3, and click Finish.

This will give you a code-editing window with a default `main` method populated. To finish our application, all you need to do is replace the comment that says "// TODO code application logic here" with a `println` statement that will write your message:

```
System.out.println("Hello Raspberry Pi");
```

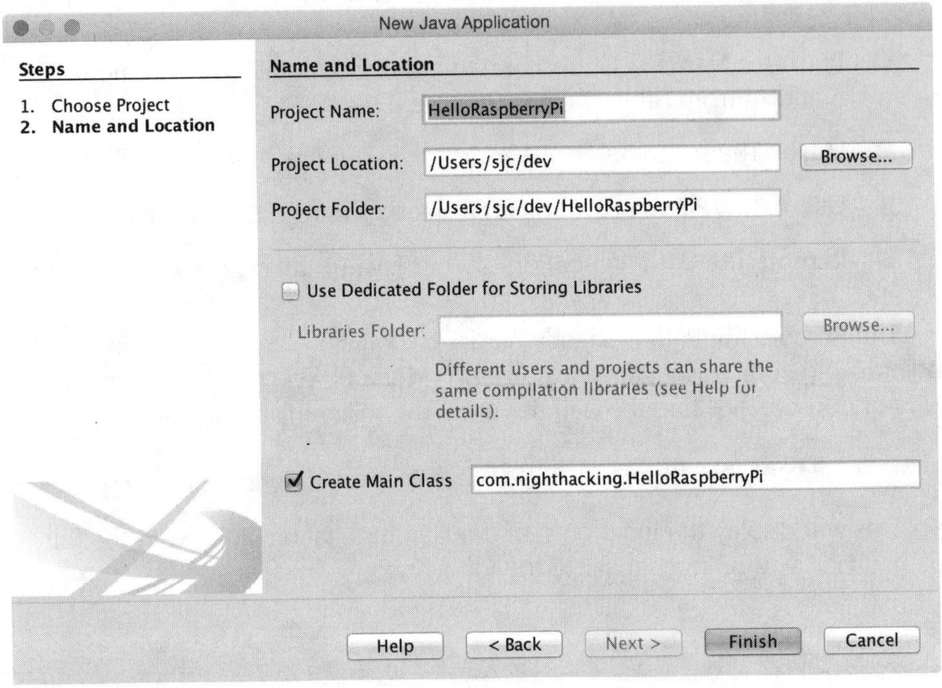

FIGURE 2-3. *New Project Wizard in NetBeans*

The program will now compile and run on the local machine fine, but our goal is to instead run it on a Raspberry Pi. Make sure that you have the Raspberry Pi that you configured in the previous section powered on and connected via Wi-Fi or Ethernet. Then, change the run options for your project to use the Remote Java SE platform by opening the Project Properties dialog (File | Project Properties (HelloRaspberryPi)). Click Run in the Categories pane on the left and change the Runtime Platform field to Raspberry Pi. This will prompt you to create a new configuration, as shown in Figure 2-4.

Choose a name for your configuration, such as Raspberry Pi, click OK to save the configuration and click OK on the Project Properties dialog to save. This will create the configuration, set it to your Remote Java SE platform,

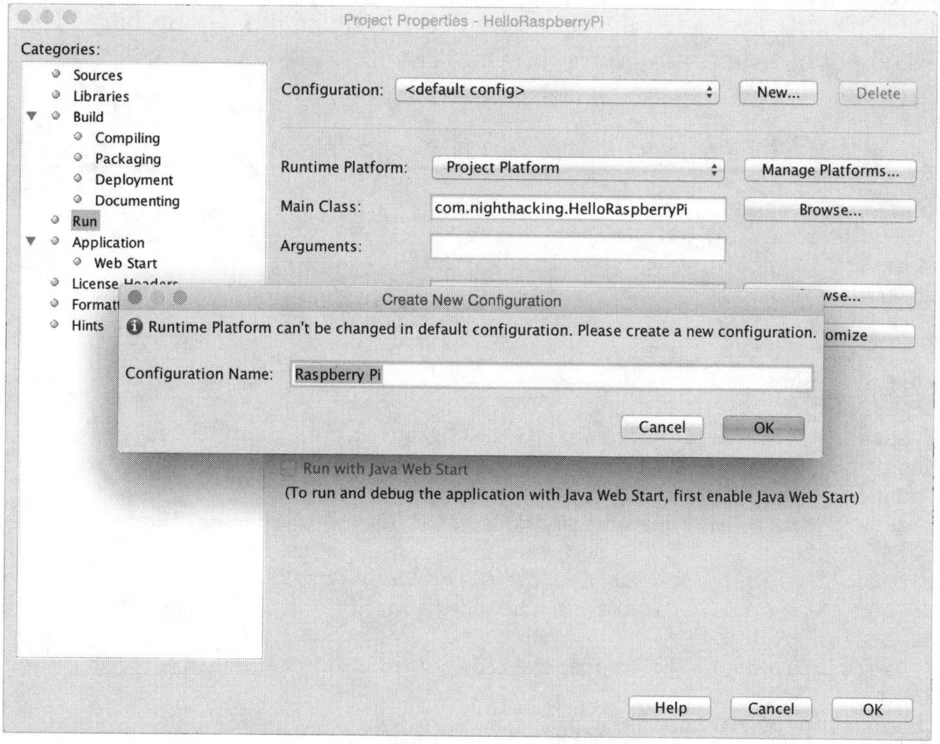

FIGURE 2-4. *Creating a new configuration in the Project Properties dialog*

and update your project to use it on subsequent runs. Now you can run your project by clicking the green arrow or choosing Run | Run Project (HelloRaspberryPi) and it will automatically do the following:

1. Compile the code

2. Build a JAR file

3. Copy the JAR file via SCP

4. Initiate an SSH connection

5. Run the application remotely

You could manually compile and copy the JAR file over and then execute it via SSH, but having the IDE take care of this is much more convenient. The full output of a successful run is shown in Listing 2-1.

Listing 2-1 *Remote execution of HelloRaspberryPi*

```
ant -f /Users/sjc/dev/HelloRaspberryPi ↵
-Dnb.internal.action.name=run ↵
-Dremote.platform.rp.target=linuxarmvfphflt-15 ↵
-Dremote.platform.password=***** ↵
-Dremote.platform.rp.filename=linuxarmvfphflt ↵
-Dremote.platform.java.spec.ver=18 run-remote
init:
Deleting: ↵
/Users/sjc/dev/HelloRaspberryPi/build/built-jar.properties
deps-jar:
Updating property file: ↵
/Users/sjc/dev/HelloRaspberryPi/build/built-jar.properties
compile:
Copying 1 file to /Users/sjc/dev/HelloRaspberryPi/build
To run this application from the command line without Ant, try:
java -jar ↵
"/Users/sjc/dev/HelloRaspberryPi/dist/HelloRaspberryPi.jar"
jar:
Connecting to nighthackingpi.local:22
cmd : mkdir -p '/home/pi/NetBeansProjects/HelloRaspberryPi/dist'
Connecting to nighthackingpi.local:22
done.
profile-rp-calibrate-passwd:
Connecting to nighthackingpi.local:22
cmd : cd '/home/pi/NetBeansProjects/HelloRaspberryPi'; ↵
'/usr/lib/jvm/jdk-8-oracle-arm-vfp-hflt//bin/java' ↵
-Dfile.encoding=UTF-8   -jar ↵
/home/pi/NetBeansProjects/HelloRaspberryPi/dist/HelloRaspberryPi.jar
Hello Raspberry Pi
```

Congratulations on remotely executing your first Java application on the Raspberry Pi! Now we will move on to a more practical example with some embedded-powered coffee brewing.

Brewing Java

The addition of Java to your Raspberry Pi wouldn't be complete without an application to help you perfect your coffee brewing skills. For the second application we write on the Raspberry Pi, we will take a scientific approach to coffee brewing in order to obtain the ideal cup of joe.

The setup includes a USB scale that will be used to measure the weight of ingredients, an Aeropress brewing device, and a portable scale as shown in Figure 2-5. All of this connects to the Raspberry Pi as a central control unit for the coffee algorithm.

Communicating with a USB Scale

To precisely measure weight for coffee brewing, we are going to use a USB shipping scale. While it is possible to create your own scale from scratch using a strain gauge, a Wheatstone bridge, and an analog amplifier (http://morf.lv/modules.php?name=tutorials&lasit=19), it turns out to be cheaper and more reliable to simply use an electronic shipping scale.

The protocol used by most shipping scales is simple one-way communication where the current scale value is repeatedly broadcast over a single endpoint on the first interface. I am going to be using a Dymo M10 scale for this project,

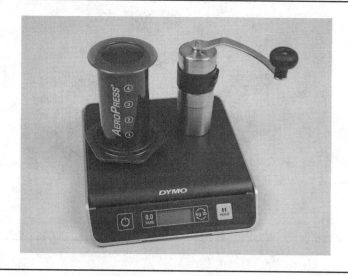

FIGURE 2-5.   *Hardware for the coffee brewing project*

as shown in Figure 2-6, but any Stamps.com or DymoStamp-compatible scale should work. To use the scale, simply plug it into one of the host ports on your Raspberry Pi and turn it on. The Dymo M10 only consumes 16mA, so it can be safely powered right off the Raspberry Pi USB bus.

TIP
When shopping for a scale, make sure you get a scale that has resolution to at least 1 or 2 grams. Scales with larger capacity typically have less resolution, and scales with smaller capacity typically have much finer resolution. If you are a real coffee connoisseur, you will want to get a professional scale that measures to 1/10 of a gram, like the Scout Pro used in Chapter 6.

To start, create a new project in NetBeans called **UsbScaleTest** and set it up for embedded development the same way you did earlier with the `HelloRaspberryPi` project. One extra step this time will be to configure a third-party library for USB communication.

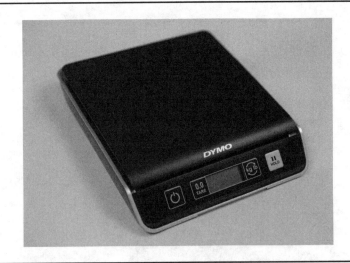

FIGURE 2-6. *Dymo M10 postal scale*

NOTE
It may also be helpful to download the full code sample for this chapter at the following GitHub repo: https://github.com/RaspberryPiWithJava/ JavaScale.

For communication with our USB scale, we are going to use the usb4java Java library. This is an open-source, JSR 80–compliant implementation of the standard javax.usb specification that has support for ARM Linux distributions like the Raspberry Pi. You can download the latest version of usb4java from the project website: http://usb4java.org/.

Make sure to download both the core library and the javax extension. From the core distribution, you will need to grab the following JAR files:

- usb4java-1.2.0.jar

- libusb4java-1.2.0-linux-arm.jar

- commons-lang3-3.2.1.jar

You also need these additional JAR files from the usb4java-javax distribution:

- usb-api-1.0.2.jar

- usb4java-javax-1.2.0.jar

Place all these files in a new folder called **lib** in your project directory, and add them to your project dependencies. You do so via the Project Properties dialog in the Libraries category. Click the Add JAR/Folder button and select all the JAR files in your lib folder for inclusion. A project with all the required JAR files included is shown in Figure 2-7.

NOTE
Make sure you select the JAR files themselves and not the outer lib folder. Using folders as a library only works when you have class files that are not inside a JAR.

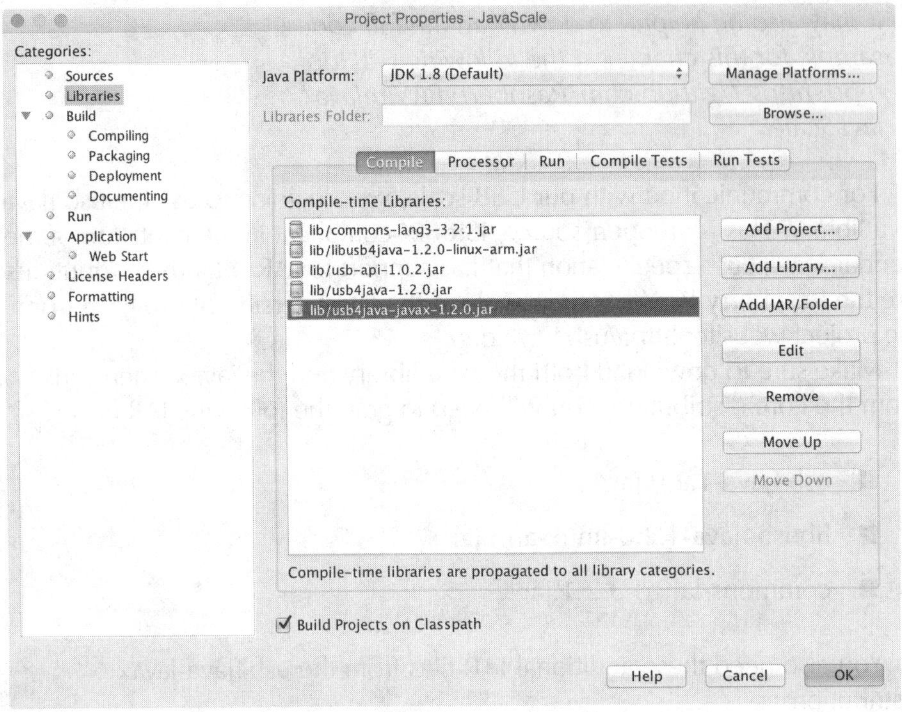

FIGURE 2-7. *Library configuration in NetBeans*

You also need to create a properties file in the root package that tells the javax.usb wrapper to use usb4java as the implementation. To accomplish this, create a file called **javax.usb.properties** in the root package (under src) and give it the following contents:

```
javax.usb.services = org.usb4java.javax.Services
```

To test the data returned from the scale, we are going to use a single-class implementation of the USB scale protocol that returns 60 data points and prints out the results on the command line. The `main` method for our application is shown in Listing 2-2 and can be summarized as follows:

1. Find a connected USB scale.

2. Open a connection to the scale.

3. For 60 data points, submit a request to retrieve data.

4. Close the scale.

Listing 2-2 *Scale test main method*

```
public static void main(String[] args) throws UsbException {
  UsbScaleTest scale = UsbScaleTest.findScale();
  scale.open();
  try {
    for (int i = 0; i < 60; i++) {
      scale.syncSubmit();
    }
  } finally {
    scale.close();
  }
}
```

The try...finally block in Listing 2-2 ensures the scale will get closed properly even in the case of an error or exception. Listing 2-3 shows the implementation of the first method, findScale, which discovers Dymo M10 or M25 scales using the javax.usb API. I have included in the code the vendorId and productId for the Dymo M10 and its sister scale, the Dymo M25. However, any scale will work just fine as long as you replace the appropriate vendorId and productId in the code, which will show up when you plug in the scale and run the dmesg command.

Listing 2-3 *Code to find USB scales*

```
public static UsbScaleTest findScale() throws UsbException {
  UsbServices services = UsbHostManager.getUsbServices();
  UsbHub rootHub = services.getRootUsbHub();
  // Dymo M10 Scale:
  UsbDevice device = findDevice(rootHub, (short) 0x0922, (short) 0x8003);
  // Dymo M25 Scale:
  if (device == null) {
    device = findDevice(rootHub, (short) 0x0922, (short) 0x8004);
  }
  if (device == null) {
    return null;
  }
  return new UsbScaleTest(device);
}
```

This calls the `findDevice` method, which contains code that traverses the USB device tree as shown in Listing 2-4.

Listing 2-4 *Locating a device*

```
private static UsbDevice findDevice(UsbHub hub, short vendorId, short productId) {
  for (UsbDevice device : (List<UsbDevice>) hub.getAttachedUsbDevices()) {
    UsbDeviceDescriptor desc = device.getUsbDeviceDescriptor();
    if (desc.idVendor() == vendorId && desc.idProduct() == productId) {
      return device;
    }
    if (device.isUsbHub()) {
      device = findDevice((UsbHub) device, vendorId, productId);
      if (device != null) {
        return device;
      }
    }
  }
  return null;
}
```

To read data from the scale, you need to connect to the correct interface and endpoint. Fortunately, the USB scale protocol is fairly simple, so you can simply grab the first interface and endpoint and then start listening to the data coming in from the scale directly, as shown in Listing 2-5.

Listing 2-5 *Code to open a connection to a USB scale*

```
private void open() throws UsbException {
  UsbConfiguration configuration = device.getActiveUsbConfiguration();
  iface = configuration.getUsbInterface((byte) 0);
  // this allows us to steal the lock from the kernel
  iface.claim(usbInterface -> true);
  final List<UsbEndpoint> endpoints = iface.getUsbEndpoints();
  pipe = endpoints.get(0).getUsbPipe(); // there is only 1 endpoint
  pipe.addUsbPipeListener(this);
  pipe.open();
}
```

Notice that we had to use the `claim` method that accepts a UsbInterfacePolicy. This allows us to force the kernel to detach from the USB interface so we can claim it for our application.

The implementation of `syncSubmit` is trivial, calling the same-named method on the `UsbPipe`:

```
private void syncSubmit() throws UsbException {
    pipe.syncSubmit(data);
}
```

However, the real work happens in the callback. To receive the callback, our class needs to implement the `UsbPipeListener` interface, which has two required methods. The first is `dataEventOccurred`, which will be called as a result of invoking `syncSubmit` and will contain the data returned from the scale. The second is `errorEventOccurred`, which will be invoked when there is a problem interfacing with the scale.

The data sent by these shipping scales is a simple byte array with six values. The protocol is not well documented but has been reverse-engineered by the open-source community. The data is as follows:

Byte 0	Unused
Byte 1	Special flags: empty = 2, overweight = 6, negative = 5
Byte 2	Unit of measure: grams = 2, ounces = 11
Byte 3	Weight scale
Byte 4	Base weight low order byte
Byte 5	Base weight high order byte

Listing 2-6 shows the implementation of `dataEventOccurred`, which takes apart the byte array returned and prints out a human-readable scale value to the command line.

Listing 2-6 *USB scale data processing function*

```
@Override
public void dataEventOccurred(UsbPipeDataEvent upde) {
    boolean empty = data[1] == 2;
    boolean overweight = data[1] == 6;
    boolean negative = data[1] == 5;
    boolean grams = data[2] == 2;
    int scalingFactor = data[3];
    int weight = (data[4] & 0xFF) + (data[5] << 8);
    if (empty) {
        System.out.println("EMPTY");
    } else if (overweight) {
```

```
    System.out.println("OVERWEIGHT");
} else if (negative) {
    System.out.println("NEGATIVE");
} else { // Use String.format since printf causes problems on remote exec
    System.out.println(String.format("Weight = %,.1f%s",
        scaleWeight(weight, scalingFactor),
        grams ? "g" : "oz"));
    }
}
```

Besides some bit shifting to get the weight magnitude, we also need to scale it by the `scalingFactor` returned in Byte 3 as follows:

```
private double scaleWeight(int weight, int scalingFactor) {
    return weight * Math.pow(10, scalingFactor);
}
```

In the case of an error, the best we can do is log it and continue:

```
@Override
public void errorEventOccurred(UsbPipeErrorEvent upee) {
    Logger.getLogger(UsbScaleTest.class.getName()).log(Level.SEVERE, "Scale Error", upee);
}
```

And the last method to finish the scale test is the `close` method. This will simply close the pipe and interface cleanly so that the next application that tries to use the scale will be able to access it:

```
public void close() throws UsbException {
    pipe.close();
    iface.release();
}
```

Before running this example, you will need to make sure that you have your remote configuration set to run with root privileges so you have access to USB devices. Here are the steps to accomplish this:

1. Choose Tools | Java Platforms.

2. Click your Raspberry Pi platform under the Remote Java SE tree.

3. Click the Exec Prefix field and enter a value of **sudo**.

You can now run the completed `UsbScaleTest` class, which will compile and deploy the JAR as before, but this time it will show some more interesting output. If you have your scale connected and turned on, it should output the first 60 readings from the scale, including information about whether the scale is empty, overweight, or negative, as shown in Listing 2-7.

Listing 2-7   *USB scale test output*

```
cmd : cd '/home/pi/NetBeansProjects/JavaScale'; '/usr/lib/jvm/jdk-
8-oracle-arm-vfp-hflt//bin/java'  -Dfile.encoding=UTF-8   -jar /
home/pi/NetBeansProjects/JavaScale/dist/JavaScale.jar
NEGATIVE
EMPTY
EMPTY
EMPTY
Weight = 64.0g
Weight = 72.0g
Weight = 72.0g
Weight = 56.0g
Weight = 56.0g
...
run-remote:
BUILD SUCCESSFUL (total time: 31 seconds)
```

To get a good feel for how the USB interface works, try adding a few objects of different weight while the scale is returning data. If you want to get a negative value, you need to add an object to the scale, press tare (to zero it), and then remove the object. To get an overweight reading, add an object that is heavier than the scale supports (for example, an 11kg object on the M10 scale). Be careful not to use an object that is too heavy, because it can break the scale's sensitive internal components.

Now that you have a good feel for how the scale works, it is time to apply this to brew some perfectly proportioned coffee, and for that we will need a coffee calculator.

Coffee Calculator

The science behind our application is that we will be applying the Specialty Coffee Association of America's (SCAA) Coffee Brewing Control Chart to select the optimal amount of coffee grounds for our beverage. This is based on research in the 1960s led by Dr. Earnest Earl Lockhart, who is best known for his graphical representation of coffee brewing parameters along with a recommended guide for optimal strength and extraction. The North American version of this chart is shown in Figure 2-8.

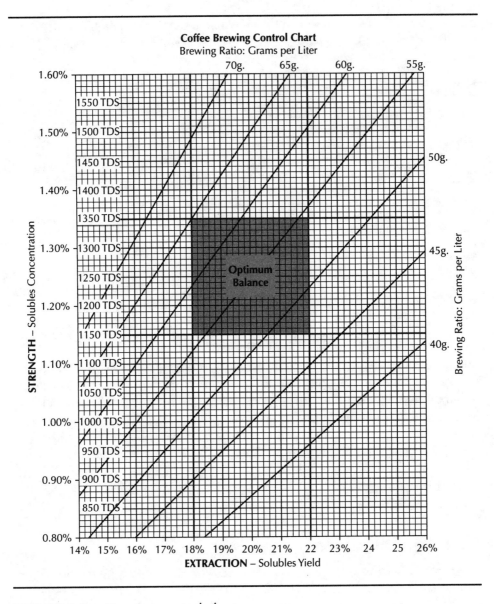

FIGURE 2-8. *Brewing control chart*

There are three different units represented on this chart, with the strength of your coffee represented on the vertical axis in percentage of total dissolved solids (TDS), the level of extraction represented on the horizontal axis in percentage, and the brewing ratio represented by the diagonal lines in grams per liter.

If you are a true coffee connoisseur, you can use this chart to precisely dial in your coffee experience by using a refractometer to measure the TDS in your coffee brew, selecting the line corresponding to your brew ratio, and solving for the extraction ratio. This lets you empirically measure the effects of grind coarseness, water temperature, and steeping time on the extraction rate. However, to keep things simple, we are going to use the chart as a guide to recommend a dosing weight of coffee for a given number of cups of coffee. This is an important starting point for brewing a cup of coffee that falls in the Optimum Balance region of the chart.

Our target density for a "normal" cup of coffee will be 55g/L, which gives the highest chance of hitting the SCAA's optimum balance for a given extraction percentage. There is also a Specialty Coffee Association of Europe (SCAE) that recommends the same 18–22 percent extraction rate, but moves the optimum strength up to 1.2 percent to 1.45 percent soluble concentration. This will define our "rich" cup of coffee at 58g/L. Finally, the Norwegian Coffee Association further moves the optimal strength up to 1.3 percent to 1.5 percent soluble concentration, for which we will define our "strong" cup of coffee at 62g/L.

Listing 2-8 shows a `CoffeeCalculator` class that takes these principles and turns them into code that will help us calculate the perfect brew.

Listing 2-8 *CoffeeCalculator class for determining grind from strength and volume*

```java
public class CoffeeCalculator {
  public static final double REGULAR = 55;
  public static final double RICH = 58;
  public static final double STRONG = 62;
  /**
   * Calculates the weight of grounds needed to reach a target coffee strength.
   *
   * @param strength Target strength in grams/liter
   * @param volume Final water volume in grams (1g = 1ml)
   * @return Amount of grounds needed in grams
   */
  public static double grindWeight(double strength, double volume) {
    return strength * (water / 1000);
  }
}
```

Given a target liquid volume (cup size), the `CoffeeCalculator` class will help us determine how much coffee grounds to use. We are assuming all values in grams since this is what most scales use and there is a straightforward conversion from volume to mass of water in the metric system.

A simple example of using this class would be to calculate how much grounds to use for a 300-gram cup of water:

```
grindWeight(REGULAR, 300)
```

This would return 17.4g, which should sound about right if you have ever followed a coffee brewing recipe from one of the popular gourmet coffee roasters.

For convenience, we are making two simplifications related to this calculation:

- **Weight of dissolved solids** The weight of coffee is slightly heavier than the weight of an equivalent volume of water due to dissolved coffee solids. Our calculation assumes the weight is equal.

- **Water trapped in grounds** Not all the water will make it through the extraction process, since the grounds absorb some of the moisture. Our calculation measures the water added rather than the volume extracted, which is much easier.

These two sources of error are relatively small and partially cancel each other out. Also, they are consistent and repeatable phenomenon, so we should be able to get very reliable results in our coffee brewing regardless.

Asynchronous Communication

While we used a synchronous algorithm for reading the scale in our earlier example, this turns out to be a poor choice for our coffee algorithm. The reason for this is that USB scale data is buffered, so reading on demand returns stale data initially. If we wait until we need to know the current weight to take a reading, it is impossible to differentiate between the stale buffered data and the current scale weight unless we read and discard a fixed amount of data. By reading data continuously, we have an instantaneous snapshot of the current scale value in memory at all times, and can simply block our thread until the next reading is available if we are waiting for a specific value.

The code in Listing 2-9 implements a new `USBPipeListener` callback that processes the returned data, submits a new request for data, and notifies any threads blocked on the `scalePhaser` that we have new data.

Listing 2-9 *USBPipeListener callback function*

```
public void dataEventOccurred(UsbPipeDataEvent upde) {
  processData();
  if (closing) {
    busy = false;
  } else {
    try {
      pipe.asyncSubmit(data);
    } catch (UsbException ex) {
      errorEventOccurred(new UsbPipeErrorEvent(upde.getUsbPipe(), ex));
    }
  }
  scalePhaser.arrive();
}
```

Phaser is one of the new thread control classes introduced in Java 7, and is ideally suited for this purpose because it allows notification of arrival from a single thread to unblock potentially multiple threads. To create a Phaser for this purpose, simply construct one with a single party like this:

```
private final Phaser scalePhaser = new Phaser(1);
```

Since there is only one registered party, the Phaser fires on each call to arrive. Then, blocking on it is as simple as calling awaitAdvance with the current phase value as shown in Listing 2-10.

Listing 2-10 *Example of waiting for a change in scale weight using a Phaser*

```
public void waitFor(DoublePredicate condition) {
  while (!condition.test(getWeight())) {
    scalePhaser.awaitAdvance(scalePhaser.getPhase());
  }
}
```

The waitFor method demonstrates the use of the DoublePredicate functional interface introduced in the Java 8 release to support lambdas. This allows it to take an arbitrary condition as a lambda expression to wait on, such as waiting for the scale to read 80 grams or more:

```
scale.waitFor(w -> w >= 80);
```

This is the basis for an improved version of the USB scale communication logic refactored into a new class called UsbScale.java. It also implements a unified Scale interface that we will use to create an alternate implementation for serial scales in Chapter 7. The full set of methods for the `Scale` interface is shown in Listing 2-11.

Listing 2-11 *Unified `Scale` interface*

```
public interface Scale {
  void connect() throws IllegalStateException;
  double getWeight();
  boolean isStable();
  void waitFor(DoublePredicate condition);
  void waitForStable(DoublePredicate condition);
  void tare() throws UnsupportedOperationException;
  void close();
}
```

There are two additional scale concepts introduced here to improve the reliability and consistency of our coffee recipe: a "stable" scale value, and a programmatic "tare." The concept of stability is important, because scales do not immediately register new weights, so the value can fluctuate quite a bit before it settles down. Some scales implement a concept of stability directly in their data reporting; however, the USB scales do not do this. As a workaround, when updating the weight we will compare the last few results to see if we have reached a steady state, as shown in Listing 2-12.

Listing 2-12 *Update of current weight value with stability calculation*

```
private void updateWeight(int newWeight) {
  boolean isStable = true;
  for (int i = 0; i < pastWeights.length - 1; i++) {
    pastWeights[i] = pastWeights[i + 1];
    if (pastWeights[i] != weight) {
      isStable = false;
    }
  }
  pastWeights[pastWeights.length - 1] = weight;
  if (weight != newWeight) {
    isStable = false;
    weight = newWeight;
  }
  stable = isStable;
}
```

This allows us to have more reliable results when executing the recipe, because we know when we hit a target value that it is no longer approaching or bouncing, but has actually stabilized. You can control the number of weights to compare for stability by the size of the `pastWeights` array. It is a trade-off between speed and accuracy, but a good number seems to be comparing two past readings against the current weight measurement:

```
private final int[] pastWeights = new int[] {-1, -1};
```

Resetting the scale value to zero or "taring" is an important part of executing our coffee recipe. Some scales allow you to send a command that programmatically tares; however, our USB scales do not, so the best we can do is to prompt the user to press the "tare" button manually. To indicate that this is not supported by our scale, we are going to reuse the built-in `UnsupportedOperationException`:

```
@Override
public void tare() {
   throw new UnsupportedOperationException();
}
```

You can download the full source code for the `Scale` and `UsbScale` classes from the following GitHub repo: https://github.com/RaspberryPiWithJava/JavaScale.

Coffee Brewing Recipe

Now that we can asynchronously communicate with a scale hooked up via USB, the next step is to build out a coffee recipe that uses our `CoffeeCalculator` and `UsbScale` classes. While you can use any coffee brewing method of your choice, I recommend trying the AeroPress brewing system. It is a simple and inexpensive coffee brewing device that also travels quite well as a portable coffee maker for on-the-go joe, as shown in Figure 2-9. The following discussion assumes you are using the AeroPress.

The way the AeroPress works is that you put your coffee grounds and a portion of the heated water into the main chamber. The extraction occurs directly in the main chamber as you stir the grounds and brew for 60 seconds. Then you insert the plunger and create a pressurized space to force the water through the filter. The resulting liquid is a concentrated form of coffee closely resembling espresso, which can then be diluted to the desired coffee strength by adding additional hot water.

FIGURE 2-9. *AeroPress coffee maker*

The AeroPress combines the benefit of uniform extraction provided by the French press with a sediment-free filtered output similar to filtered brewing. As a result, it is much less sensitive to grind size and uniformity; however, I still recommend using a high-quality conical burr grinder that will not heat up your beans. If you don't have an electric grinder already, a good start that pairs well with the travel-friendly nature of the AeroPress is to get a Japanese-made hand grinder, such as the Porlex Mini shown in Figure 2-10. Not only does it produce very fine and consistent coffee grind, but it also perfectly fits in the AeroPress chamber once the rubber is removed.

In order to support reusable recipes, we are going to build out a little bit of infrastructure first. To start with, we need a `Recipe` interface to describe how we are going to specify our AeroPress brewing method and other recipes we will create in future chapters. The `Recipe` interface shown in Listing 2-13 has four methods.

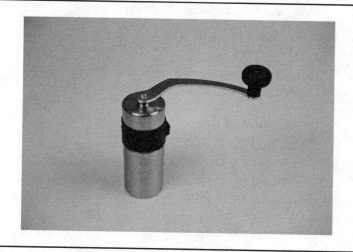

FIGURE 2-10.   *Porlex Mini travel grinder*

Listing 2-13   *Recipe interface*

```
public interface Recipe {
  String name();
  String description();
  Ingredient[] ingredients();
  Step[] steps();
}
```

The first two methods provide the name and description of the Recipe we will be making. The third method returns a list of ingredients using a wrapper class, and the final method is the actual set of steps. While it would be possible to simply write the steps as straight Java code, this allows us to later do improvements in recipe flow, such as skipping or repeating steps.

The Ingredient and Step classes are fairly straightforward, and both follow a factory pattern where they supply static methods that can be used to construct an instance of the class. In the case of ingredients, we will be specifying them by weight, making use of our CoffeeCalculator class as shown in Listing 2-14.

Listing 2-14 *Initialization of ingredients for the* `AeroPressCoffee` *recipe*

```
public AeroPressCoffee(double strength) {
  beans = Ingredient.byWeight(CoffeeCalculator.grindWeight(strength,
    CUP_SIZE), "Coffee Beans");
  brewingWater = Ingredient.byWeight(beans.getWeight() / BREW_RATIO, "Water");
  extraWater = Ingredient.byWeight(CUP_SIZE - brewingWater.getWeight(), "Water");
}
@Override
public Ingredient[] ingredients() {
  return new Ingredient[]{beans, brewingWater, extraWater};
}
```

This algorithm is designed to create a fixed volume of liquid, which is set by the CUP_SIZE constant in grams/ml, and will use the strength passed in to the constructor, which should be one of the constants defined in the `CoffeeCalculator` class for a medium, rich, or strong cup of coffee. Since we are using an AeroPress, there is an additional constant called BREW_RATIO that determines how much water we mix with the grounds initially and will affect the extraction process. If you notice that your coffee is bitter (over-extracted, too much water) or sour (under-extracted, not enough water), you can tweak this parameter to change the volume of water pressed through the grounds.

My recommended targets for these constants are as follows:

```
private static final double CUP_SIZE = 300; // grams
private static final double BREW_RATIO = .2; // beans / water
```

And finally, we come to the important part, the `AeroPressCoffee` recipe. This consists of 19 steps that walk you through the process of creating the perfect cup of java, as shown in Listing 2-15.

Listing 2-15 *List of steps for the* `AeroPressCoffee` *recipe*

```
@Override
public Step[] steps() {
  return new Step[]{
    Step.say("Add " + beans),
    Step.waitFor(beans),
    Step.say("Great, take your beans off the scale now."),
    Step.waitForClear(),
    Step.say("Put your AeroPress filled with grounds on"),
    Step.waitForContents(),
    Step.tare(),
    Step.say("Pour " + brewingWater + " at 200F"),
    Step.waitFor(brewingWater),
    Step.say("Brewing time!  Stir for 10 seconds and wait for countdown to finish."),
```

```
        Step.countdown(60),
        Step.say("Done!  Take the AeroPress off the scale before proceeding."),
        Step.waitForClear(),
        Step.say("Now press it down firmly until all the liquid is extracted.\n"
        + "After you are done, place your cup on the scale"),
        Step.waitForContents(),
        Step.tare(),
        Step.say("Now add " + extraWater),
        Step.waitFor(extraWater),
        Step.say("Enjoy your Java brew!")
    };
}
```

To give this a try yourself, download the full source code from the
following repo: https://github.com/RaspberryPiWithJava/JavaScale.

The main class is called JavaScale and executes a
CommandLineRecipeRunner that will fire off our AeroPressCoffee
recipe for a strong cup of coffee:

```
public static void main(String[] args) throws InterruptedException {
    CommandLineRecipeRunner runner = new CommandLineRecipeRunner();
    runner.runRecipe(new AeroPressCoffee(CoffeeCalculator.STRONG));
    runner.close();
}
```

Listing 2-16 shows the output of running the JavaScale application
with the default settings.

Listing 2-16   *Brewing a cup of java with the default settings*

```
Precisely brews 1 cup of coffee using an AeroPress Coffee Maker and a scale.
Add 18.6g of Coffee Beans
Great, take your beans off the scale now.
Put your AeroPress filled with grounds on
Press the 'tare' button on the scale.
Pour 93.0g of Water at 200F
Brewing time!  Stir for 10 seconds and wait for countdown to finish.
60 seconds left
...
1 second left
Done!  Take the AeroPress off the scale before proceeding.
Now press it down firmly until all the liquid is extracted.
After you are done, place your cup on the scale
Press the 'tare' button on the scale.
Now add 207.0g of Water
Enjoy your Java brew!
```

Once you have tried it with the default settings, here are some things you may want to try tweaking:

- Change the strength of the cup of coffee (REGULAR or RICH).

- Adjust the volume of coffee created (although remember that the AeroPress has a physical limit on how much liquid it can use during the extraction process).

- Fine-tune the BREW_RATIO for your bean type and preference.

I hope you have enjoyed programming your brew as much as you did drinking it! The next chapter will show you some additional recipes that you can create using the GPIO bus on the Raspberry Pi to hook up additional sensors and devices.

Commercial Licensing

The Raspberry Pi foundation does an excellent job making sure that all the software that ships is free for use in an educational or noncommercial setting. However, if you have plans to use Raspberry Pi as a commercial device, there are a few things you should be aware of.

NOTE
Please consider any advice offered here to be general guidance to use as a starting place for further research. Consult a lawyer or professional legal advisor before making any business decisions.

The Raspberry Pi Foundation licenses the hardware for personal use only. However, the Raspberry Pi Foundation has publicly stated that it is supportive of commercial use of the Raspberry Pi and only asks that you include the words "Powered by Raspberry Pi" on your packaging. The Raspberry Pi Foundation also encourages you to consider donating a portion of your profits if your commercial venture is successful, but that is up to you. Full details are available here: www.raspberrypi.org/starting-a-business-with-a-raspberry-pi/.

If you plan to build a commercial product, you may want to consider using the Raspberry Pi Compute Module. This is a full Raspberry Pi processor complete with memory and integrated storage on a board the size of a DIMM module. In fact, it uses a standard DIMM socket, making it easier to build compatible PCBs for a custom product.

Something else to be careful about is use of the Raspberry Pi logo or word mark. If you include the words "Raspberry Pi" as part of your company name, product, or logo, you could be in violation of the Raspberry Pi Foundation's trademark. Also, if you use the Raspberry Pi logo or a derivative graphic, you may also be in violation. However, there are some cases in which you can use the word mark, such as with a referential phrase like "runs on," "for use with," or "compatible with." The Raspberry Pi Foundation has put out guidelines with more details here: www.raspberrypi.org/trademark-rules/.

Also, many of the packages in the Raspbian repository are licensed on personal use terms, such as Mathematica. Before shipping a commercial product, you need to check the license on packages you plan to install to ensure that you are not in violation of the terms.

Finally, Oracle Java comes with licensing terms as well, which are fully spelled out in the Oracle Binary Code License Agreement (www.oracle.com/ technetwork/java/javase/terms/license/index.html). Oracle Java is free for development, evaluation, and for production usage on a general-purpose computer. This means if you are using the Raspberry Pi to replace a PC (for example, as a web server or desktop computer equivalent), then you don't have to pay a license. Also, if you are a developer, hobbyist, or educational institution, you don't have to worry about license fees. However, if you are building a commercial product for embedded use (such as a kiosk, game console, etc.), then you may have to pay a volume license based on the number of units you sell. The price list is publicly posted here: www.oracle .com/us/corporate/pricing/price-lists/java-embedded-price-list-1977272.pdf.

If you happen to fall into the commercial use category for Oracle Java, another option is to use OpenJDK, which is released under a fully open-source license and free for use in embedded commercial projects. The main disadvantage to OpenJDK over Oracle Java is performance. Right now OpenJDK does not support a just-in-time (JIT) compiler for Java 7 or 8, and the available JIT for Java 6 (Cacao) is significantly slower than the Oracle JIT. The other disadvantage is that you are on your own as far as support with OpenJDK, so if you have a bug or blocking issue, you will have to fix it yourself in the open-source repo. Other than that, OpenJDK can often be a good alternative to licensing Oracle Java if you do not require the performance or commercial support.

CHAPTER
3

Binary Timer

While the Raspberry Pi can be used as a miniature, general-purpose computer, its utility really shines when you take advantage of the general purpose I/O (GPIO) pins. The GPIO pins can be used to read digital signals, power small components, and talk to a variety of devices ranging from temperature sensors to accelerometers to radio frequency identification (RFID) readers.

Depending upon the model of the Raspberry Pi you are using, the number of available GPIO pins and the pin layout vary. Here is a quick summary of the differences you will find on different boards:

- **Raspberry Pi B (rev 1)**   26-pin header with 17 available GPIO pins

- **Raspberry Pi B (rev 2), A**   26-pin header with 17 available GPIO pins + 4 additional on the P5 header

- **Raspberry Pi B+, A+, 2**   40-pin header with 26 available GPIO pins

So, the number of GPIO pins available for connecting devices ranges from 17 to 26 based on the board and revision. Several of these pins are designated for special protocols such as Serial Peripheral Interface (SPI) or Inter-Integrated Circuit (I²C), although they can be used as simple digital input/output pins as well.

For the purpose of this book, Model B revision 1 boards are considered to be "legacy" and not recommended for use. The pinouts differ slightly from the revision 2 boards, requiring different pin configurations, and they lack the additional P5 header, limiting the number of usable GPIO pins. The easiest way to identify if you have a revision 1 board is to look for the absence of mounting holes.

TIP
The pins to watch out for are 3, 5, and 13 (by header order), so if you don't use these, your program will be compatible with the earliest board revisions. Also, if you use the Pi4J library's pin numbering scheme, you are insulated from GPIO pin differences on the revision 1 board.

The goal of this chapter is to learn how to use the GPIO libraries by implementing a timer that counts down in binary. This is a great way to learn how to do simple input (switches) and simple output (light emitting diodes or LEDs) using Java libraries.

Bill of Materials

To finish the project in this chapter, you will need a few items besides your Raspberry Pi. All of the items are fairly inexpensive and can be purchased online or in small electronic hobby shops that you may have in your neighborhood.

Here is the full list of everything you will need:

■ **Raspberry Pi**   Your choice of Raspberry Pi, but one of the newer models with a 40-pin header is preferred (Model B+, A+, or 2).

■ **Pi Cobbler**   This is a clever little invention by the Adafruit folks that provides an easy way to mirror the Pi GPIO header onto a breadboard for prototyping. Make sure to pick up the right one for your Pi (either 26 or 40-pin): https://www.adafruit.com/products/2029.

■ **Full-size breadboard**   Breadboards are really handy for prototyping circuits quickly and are fairly inexpensive. Adafruit carries these as well: https://www.adafruit.com/products/239.

■ **LEDs**   For output we will be using LEDs to show the count. You will need 17 total, and having a few different colors will make it easier to read the output. I ended up using three blue, six green, six yellow, and two red LEDs purchased from Adafruit: https://www.adafruit.com/products/297.

■ **Switches**   Tactile switches are a great way to take user input and very easy to wire up. A pack of colorful switches like this set from Adafruit will go a long way: https://www.adafruit.com/products/1009.

■ **Resistors**   These are handy to have around in a variety of sizes. For this project, you will need 17 identical resistors of 68Ω or larger value, so pick up a large pack of resistors like this one: www.amazon.com/480-pack-5-tolerance-resistors-Assorted-Values/dp/B000TAAIIA.

■ **Breadboard cables**   To hook up everything in this project you will need a lot of wires. If you are clever in the layout you can save a few connections, but expect to use around 30–40 wires: https://www.adafruit.com/product/153.

■ **Hookup wire (optional)**   I prefer to breadboard with short wires cut to size to keep things neat. A pack of colored wire that will last for a very long time is not expensive: https://www.adafruit.com/products/1311.

Accessing GPIO from Java

Two libraries are commonly used for accessing the GPIO pins on the Raspberry Pi: Device I/O and Pi4J. The Device I/O library, which is part of the OpenJDK project, provides a standard library for accessing I/O pins across any embedded platform, including the Raspberry Pi. The Pi4J library is an open-source library that is exclusive to the Raspberry Pi. We will make use of both of these libraries throughout the book, but here is a quick comparison of the two libraries:

Device I/O benefits:

- Supports multiple embedded boards (although presently just the Raspberry Pi)

- Portable to Java ME

- API optimized for Java 8 (lambdas, try-with-resources, and so on)

Pi4J benefits:

- Better support for different Raspberry Pi boards

- Advanced features, such as button debouncing and interrupt-based listening

- Extensible providers for add-on boards

- Direct access for faster GPIO support

The easiest way to relate the two libraries is that Device I/O is a Java standard providing baseline GPIO access across a range of embedded devices, while Pi4J is a specialized library for the Raspberry Pi with additional performance enhancements and features. If you are targeting only Raspberry Pi devices as your platform, using Pi4J makes a lot of sense. Also, presently, setting up and using the Device I/O library is a bit of a chore. However, other projects in the Java community, such as Eclipse Kura, are standardizing on it, so the Device I/O library is likely to get better over time.

This chapter presents the code for both a Device I/O version and a Pi4J version of exactly the same project. This will help you learn how to set up both libraries and also provide you with an equivalent comparison. Later chapters focus on one library or the other based on the project requirements.

While it is useful to know how to use both libraries, I don't recommend mixing them in the same project since it can be difficult to deal with conflicts between port usages across the two libraries.

Installing the Device I/O Library

Currently, the Device I/O library is not released with the version of Java on the Raspberry Pi. Also, there are no binary builds available, so you have to build the library from source. Fortunately, this is a fairly easy process and can be accomplished directly on the Raspberry Pi.

TIP

In case the availability of binaries or the build process changes after the time of this writing, you are advised to check the official OpenJDK Device I/O page and wiki at the following links:
http://openjdk.java.net/projects/dio/
https://wiki.openjdk.java.net/display/dio/Main

To start, download the source code from the OpenJDK Mercurial repository by executing the following command from an SSH prompt or the console on your Raspberry Pi:

```
sudo apt-get install mercurial
```

Next, clone the Device I/O library source code to your Raspberry Pi. The following command creates a folder called dio in your current working directory with the latest source code:

```
hg clone http://hg.openjdk.java.net/dio/dev dio
```

To build the source code, you need to run the make command on the newly downloaded code. The build script also requires a few variables to be set up so it knows where to access the Raspberry Pi native libraries and the Java 8 JDK:

```
cd dio
export PI_TOOLS=/usr
export JAVA_HOME=/usr/lib/jvm/jdk-8-oracle-arm-vfp-hflt
make
```

NOTE
*Make sure the JAVA_HOME path is correct for
your installation of Java. If you need help with
locating your JDK 8 installation directory, refer
to Chapter 2.*

Next, install it into the local Java Runtime Environment (JRE):

```
sudo cp -r build/deviceio/lib/* $JAVA_HOME/jre/lib
```

You will also need the libraries locally for your project. To do this you can use any visual Secure Copy (SCP) or Secure FTP (SFTP) client, such as Cyberduck. However, real geeks will do it from the command line (this works out of the box in OS X or Linux). Unlike the other commands, this one must be run from your desktop or laptop that is connected to your Raspberry Pi:

```
scp pi@timerpi.local:~/dio/build/deviceio/lib/ext/dio.jar dio.jar
```

NOTE
*Substitute your Pi IP address or hostname for
timerpi.local. Also, this command assumes that the
dio folder was created in your user home directory
on the Raspberry Pi. If not, adjust the path as
appropriate.*

To use the Device I/O library in your project, create a new Java project called **DioLed** in NetBeans (see Chapter 2 for more details on this) and add **dio.jar** as a compile-time library. To access the library settings, choose File | Project Properties (DioLed), click Libraries in the Categories pane, and make sure the Compile tab is selected. Then click Add JAR/Folder and choose the dio.jar file you copied over from the Raspberry Pi. The configured project is shown in Figure 3-1.

Device I/O Pin Assignments

The Java Device I/O library uses the standard GPIO port assignments as specified by the Motorola Broadcom chipset. Figure 3-2 shows a full list of all the ports, their numbers, and what their functions are for the Raspberry Pi B+, A+, and 2.

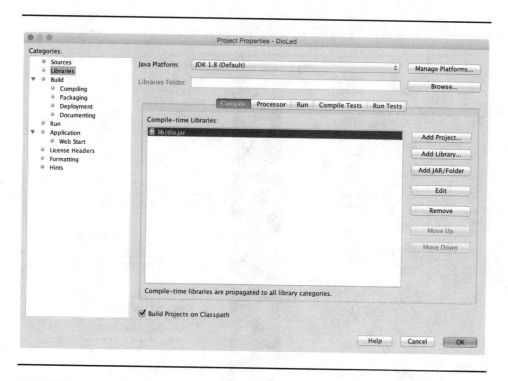

FIGURE 3-1.   *Project with correctly configured Device I/O library*

NOTE
If you have a Raspberry Pi B (revision 2) or A, the ports are exactly the same from 1 through 26, so you can use the same diagram and ignore pins 27 through 40.

In the diagram notice that the top-left pin (pin 1) has a square border. This is also the easiest way to tell the orientation of the pins on the Raspberry Pi. If you flip the board upside down, you will notice that one of the mounting holes is square, while the rest are perfectly round. This square hole is pin 1 in Figure 3-2.

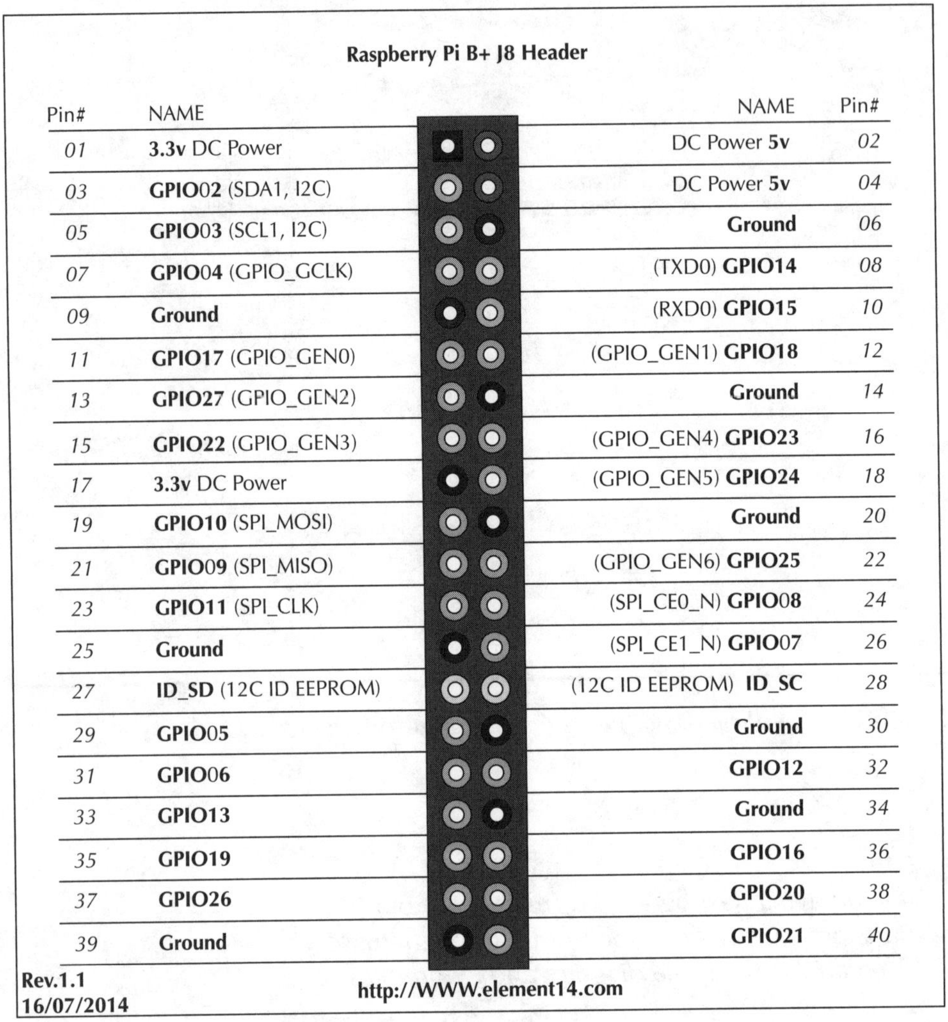

Raspberry Pi B+ J8 Header

Pin#	NAME			NAME	Pin#
01	3.3v DC Power	■ ○		DC Power 5v	02
03	GPIO02 (SDA1, I2C)	○ ○		DC Power 5v	04
05	GPIO03 (SCL1, I2C)	○ ○		Ground	06
07	GPIO04 (GPIO_GCLK)	○ ○		(TXD0) GPIO14	08
09	Ground	○ ○		(RXD0) GPIO15	10
11	GPIO17 (GPIO_GEN0)	○ ○		(GPIO_GEN1) GPIO18	12
13	GPIO27 (GPIO_GEN2)	○ ●		Ground	14
15	GPIO22 (GPIO_GEN3)	○ ○		(GPIO_GEN4) GPIO23	16
17	3.3v DC Power	● ○		(GPIO_GEN5) GPIO24	18
19	GPIO10 (SPI_MOSI)	○ ●		Ground	20
21	GPIO09 (SPI_MISO)	○ ○		(GPIO_GEN6) GPIO25	22
23	GPIO11 (SPI_CLK)	○ ○		(SPI_CE0_N) GPIO08	24
25	Ground	● ○		(SPI_CE1_N) GPIO07	26
27	ID_SD (I2C ID EEPROM)	○ ○		(I2C ID EEPROM) ID_SC	28
29	GPIO05	○ ●		Ground	30
31	GPIO06	○ ○		GPIO12	32
33	GPIO13	○ ○		Ground	34
35	GPIO19	○ ○		GPIO16	36
37	GPIO26	○ ○		GPIO20	38
39	Ground	● ○		GPIO21	40

Rev.1.1
16/07/2014

http://WWW.element14.com

FIGURE 3-2. *GPIO ports for the Raspberry Pi B+, A+, and 2 (Diagram by Christopher G. Stanton; source: www.element14.com/raspberrypi.)*

Even though there are 40 pins total, several of them are not usable for GPIO since they supply power (3.3v/5v) or ground.

Most of the remaining pins can be used for GPIO, but may require some configuration before they are accessible, as noted in the following list.

- **Pins 3 and 5 are for I²C** By default, the I²C bus is disabled and these pins can be used for GPIO. However, these have hard-wired internal 1.8kΩ pull-up resistors to 3.3V.

- **Pins 8 and 10 are for Serial UART** These pins are reserved for console serial communication by default, which needs to be disabled if you want to use them for GPIO or to connect to a serial device.

- **Pins 19, 21, 23, 24, and 26 are for SPI** This is another communication bus for devices that is disabled by default, so these pins can be used for GPIO.

- **Pins 27 and 28 are for EEPROM** These pins are designed for identifying add-on boards stacked on top of the Raspberry Pi and can't be used for GPIO.

Also, regarding pin numbering, it is important to note that there are several different ways to refer to the same GPIO pins, which can be very confusing:

- **Header pin order** Sometimes the location of the pin on the P5 header is referenced. This is handy to know when connecting devices, but is rarely the number your program will use.

- **Broadcom GPIO pin number** This is the most common numbering scheme, which matches the GPIO pinouts. However, since this depends on the wiring on the Raspberry Pi, the physical pin locations may change (which happened between revisions 1 and 2 of the Model B board).

- **Pi4J/WiringPi numbers** To try to standardize on a simpler numbering scheme, the Pi4J and WiringPi libraries define an alternate set of numbers that is constant between different board revisions.

In summary, know your pin assignments and be careful which numbering standard you are using. Since there is no overcurrent protection on the Pi, hooking up the wrong GPIO pins in your circuit can be disastrous, so wire once and check twice.

What Is the Worst You Can Do to Your Raspberry Pi?

Raspberry Pis are actually pretty reliable, and despite my best efforts going through around 100 Raspberry Pis, I have only had a couple go bad. Here are a few things that I wouldn't recommend doing, though none of them damaged my hardware:

- **Ejecting the SD card while it is running** This immediately unmounts your entire filesystem and can cause minor filesystem corruption. Usually recoverable.

- **Shorting 3V to ground** Not such a good idea, but about all it does is overload and reset your Pi.

- **Full immersion in coffee** I had the good sense to do this when it was powered off, and to rinse it in distilled water and fully dry it before turning it back on. It is still working to this day.

Device I/O Library LED Test

To demonstrate how to use the Device I/O library for output, we are going to blink a light-emitting diode (LED). This is a great way to test out your GPIO pins since it is a visible device that can be powered by the current from the pins.

Connecting an LED to the Raspberry Pi GPIO pins just requires a few jumper cables. To prevent the LED from being overloaded, we also need a resistor that we can hook up in serial.

To choose an appropriate resistor, you will need to know the voltage drop and target current of your LED. This depends on the manufacturer, type, and even the color of your LED. However, 99 percent of the LEDs you will encounter in hobby electronics can take a 20mA current with no problem, and will have a forward voltage drop varying from 2V to 3V.

Since the GPIO pins operate at 3.3V, you can calculate the maximum resistance using Ohm's law: voltage (V) = current (I) × resistance (R). Here is an example based on the worst-case scenario of a 2V forward voltage and a 20mA current limit:

$$V = I \times R$$
$$R = V / I$$
$$R = (3.3V - 2V) / .02A$$
$$R = 65\Omega$$

Therefore, you should be pretty safe using a common 68Ω resistor for most LEDs plugged into the Raspberry Pi. It is not unusual to use larger resistors to reduce power consumption in embedded projects, so feel free to use bigger ones. However, remember that this will reduce the brightness of your LEDs.

TIP

Some LEDs are more resilient to current spikes than others, and will work fine when connected directly. However, even if the LED works, connecting it directly is a great way to shorten its life, so it is always recommended to pair your LED with a suitable resistor.

You can tell the value of a resistor by the colored bands and a lookup chart. Most resistors have four to five bands, with the three to four bands closest together being the actual resistance value, and the final band being the tolerance. For the 68Ω resistor we calculated, the colors would be blue, gray, black. You could get up to a 5 percent tolerance resistor and still be fine, which would be a fourth, gold band. To quickly look up resistors by color code, the easiest way is to use a web calculator like this one from DigiKey: www.digikey.com/en/resources/conversion-calculators/conversion-calculator-resistor-color-code-4-band.

For our circuit diagrams in this book, we are going to be using the open-source Fritzing layout application (http://fritzing.org/). This tool was originally designed by the Interaction Design Lab at the University of Applied Sciences Potsdam, Germany, and is a great way to do your own circuit designs with a huge library of components from different online vendors, as well as the ability to design simple printed circuit boards (PCBs) for fabrication. Figure 3-3 shows a simple circuit diagram built using the Fritzing layout application.

This is a simple circuit with a resistor, LED, and some wires. Note that LEDs have a positive side and a negative side, usually indicated by the positive lead (the anode) being slightly longer than the negative lead (the cathode). If you hook up the LED backward, it won't damage it, but it won't light up either, so make sure that you hook up the longer end to the GPIO pin.

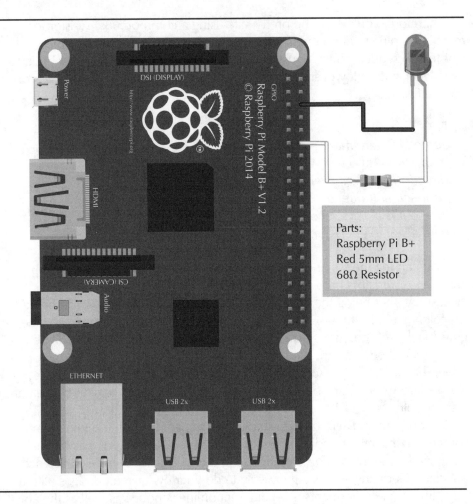

FIGURE 3-3. *Circuit diagram for a single LED*

To turn this on and off with the Device I/O library, we need to create three files:

- **java.policy**   The policy file that grants permissions for us to use GPIO
- **dio.properties**   Defines the pin setup for our application
- **LedDio.java**   Our main Java code that will blink the LED

The policy file is really a legacy from the Java ME Device I/O API and is intended for highly restricted environments where you want to limit the access to peripherals, such as cell phones. For applications running on small, embedded systems like the Raspberry Pi, you will most often have control of the entire embedded device and not be competing with other applications installed by end users, so a permissive policy file is fine. Listing 3-1 is a great boilerplate permissions file to use for all your projects.

Listing 3-1 *Highly permissive policy file for the Device I/O library*

```
// grant all permissions for the DIO framework
grant {
    permission jdk.dio.DeviceMgmtPermission "*:*", "open";
    permission jdk.dio.gpio.GPIOPinPermission "*:*", "open,setdirection";
    permission jdk.dio.gpio.GPIOPortPermission "*:*";
    permission jdk.dio.i2cbus.I2CPermission "*:*";
    permission jdk.dio.spibus.SPIPermission "*:*";
    permission jdk.dio.uart.UARTPermission "*:*";
};
```

The pin configuration file requires a little bit more customization since you will often want to change which pins are used for input/output and possibly add or remove features like serial, I²C, and SPI. You can often take an existing pin configuration file and customize it or pare it down to the features you need. For the simplest cases, it is easy enough to create one from scratch as well. Listing 3-2 shows a single file that will open a single pin for output.

Listing 3-2 *Simple device I/O properties file to open Pin 18 for digital output*

```
gpio.GPIOPin = initValue:0, deviceNumber:0, direction:1, mode:4,
trigger:3, predefined:true
1 = deviceType: gpio.GPIOPin, pinNumber:18
```

The first line defines the defaults for the `gpio.GPIOPin` device type. Unfortunately, you have to know what the integer values are for different constants to figure this out—something that is noticeably absent from the Device I/O Javadocs as well. However, I did the hard work and mined the constants out of the code to create Listing 3-3, so you know all the possible values for direction, mode, and trigger.

Listing 3-3 *Possible constants for direction (dir), mode, and trigger in Device I/O property files*

```
DIR_BOTH_INIT_INPUT = 2;
DIR_BOTH_INIT_OUTPUT = 3;
DIR_INPUT_ONLY = 0;
DIR_OUTPUT_ONLY = 1;
MODE_INPUT_PULL_DOWN = 2;
MODE_INPUT_PULL_UP = 1;
MODE_OUTPUT_OPEN_DRAIN = 8;
MODE_OUTPUT_PUSH_PULL = 4;
TRIGGER_BOTH_EDGES = 3;
TRIGGER_BOTH_LEVELS = 6;
TRIGGER_FALLING_EDGE = 1;
TRIGGER_HIGH_LEVEL = 4;
TRIGGER_LOW_LEVEL = 5;
TRIGGER_NONE = 0;
TRIGGER_RISING_EDGE = 2;
```

There is also a bit of ceremony around how you need to configure your NetBeans project to properly deploy the Device I/O configuration files and refer to them from the run command. To make sure your property and permission files are copied to the output directory, you need to add an extra build post-compile step to your NetBeans build.xml file as shown in Listing 3-4.

Listing 3-4 *NetBeans post-compile step to copy over resources in the config directory*

```
<target name="-post-jar">
    <copy todir="${dist.jar.dir}">
        <fileset dir="config" includes="**"/>
    </copy>
</target>
```

The ant target assumes that both your java.policy and dio.properties files are in a folder called config under the project root.

Once these files are configured to copy over to the build folder after compilation, you also need to modify the `java run` command to make use of them. To do this, open the Project Properties dialog, click Run in the Categories pane, and enter the following VM Options:

```
-Djdk.dio.registry=dist/dio.properties -Djava.security.policy=dist/java.policy
```

TIP
Unlike in the previous chapter where we were accessing native USB libraries, we don't need to run the application as the root user by adding "sudo" as an exec prefix. However, if you already have your remote Java platform configured this way, it is fine to run it as root as well.

The last step is to write the code that will turn on and off the LED. Ironically, this is the simplest and shortest part of the process, and can be accomplished in only a few lines of code. Listing 3-5 shows a sample program that will turn the LED on and off five times, one cycle per second.

Listing 3-5 *Example of using Device I/O to blink an LED*

```
public class DioLed {
  public static void main(String[] args) throws IOException, InterruptedException {
    try (GPIOPin led = DeviceManager.open(1);) {
      for (int i = 0; i < 10; i++) {
        led.setValue(i % 2 == 0);
        Thread.sleep(500);
      }
    }
  }
}
```

Notice that this code is fairly clean and succinct. It uses a `try-with-resources` block to open the `GPIOPin` as well as automatically close it at the end. The function for setting the LED value is very straightforward as well. One important thing to note is that the GPIO number referenced in the `open` method is the ID in our dio.properties file, not the Broadcom GPIO number!

Using Pi4J

The Pi4J library is written by Robert Savage and based on the very widely used WiringPi C library. Compared to the Device I/O library, Pi4J has lots of features and is very easy to get started with.

To use Pi4J you just require one JAR file (`pi4j-core.jar`)—no permissions, no property files, no custom JVM arguments. However, you do require root access (which you learned how to set up in NetBeans in Chapter 2).

NOTE
Pi4J can use Sysfs GPIO access like the Device I/O library (see the "GPIO Performance Hacking" section at the end of this chapter for details). However, this is harder to set up and takes a big performance hit, so I recommend sticking with the default /dev/mem implementation.

Pi4J Pin Assignments

By default, Pi4J uses the WiringPi pin assignments. The advantage of these are that they are sequential and in the same location from revision to revision of the Raspberry Pi boards. In practice this only matters between revisions 1 and 2 of the Raspberry Pi B, because the Raspberry Pi Foundation has standardized on the main header pin layout for all subsequent boards, opting to add more pins to the header instead. Figure 3-4 shows the pin assignments to use with Pi4J.

Pi4J also has the option to initialize pin assignments to the Broadcom GPIO pin numbering. However, I don't recommend changing this, since it will confuse others who are familiar with the Pi4J library and assume certain pin assignments. The only reasons you may want to do this is if you need to run as non-root (in which case Sysfs access is by Broadcom numbering) or if you are running mixed Device I/O and Pi4J code.

Pi4J LED Test

To demonstrate the usage of the Pi4J library, we are going to recode exactly the same LED test using the Pi4J library instead. However, the setup of Pi4J is much simpler and the number of changes is minimal, so this will be a breeze!

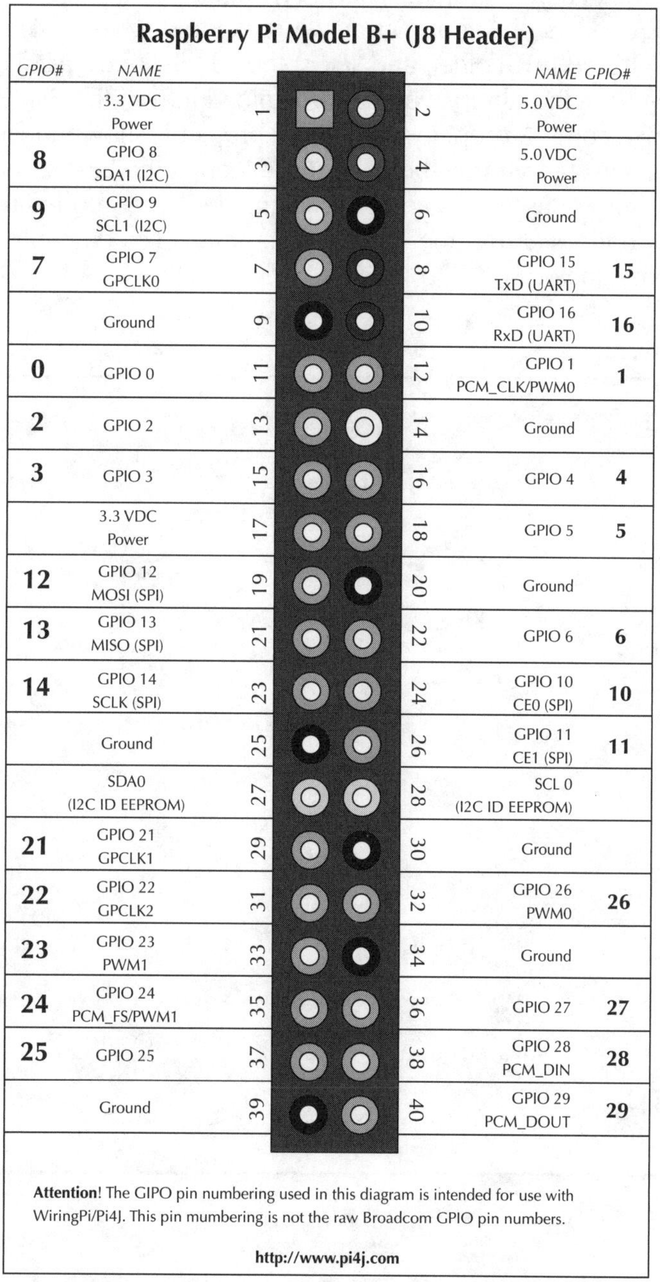

Raspberry Pi Model B+ (J8 Header)

GPIO#	NAME	#	#	NAME	GPIO#
	3.3 VDC Power	1	2	5.0 VDC Power	
8	GPIO 8 SDA1 (I2C)	3	4	5.0 VDC Power	
9	GPIO 9 SCL1 (I2C)	5	6	Ground	
7	GPIO 7 GPCLK0	7	8	GPIO 15 TxD (UART)	15
	Ground	9	10	GPIO 16 RxD (UART)	16
0	GPIO 0	11	12	GPIO 1 PCM_CLK/PWM0	1
2	GPIO 2	13	14	Ground	
3	GPIO 3	15	16	GPIO 4	4
	3.3 VDC Power	17	18	GPIO 5	5
12	GPIO 12 MOSI (SPI)	19	20	Ground	
13	GPIO 13 MISO (SPI)	21	22	GPIO 6	6
14	GPIO 14 SCLK (SPI)	23	24	GPIO 10 CE0 (SPI)	10
	Ground	25	26	GPIO 11 CE1 (SPI)	11
	SDA0 (I2C ID EEPROM)	27	28	SCL 0 (I2C ID EEPROM)	
21	GPIO 21 GPCLK1	29	30	Ground	
22	GPIO 22 GPCLK2	31	32	GPIO 26 PWM0	26
23	GPIO 23 PWM1	33	34	Ground	
24	GPIO 24 PCM_FS/PWM1	35	36	GPIO 27	27
25	GPIO 25	37	38	GPIO 28 PCM_DIN	28
	Ground	39	40	GPIO 29 PCM_DOUT	29

Attention! The GIPO pin numbering used in this diagram is intended for use with WiringPi/Pi4J. This pin mumbering is not the raw Broadcom GPIO pin numbers.

http://www.pi4j.com

FIGURE 3-4. *Pin assignments for the Pi4J library (Diagram by Robert Savage; source: pi4j.com/pins/model-b-plus.html.)*

To start, create a new project called **Pi4JLed** as a Java project type. Open the Project Properties dialog of your new project and go to the Libraries category. Click Add JAR/Folder, and select the `pi4j-core.jar` file. If you don't already have this library, you can download it from the Pi4J Project site here: http://pi4j.com/. A properly configured project is shown in Figure 3-5.

Now you can start writing the code for triggering the LED. Listing 3-6 shows the same example with an LED blinking five times, coded using Pi4J libraries. The code is almost the same, but has a few key differences. How many of them can you spot?

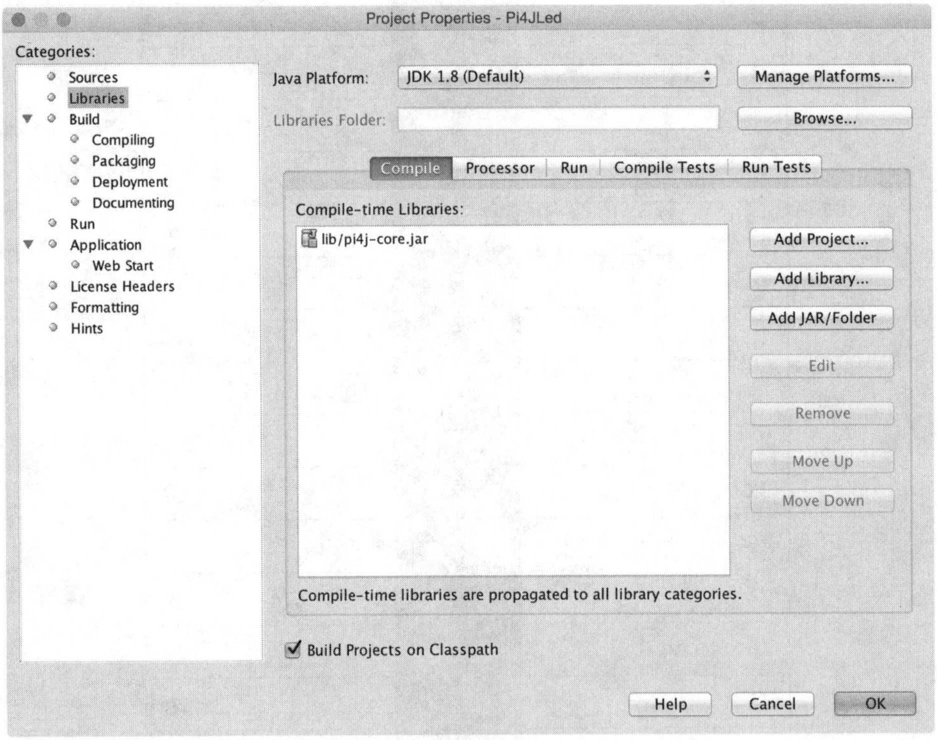

FIGURE 3-5. *Properly configured Pi4J project*

Listing 3-6   *Pi4J version of the blinking LED code*

```
public class Pi4JLed {
  public static void main(String[] args) {
    GpioController gpio = GpioFactory.getInstance();
    GpioPinDigitalOutput led = gpio.provisionDigitalOutputPin(RaspiPin.GPIO_01);
    for (int i = 0; i < 10; i++) {
      led.setState(i % 2 == 0);
      Gpio.delay(500);
    }
    gpio.shutdown();
  }
}
```

Here are some of the differences that you should take note of:

■   There is no `try` block, because Pi4J doesn't support the `AutoClosable` interface for use with `try-with-resources`. However, it does register shutdown hooks for you, so you can be lazy and let it do the work for you.

■   Pi4J requires initialization before the use of the first pin. Shutdown is optional, but recommended if you don't want the system to wait for threads to time out, which can take up to 30 seconds.

■   There are no exceptions in the Pi4J version! Pi4J doesn't throw `IOExceptions` that we have no idea how to recover from (thankfully!) Also, rather than using `Thread.sleep`, there are some nice convenience methods for this on the Pi4J GPIO class.

■   The GPIO port is the same. Well, this is not a difference, but it is a very important similarity by coincidence. We are referring to Broadcom GPIO port 18 in both cases. This maps to WiringPi port 1 (per the diagram in the previous section), and we also happen to have slotted it into configuration 1 in the dio.properties file. However, don't rely on ports being the same in general.

And there you have it. In a single section you were able to replicate the same LED blinking code that took three sections of this chapter to explain using the Device I/O library. Now we will move on to a more realistic example making use of more of the GPIO capabilities of the Raspberry Pi.

Counting Down in Binary

The simplest and least expensive device to hook up to GPIO pins on a Raspberry Pi is an LED. In this project we are going to hook up a whole bunch of LEDs to create a binary clock that ticks down from our target time to 0. Since most time is represented using hours, minutes, and seconds in base-10, a binary representation requires a little bit of conversion that can be done in several different ways, so we'll tackle that topic first.

Implementing a Binary Timer

This section presents three different ways to implement a binary timer or clock, all of which have advantages and disadvantages.

Binary Coding of Sexagesimal Digits

The current time system of hours, minutes, and seconds dates back to the ancient Sumerians in 3rd millennium B.C. They had a numerical system based on 60, which is a convenient factor to use for angles and fractions since it is evenly divisible by so many factors (http://en.wikipedia.org/wiki/Sexagesimal). The same is true of time, where hours and minutes are evenly subdivided into halves, thirds, quarters, and even sixths. The subdivision of a day into 24 hours doesn't follow this rule, but it is thought to have originated from either the annual lunar cycle or early finger counting using the 12 bone joints. Since time was originally subdivided using sundials and constellations, dividing the light and dark portions of the day into 12 parts led to a 24-hour day (www.scientificamerican.com/article/experts-time-division-days-hours-minutes/).

Simple binary encoding of the digits on a digital clock is the most common way of implementing binary clocks, because it is fairly easy to read. You only need to know your binary digits up to 9 and can simply convert in your head to sexagesimal hours/minutes/seconds. However, this lacks true "geekiness" since you are re-encoding a base-10 representation of a base-60 subdivision. An example of a clock using a binary encoding of sexagesimal digits is shown in Figure 3-6.

A truer interpretation of binary sexagesimal encoding would be to encode each of the time units as its own six-digit binary number, as shown in Figure 3-7.

However, this makes it much more difficult to read, and still does not do away with the historic baggage of representing time in sexagesimal divisions.

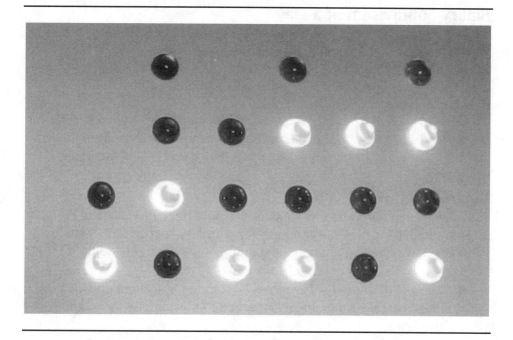

FIGURE 3-6. *Example of a binary clock showing the time 12:15:45*

FIGURE 3-7. *Example of a binary clock circuit showing the time 13:49:37 ("Digiclock cropped" by Zachzink – own work. Licensed under CC BY 3.0 via Wikimedia Commons; http://commons.wikimedia.org/wiki/File:Digiclock_cropped.png#/media/File:Digiclock_cropped.png.)*

Binary Subdivision of a Day

A more accurate interpretation of binary time would be to simply subdivide the day in halves until you reach a suitable time unit. By dividing a day into 65,536 units (2 to the 16th power), you get a unit that is slightly larger than 1 second (1.318359375 seconds). An example of a binary day clock is shown in Figure 3-8.

If the earth were ruled by computers, this is the system we would all be using! However, this subdivision turns out to be impractical for most timing purposes that standardize on the second as the core unit of time.

Binary Multiples of a Second

The next level of hardcore time geekiness would be to question the basic assumption that a day is a useful basis for a time system. In fact, there are a lot of issues with basing time on the rotation of the earth, including

■ *The length of days varies throughout the year.* Hence, odd systems like daylight saving time (DST) are used to shift time to match the sunrise.

■ *The number of days per year varies.* Leap years attempt to account for this by adding an extra day every four years, but even this is inaccurate, so every 400 years a leap day has to be removed (http://en.wikipedia.org/wiki/Leap_year).

FIGURE 3-8. *The current time in binary subdivisions of a day, from www.abulsme.com/binarytime/*

■ *The length of a year is slowly increasing!* Through astronomical observations in the 19th and 20th centuries, scientists have discovered that the solar year is not consistent, and on average is slowly lengthening (http://en.wikipedia.org/wiki/Second).

For the preceding reasons, the International System of Units (SI) in 1967 defined the unit for a second as "...the duration of 9 192 631 770 periods of the radiation corresponding to the transition between the two hyperfine levels of the ground state of the caesium 133 atom." Reference: *SI Brochure*, 8th edition, "Unit of time (second)" (www.bipm.org/en/publications/si-brochure/second.html).

If the earth were populated by alien colonists, this is the sort of time system they would most likely employ (with a different arbitrary constant based on their home planet). Anchoring our binary counting algorithm on an atomic reaction also is the highest level of geekiness attainable, so we are going to go with this as the baseline. It also happens to be practical since stopwatches and timers are typically based on seconds.

To make this possible, we are going to set up a multicolor LED display arranged as follows:

■ **2 red LEDs** 4096–16,383 seconds [1.14 to 4.55 hours]

■ **6 yellow LEDs** 64–4095 seconds [1.07 to 68.25 minutes]

■ **6 green LEDs** 0–63 seconds

■ **3 blue LEDs** 0.125–0.875 subseconds

So with the baseline model of the Raspberry Pi (Model B revision 1), which only has 17 GPIO pins, we can represent quite a reasonable range of time for the purposes of our timer (4.5 hours with 0.125-second precision). In practice, you will probably have at least a Model B revision 2 with 21 pins available or, more likely, one of the new A+, B+, or 2 models with a full 26 GPIO pins. Finally, the color-coding is a helpful guide to approximate remaining time in hours or minutes for large values.

Wiring the Breadboard

Using a breadboard is a great way to start with your embedded designs and projects, because it allows you to quickly prototype different ideas. Unlike soldering components or designing printed circuit boards, solderless breadboards are very easy to change and tweak as you are in the prototyping phase of the project. Also, it is fairly easy to transfer your breadboard design into a more permanent format using a breadboard form-factor prototype board.

Breadboards come in a wide variety of sizes, but they all share similar properties. The holes are a standard size, allowing for 21–26 AWG wire or pins to be used, as is the spacing, which allows for common components to be used on any breadboard. Also, the holes are electrically connected in rows and columns, allowing you to make connections between components with a minimal number of hookup wires. Figure 3-9 shows how the holes are wired on a full-size breadboard.

The pair of horizontal rails on the top and bottom is electrically connected, and marked for ground and power, which is a common requirement on wiring designs. The center of the board is wired vertically with groups of five holes connected electronically and separated by the center horizontal line. This makes it possible for a square component with four pins (such as a button) to straddle the center of the breadboard and have each of its leads on a different pin grouping.

Button Pin Assignments

Speaking of buttons, we are going to use a common type of button called a momentary switch in this project. Momentary switches have four terminals that are electrically connected in pairs. The adjacent terminals are permanently connected, while the opposing terminals are only connected

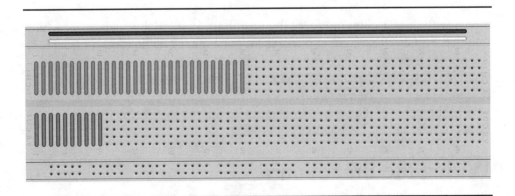

FIGURE 3-9. *Wiring on a full-size breadboard*

when the switch is depressed. To identify which terminals the switch controls, they are typically numbered on the back with 1 through 4, where leads 1 and 2 are permanently connected, as are leads 3 and 4. The circuit diagram for this, as well as some examples of correct button wirings, is shown in Figure 3-10.

Wiring diagonally across the button is always safe. Also, switches typically have bumps in the bottom so that they will only fit in the center rails in one direction, and in this orientation it is safe to wire across pins on the same side of the breadboard. In contrast, if you wired up components across pins 1 and 2 on the left side in Figure 3-10, it would cause a short. This would be the same as if the button were held down permanently, which would defeat the purpose of wiring in a button since it would always appear to be on.

Completing the Wiring

Now that you know how to wire up LEDs and buttons, we are going to complete the wiring so that we have all 17 LEDs for our time and four control buttons hooked up to individual GPIO pins. The wiring diagrams and pin assignments in this example assume that you have one of the newer Raspberry Pi boards, such as the B+, A+, or 2.

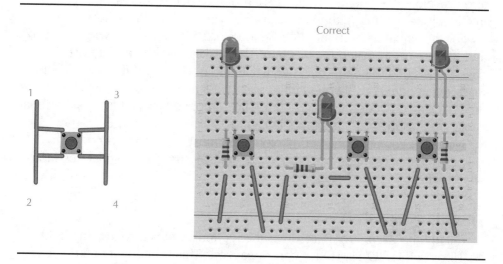

FIGURE 3-10. *Typical button connections and examples of correct wiring*

NOTE
If you have a Raspberry Pi B revision 2, or Raspberry Pi A, then you can still accomplish this exercise; however, you will need to supplement pins on the main header with ones on the P5 pinout. This is directly next to the P1 header and contains eight pins (in two rows of four) that you will need to solder a header onto.

We will also be making use of a Raspberry Pi Cobbler from Adafruit. This is a handy device that has a small PCB with labeled headers for all of the GPIO pins. On one side is a header that is a perfect fit for a serial cable you can use to connect to the Raspberry Pi, and on the other side are headers that are perfectly spaced to slide into a breadboard when straddling the center gap. The Pi Cobbler comes in two flavors, a B/A version with 26 pins and a B+/A+/2 version with 40 pins, so make sure to get the right one for your board.

To make it easier to follow along on the wiring, Figures 3-11 and 3-12 show a Fritzing breadboard diagram and a photo of a completed breadboard, respectively. The Fritzing diagram in Figure 3-11 shows the placement of LEDs and resistors as well as the electrical connections for my prototype. You can also download the Fritzing model as part of the source code for this chapter in GitHub here: https://github.com/RaspberryPiWithJava/BinaryTimer.

For the actual breadboard, I chose to use 22 AWG hookup wire cut to size and with colors to match the diagram. This makes it a little easier to see the connections on the board, but is equivalent to using simple jumper wires to make the connections if you want to spend less time stripping wires and more time hacking on your timer algorithm. The completed project (minus the serial cable and Raspberry Pi) is shown in Figure 3-12.

Now that you are done wiring, you are almost ready to start coding. However, we have made use of a couple special-purpose pins that need to be disabled first.

Disabling Serial

By default the Raspberry Pi reserves the Rx and Tx pins (Broadcom GPIO 14/15 or Pi4J GPIO 15/16) for console access. This is handy if you don't have a display to hook up to the Raspberry Pi for troubleshooting, but our project uses a lot of pins, so we need every available GPIO!

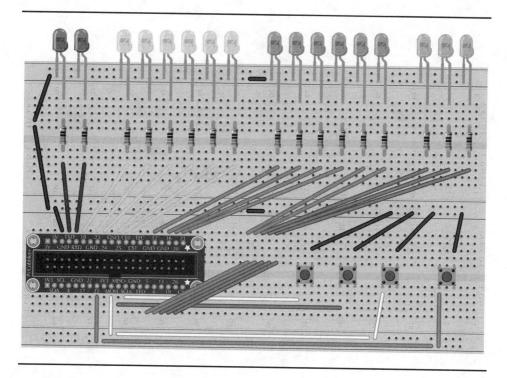

FIGURE 3-11.   *Fritzing model for the binary timer LCD project*

To free up the serial pins, you can disable the serial console from the raspi-config utility via SSH. Once you have logged in to the Raspberry Pi using the terminal or PuTTY, simply type

```
sudo raspi-config
```

From the menu, choose 8 Advanced Options and then the submenu A8 Serial, as shown in Figure 3-13.

After finishing the configuration changes, reboot the Raspberry Pi using the following command:

```
sudo shutdown -r now
```

Now you are ready to start coding against all the GPIO pins, including the special RX/TX pins normally reserved for the serial console.

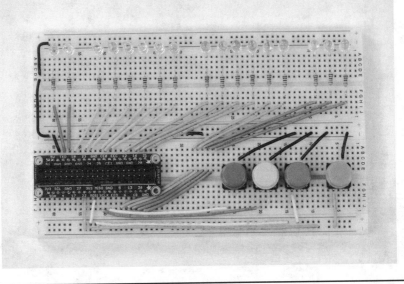

FIGURE 3-12. *Completed wiring for the binary timer using two full-size breadboards*

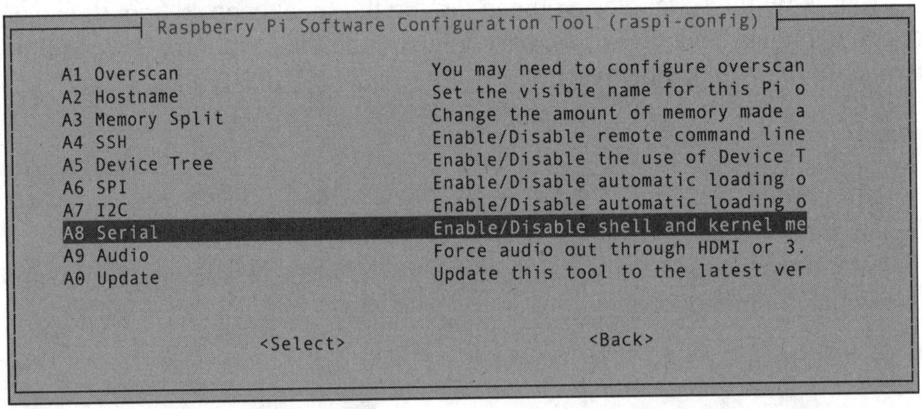

```
┌───────┤ Raspberry Pi Software Configuration Tool (raspi-config) ├───────┐
│                                                                          │
│   A1 Overscan              You may need to configure overscan            │
│   A2 Hostname              Set the visible name for this Pi o            │
│   A3 Memory Split          Change the amount of memory made a            │
│   A4 SSH                   Enable/Disable remote command line            │
│   A5 Device Tree           Enable/Disable the use of Device T            │
│   A6 SPI                   Enable/Disable automatic loading o            │
│   A7 I2C                   Enable/Disable automatic loading o            │
│   A8 Serial                Enable/Disable shell and kernel me            │
│   A9 Audio                 Force audio out through HDMI or 3.            │
│   A0 Update                Update this tool to the latest ver            │
│                                                                          │
│                  <Select>                        <Back>                  │
│                                                                          │
└──────────────────────────────────────────────────────────────────────────┘
```

FIGURE 3-13. `Raspi-config` *menu for disabling the serial console on the Raspberry Pi*

Binary Timer Algorithm

Now we are ready to start on the main coding of this project. Two full implementations using the Device I/O library and Pi4J are available in the chapter GitHub repo here: https://github.com/RaspberryPiWithJava/ BinaryTimer. However, there is not all that much code, with both implementations coming in well below 200 lines including imports and comments.

The run routine breaks the program down into four main sections, which we will tackle in succession:

```
public void run() {
    initPins();
    addListeners();
    updateLeds();
    runClock();
}
```

Initializing GPIO

Initialization in the Device I/O libraries and Pi4J is similar to how we approached it earlier in the chapter when setting up LEDs. The main difference is the sheer volume of input and output pins we need to configure (21 in total).

The Device I/O library gives us a convenient way to break this out as a separate property file with all the configuration abstracted from the code. The full listing of the dio.properties file with pins to match our Fritzing wiring diagram is shown in Listing 3-7.

Listing 3-7 *Device I/O property file with input and output pins configured for the binary timer*

```
gpio.GPIOPin = initValue:0, deviceNumber:0, direction:1, mode:4, ↵
trigger:3, predefined:true
# LEDs:
1 = deviceType: gpio.GPIOPin, pinNumber:14
2 = deviceType: gpio.GPIOPin, pinNumber:15
3 = deviceType: gpio.GPIOPin, pinNumber:18
4 = deviceType: gpio.GPIOPin, pinNumber:23
5 = deviceType: gpio.GPIOPin, pinNumber:24
6 = deviceType: gpio.GPIOPin, pinNumber:25
7 = deviceType: gpio.GPIOPin, pinNumber:08
8 = deviceType: gpio.GPIOPin, pinNumber:07
```

```
 9 = deviceType: gpio.GPIOPin, pinNumber:12
10 = deviceType: gpio.GPIOPin, pinNumber:16
11 = deviceType: gpio.GPIOPin, pinNumber:20
12 = deviceType: gpio.GPIOPin, pinNumber:21
13 = deviceType: gpio.GPIOPin, pinNumber:05
14 = deviceType: gpio.GPIOPin, pinNumber:06
15 = deviceType: gpio.GPIOPin, pinNumber:13
16 = deviceType: gpio.GPIOPin, pinNumber:19
17 = deviceType: gpio.GPIOPin, pinNumber:26
# Buttons:
18 = deviceType: gpio.GPIOPin, pinNumber:11, direction:0, mode:1
19 = deviceType: gpio.GPIOPin, pinNumber:09, direction:0, mode:1
20 = deviceType: gpio.GPIOPin, pinNumber:10, direction:0, mode:1
21 = deviceType: gpio.GPIOPin, pinNumber:22, direction:0, mode:1
```

The only difference in the input and output pins is that the output pins override the direction to be 0 (DIR_INPUT_ONLY) and the mode to be 1 (MODE_INPUT_PULL_UP).

 TIP
The reason why we are using pull-up resistors is so that the pin will have a value of 1 until we press it, which connects it to ground (0). Even though the logic is inverted (button pressed is 0), this is the preferred way to wire up buttons, because it reduces power consumption when the switch is active, which is important in battery-powered projects.

The setup for Pi4J is similar, but with the WiringPi pin numbers instead of the Broadcom GPIO numbers. Also, we have to set it up in code with a few constant arrays, which is less code separation but has the advantage of giving us code completion and type safety, as shown in Listing 3-8.

Listing 3-8 *Constant setup for Pi4J GPIO inputs and outputs*

```
private static final Pin[] LED_PINS = {
  RaspiPin.GPIO_15,
  RaspiPin.GPIO_16,
  RaspiPin.GPIO_01,
  RaspiPin.GPIO_04,
  RaspiPin.GPIO_05,
  RaspiPin.GPIO_06,
```

```
    RaspiPin.GPIO_10,
    RaspiPin.GPIO_11,
    RaspiPin.GPIO_26,
    RaspiPin.GPIO_27,
    RaspiPin.GPIO_28,
    RaspiPin.GPIO_29,
    RaspiPin.GPIO_21,
    RaspiPin.GPIO_22,
    RaspiPin.GPIO_23,
    RaspiPin.GPIO_24,
    RaspiPin.GPIO_25
};

private static final Pin[] BUTTON_PINS = {
    RaspiPin.GPIO_14,
    RaspiPin.GPIO_13,
    RaspiPin.GPIO_12,
    RaspiPin.GPIO_03
};
```

Once all of the pin configuration is set up, the actual initialization step in the code is quite straightforward. Listing 3-9 shows the `initPins` implementation for Pi4J, which is very similar to the Device I/O code.

Listing 3-9   *Binary timer pin initialization for Pi4J*

```
private void initPins() {
  gpio = GpioFactory.getInstance();
  for (int i = 0; i < 17; i++) {
    leds[i] = gpio.provisionDigitalOutputPin(LED_PINS[i]);
  }
  for (int i = 0; i < 4; i++) {
    buttons[i] = gpio.provisionDigitalInputPin(BUTTON_PINS[i],
PinPullResistance.PULL_UP);
  }
}
```

Updating the LEDs
Once the pins are configured, setting the LEDs is as simple as running through the current time and setting each pin to the bit value for its respective place. To handle the subsecond divisions, we simply make the lowest bit the 1's place for the timer. The algorithm for updating the LEDs using the Pi4J library is shown in Listing 3-10.

Listing 3-10 *Code for updating the LEDs using Pi4J*

```
private void updateLeds() {
  for (int i = 0; i < 17; i++) {
    GpioPinDigitalOutput pin = leds[16 - i];
    boolean newValue = (counter >> i & 0x1) != 0;
    if (pin.getState().isHigh() != newValue) {
      pin.setState(newValue);
    }
  }
}
```

Since we changed the counter to reflect three subsecond places, rather than updating once every second, it needs to tick once every 1/8 second. This means that we will get a new LED combination every 125 milliseconds.

By using a ScheduledExecutorService, we can ensure that the LED update function will be called at a fixed interval. It is also smart enough to ignore the run time of the task passed in, which will allow us to keep an accurate countdown timer. Listing 3-11 shows the Pi4J implementation of the scheduled executor task.

Listing 3-11 *Pi4J task for scheduling LED updates*

```
private void runClock() {
  executor.scheduleAtFixedRate(() -> {
    if (!paused) {
      if (counter <= 0) {
        if ((System.currentTimeMillis() / 250) % 2 == 0) {
          setAllLeds(false);
        } else {
          updateLeds();
        }
      } else {
        updateLeds();
      }
      counter--;
    }
  }, 0, 125, TimeUnit.MILLISECONDS);
}
```

Setting the Timer

Now that we have a way to show a countdown on the LEDs, we also need a way to set the timer using the four buttons. Normally, this is a challenging UI for typing 0 through 9 on a device without a full numeric keypad. However, since we are using binary, we only have to worry about two digits!

Here is the arrangement I used for my buttons:

- **Button 0 [blue]: Binary 1**   Shifts the entire number left (multiply by 2) and adds a 1 to the digit representing seconds.

- **Button 1 [gray]: Binary 0**   Shifts the entire number left (multiply by 2) and adds a 0 to the digit representing seconds.

- **Button 2 [red]: Clear digit/pause timer/shut down**   Shifts the entire number right (divide by 2), removing what was in the digit representing seconds. Also used to pause the timer if it is running, and to shut down the entire application if it is held for three seconds.

- **Button 3 [green]: Go/pause**   Start the timer if it is not running or pause it if it is already running.

This lets you easily enter a new time while the clock is paused using binary digits plus bit shifting. The Pi4J implementation for my button control logic is shown in Listing 3-12.

Listing 3-12   *Pi4J control logic for the binary timer*

```
private void addListeners() {
  buttons[0].addListener((GpioPinListenerDigital) event -> {
    if (event.getState().isLow() && paused) { // Blue Button: Add 1 (and then x2)
      prepareEdit();
      counter <<= 1;      // shift the bits (time x2)
      counter |= 0x8;     // turn on the second bit (+1)
      updateLeds();
    }
  });
  buttons[1].addListener((GpioPinListenerDigital) event -> {
    if (event.getState().isLow() && paused) { // Gray Button: Add 0 (and then x2)
      prepareEdit();
      counter <<= 1;      // shift the bits (time x2)
      updateLeds();
    }
  });
  buttons[2].addListener((GpioPinListenerDigital) event -> {
    if (event.getState().isLow()) { // Red Button: Divide by 2, Pause, Shutdown
      shutdownFuture = executor.schedule(this::shutdown, 3, TimeUnit.SECONDS);
      if (!paused) {
        paused = true;
      } else {
```

```
        prepareEdit();
        counter >>>= 1;      // shift the bits (time /2)
        counter &= ~0x4;     // clear the bit shifted off
      }
      updateLeds();
    } else {
      shutdownFuture.cancel(false);
    }
  });
  buttons[3].addListener((GpioPinListenerDigital) event -> {
    if (event.getState().isLow()) { // Green Button: Run/Pause
      if (paused && counter >= 0) {
        counter &= 0x1FFFF; // clip to max leds
      }
      paused = !paused;
      updateLeds();
    }
  });
}
```

Button Debouncing   Buttons are mechanical switches that approximate a digital on/off, but do not do so perfectly. A common occurrence with switches is that they experience a bit of signal bounce when they transition from on to off and vice versa. It should not be too much of a surprise that there is a bit of jitter in the signal, since there is a physical contact that is being pressed together and released.

The Pi4J library has very clean event triggering and built-in button debouncing, which can be set on the GPIOPinDigitalInput and will reduce the spurious events that you would otherwise receive. Here is an example of how to provision a pin in Pi4J with button debouncing enabled:

```
GpioPinDigitalInput button = gpio.provisionDigitalInputPin(RaspiPin.
GPIO_03, PinPullResistance.PULL_UP);
button.setDebounce(20);
```

For the Device I/O library, you are receiving raw events with some spurious artifacts such as bouncing switches, duplicate states, and even extra events on startup for pins with pull-up resistors. None of these are what your application is probably expecting to receive, so you have a little bit of work to clean up the input.

To simplify things, I put together a simple debouncing algorithm, presented in Listing 3-13.

Listing 3-13 *Device I/O button debouncing helper library*

```java
public class DioDebouncer implements PinListener {
  private static final int STARTUP_INTERVAL = 200;
  private static final int DEBOUNCE_INTERVAL = 20;

  private final PinListener action;
  private int pin = -1;
  private PinEvent lastPE;
  private Future future;
  // Note: can't use the default thread pool since it is non-daemon
  private final ScheduledExecutorService executor =
Executors.newScheduledThreadPool(1, target -> {
    Thread t = new Thread(target, "Debouncer for pin[" + pin + "]");
    t.setDaemon(true);
    return t;
  });

  public DioDebouncer(PinListener action) {
    this.action = action;
    // Get rid of startup wobble from DIO library
    future = executor.schedule(() -> {}, STARTUP_INTERVAL, TimeUnit.MILLISECONDS);
  }

  @Override
  public void valueChanged(PinEvent pe) {
    checkPin(pe);
    // Remove spurious events with the same value:
    if (lastPE != null && lastPE.getValue() == pe.getValue()) {return;}
    lastPE = pe;
    if (!future.isDone()) {return; /* Debounced! */}

    action.valueChanged(pe);
    future = executor.schedule(() -> {
      if (pe.getValue() != lastPE.getValue()) {
        // Value changed during the debounce interval:
        action.valueChanged(lastPE);
      }
    }, DEBOUNCE_INTERVAL, TimeUnit.MILLISECONDS);
  }

  // Make sure the same Debouncer is not used for multiple pins
  private void checkPin(PinEvent pe) {
    int id = pe.getDevice().getDescriptor().getID();
    if (pin == -1) {
      pin = id;
    } else if (pin != id) {
      throw new IllegalStateException("Debouncer pin[" + pin + "] != event pin[" + id +
"]. Use a new debouncer per listener.");
    }
  }
}
```

The basic design of this debouncer is to fire the first new event it receives immediately, and then wait for the debounce interval (20 ms) before firing any subsequent events. If the final state after 20 ms is the same, then it has done its job and suppressed bouncing. However, if the state changes during this time period (for example, a very quick flick of the switch), then the scheduled task will fire the last event to your application.

Also, even though it is using a `ScheduledExecutorService`, all events are guaranteed to be scheduled sequentially as long as `valueChanged` is called from the same thread. This avoids unnecessary synchronization, and is a perfect match for the expected usage in DIO `setInputListener` blocks, such as this example:

```
button.setInputListener(new DIODebouncer(event -> {
   try {
      led.setValue(!event.getValue());
   } catch (IOException ex) {
      Logger.getLogger(BinaryTimerDio.class.getName()).log(Level.SEVERE, null, ex);
   }
}));
```

This will turn on an LED when the button is pressed, and turn off the LED when the button is released. If you are like me, however, there is way too much "ceremony" in this simple example, because we were forced to deal with an `IOException` that is neither throwable nor recoverable. To simplify this, I have another little helper class called `PLHelper` that is shown in Listing 3-14.

Listing 3-14. *Pin listener helper class (`PLHelper`)*

```
public class PLHelper implements PinListener {
  private final PinListenerWithThrows listener;
  public static interface PinListenerWithThrows extends DeviceEventListener {
    public void valueChanged(PinEvent pe) throws IOException;
  }
  public PLHelper(PinListenerWithThrows listener) {
    this.listener = listener;
  }
  @Override
  public void valueChanged(PinEvent pe) {
    try {
      listener.valueChanged(pe);
    } catch (IOException ioe) {
      throw new RuntimeException(ioe);
    }
  }
}
```

This simple little class lets us ignore the exception in our callback, and it will throw a `RuntimeException` with the original `IOException` wrapped in the unlikely scenario our GPIO port is inaccessible (most likely a configuration or resource contention issue).

This allows us to shorten our listener callback to the following:

```
button.setInputListener(new DIODebouncer(new PLHelper(event -> {
    led.setValue(!event.getValue());
}))));
```

And now we have a simple callback that handles button debouncing and exception wrapping for us!

Remember when running the Device I/O version of the Binary Timer that you have to set up the correct run options. To do this, open the Project Properties dialog, go to the Run category, and enter the following VM Options:

```
-Djdk.dio.registry=dist/dio.properties -Djava.security.policy=dist/java.policy
```

Completed Binary Timer

Now you have all the tools at your disposal to finish the full binary timer implementation in your choice of Java GPIO libraries. Besides the pure geek factor of having a timer that counts in binary, you have also finished an embedded project that can be used as part of another, larger project.

Again, you can find the full reference implementation of these examples in the GitHub repo for this chapter: https://github.com/RaspberryPiWithJava/ BinaryTimer.

Here are some ideas to consider for your own version of a binary timer:

■ Program your timer to keep track of "overtime" after the timer has expired.

■ Add an LED screen to show the time in base-10 for the uninitiated.

■ Add a clock mode that will show the current time in base-2.

■ Program your timer to count in millisecond resolution.

To help you with the last idea, the following bonus section goes into full details on performance of GPIO libraries in Java on the Raspberry Pi.

Bonus: GPIO Performance Hacking

For most projects, even the Binary Timer we built in this chapter with a 125-ms resolution, any normal API will provide sufficient performance. However, when you need precise and fast timings in the single-digit millisecond range, you are pushing the limit of most high-level libraries.

Let's start with a quick comparison of the Device I/O and Pi4J libraries. I wrote a simple test application that turns an LED on and off as fast as possible in a tight loop. During this loop, the application times the duration of the loop and, using the number of iterations, figures out the period (duration for turning the GPIO on and off once) and the frequency of the LED.

The calculation for period is simple:

Period = Duration / Iterations

And the calculation for frequency is the inverse of period:

Frequency = 1 / Period

The trickiest part of this calculation is probably units, so I standardized on kilohertz (kHz) since that is the useful range when discussing GPIO speed. Around 1 kHz is an acceptable speed for most applications where the GPIO is no longer the bottleneck on performance. Getting performance in the megahertz (MHz) range is nice, but not required unless you are bit-banging serial or some other low-level bus protocol. At that point you should just be using the built-in serial, I²C, and SPI buses, rather than reimplementing low-level protocols in a high-level language.

The code for the Device I/O timing test is shown in Listing 3-15 (with the Pi4J differences shown in comments).

Listing 3-15   *Device I/O timing micro-benchmark*

```
public class TimerDio {
  public static void main(String[] args) throws IOException {
    GPIOPin led = DeviceManager.open(1);
//    final GpioController gpio = GpioFactory.getInstance();
//    final GpioPinDigitalOutput pin = gpio.provisionDigitalOutputP
in(RaspiPin.GPIO_01, PinState.LOW);
    final int ITERATIONS = 100000;
    long start = System.nanoTime();
    for (int i = 0; i < ITERATIONS; i++) {
      led.setValue(true);
      led.setValue(false);
```

```
//      pin.setState(true);
//      pin.setState(false);
    }
    long duration = System.nanoTime() - start;
    System.out.println("Duration = " + duration);
    double period = (duration / 1000000d / ITERATIONS);
    System.out.println("Period (in ms) = " + period);
    System.out.println("Frequency (in kHz) = " + 1d / period);
    led.close();
//    gpio.shutdown();
  }
}
```

I performed the testing on a stock Raspberry Pi B+ running Raspbian, with no overclocking or other modifications. I tracked the timings both in code and empirically using a multimeter as shown in Figure 3-14. Not surprisingly, the value returned by the code timings was within a few percentage points of the observed frequency (which is within the tolerance range of the equipment being used to test).

FIGURE 3-14. *Fluke 87V multimeter used to test frequency*

The test gave the following results for 100,000 iterations:

- Pi4J: 0.751 kHz

- Device I/O: 3.048 kHz

Feel free to retest this on your own to see what your observed speeds are. However, as you can see, both Pi4J and DIO provide reasonable performance for being fairly high-level APIs with lots of error checking, caching, and so forth each time you set a pin value. And even in this chapter's example of flipping 17 pins at eight times per second, we are not even close to stressing the GPIO performance:

- 17 pins × 8 flips/s = 136 flips/s

- 136 flips/s × (1 cycle / 2 flips) = 68 Hz

- 68 Hz × (1 kHz / 1000 Hz) = 0.068 kHz

So we have plenty of headroom with either of the APIs. However, you might be wondering if you can do better. Occasionally, you may need to really drive the GPIO pins hard. For example, we might want to build a timer with millisecond accuracy:

- 17 pins × 8 flips/ms = 136 flips/ms

- 136 flips/ms × (1 cycle / 2 flips) = 68 kHz

So at this speed we are way over the limit of what Pi4J or Direct I/O can handle, and this is not even accounting for other logic that has to run in between GPIO cycles to update the timer state.

However, we do have another option that supports even faster GPIO performance. Pi4J gives us access to the raw Java Native Interface (JNI) to the underlying C library (WiringPi), allowing us to bypass all of the safety checks and high-level API features that introduce overhead. Listing 3-16 shows the same performance test coded up for the Pi4J raw access API.

Listing 3-16   *Pi4J raw GPIO micro-benchmark*

```
public class TimerPi4JRaw {
  public static void main(String[] args) throws IOException {
    Gpio.wiringPiSetup();
    if (!GpioUtil.isExported(1)) {
      GpioUtil.export(1, GpioUtil.DIRECTION_OUT);
    } else {
      GpioUtil.setDirection(1, GpioUtil.DIRECTION_OUT);
    }
    Gpio.pinMode(1, Gpio.OUTPUT);
    final int ITERATIONS = 100000000;
    long start = System.nanoTime();
    for (int i = 0; i < ITERATIONS; i++) {
      Gpio.digitalWrite(1, 1);
      Gpio.digitalWrite(1, 0);
    }
    long duration = System.nanoTime() - start;
    System.out.println("Duration = " + duration);
    double period = (duration / 1000000d / ITERATIONS);
    System.out.println("Period (in ms) = " + period);
    System.out.println("Frequency (in kHz) = " + 1d / period);
    GpioUtil.unexport(1);
  }
}
```

This code is a little bit more difficult to understand, and leaves us exposed for more coding errors. For example, we would need to remember to change the pin number in every location that it is used explicitly, which already added up to seven references in this small test. In a real application you would probably have a lot more maintenance than this to keep your pin numbers straight. The pin initialization and cleanup is also very specific, and if you don't do it correctly, you will have nonworking GPIO pins. Also, I used the int (0/1) version of the `digitalWrite` method to avoid an extra method dispatch required for the boolean version of the same function.

However, the performance gains are real, with a timed speed that far exceeds either of the high-level APIs:

Pi4J Raw: 1662 kHz (or 1.7 MHz)

Since these frequencies exceed the accuracy of my multimeter, I switched to my high-resolution digital oscilloscope, a PicoScope 3206D MSO. This has a maximum bandwidth of 200 MHz, which is more than enough to confirm the timed speed. Figure 3-15 shows the output of the PicoScope with an observed frequency of 1.716 MHz, which confirms the tested speed.

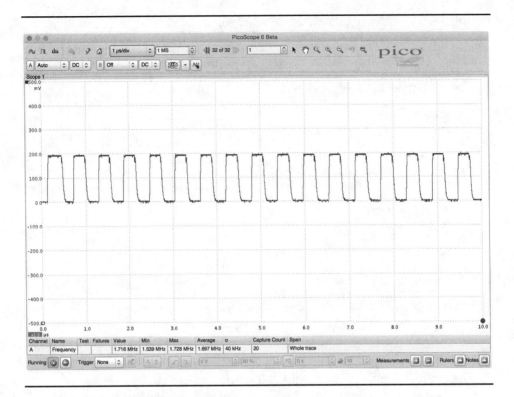

FIGURE 3-15. *Digital oscilloscope output for the Pi4J low-level API*

This is three orders of magnitude faster than the high-level APIs of Pi4J and Device I/O, and sufficiently fast to support a millisecond timer. Just for kicks, I included the millisecond timer implementation using the raw Pi4J API in the GitHub repo (https://github.com/RaspberryPiWithJava/BinaryTimer) under the name BinaryMillisecondTimerPi4JRaw.java.

For true performance gurus, it is important to know why the raw Pi4J API is so much faster. To understand this, we have to back up and talk about the different ways you can access GPIO on the Raspberry Pi. There are two primary ways of accessing GPIO, each with different trade-offs:

- ■ **Memory-mapped access (/dev/mem)** This is the lowest-level API for accessing GPIO provided by the Linux kernel. It requires root access, and the ability to memory-map the virtual device file, but it will give you direct access to set one or multiple GPIO pins extremely quickly.

■ **Sysfs access (/sys/class/gpio/)** This is a higher-level API that allows for access to only GPIO in a safer, easier way. Since it is less direct, it is also a little slower, but it has the advantage of not requiring root access.

Pi4J usually requires root access because it prefers memory-mapped access to GPIO pins (although it does have the ability to use sysfs access without root permissions). Device I/O exclusively uses filesystem access for all GPIO access.

An easy way to compare these two methods of access is to modify our earlier raw Pi4J access program to use the sysfs GPIO access method. The code for this version of the performance harness is shown in Listing 3-17.

Listing 3-17 *Pi4J Sysfs GPIO micro-benchmark*

```java
public class TimerPi4JRawSysfs {

  public static void main(String[] args) throws IOException {
    exportPin("18");
    Gpio.wiringPiSetupSys();
    final int ITERATIONS = 1000000;
    long start = System.nanoTime();
    for (int i=0; i<ITERATIONS; i++) {
      Gpio.digitalWrite(18, 1);
      Gpio.digitalWrite(18, 0);
    }
    long duration = System.nanoTime() - start;
    System.out.println("Duration = " + duration);
    double period = (duration / 1000000d / ITERATIONS);
    System.out.println("Period (in ms) = " + period);
    System.out.println("Frequency (in kHz) = " + 1d / period);
    unexportPin("18");
  }

  private static void exportPin(String port) throws IOException {
    FileWriter exportFile = new FileWriter("/sys/class/gpio/export");
    exportFile.write(port);
    exportFile.flush();
    FileWriter directionFile = new FileWriter("/sys/class/gpio/gpio" + port + "/direction");
    directionFile.write("out");
    directionFile.flush();
  }

  private static void unexportPin(String port) throws IOException {
    FileWriter unexportFile = new FileWriter("/sys/class/gpio/unexport");
    unexportFile.write(port);
    unexportFile.flush();
  }
}
```

To use the Sysfs GPIO access, there are some additional steps needed to export the pins in advance, and it forces us back to using Broadcom pin numbers for the entire program. Another issue to watch out for is that if the test does not complete successfully due to an exception or abnormal termination, the GPIO pin will remain exported, which requires a little bit of clean-up before the next run.

Running this version, we get the following performance: 82.1 kHz. This is quite a performance reduction from the 1.7 MHz we got earlier by using the memory-mapped access, and gives us a nice upper bound on the Device I/O library. Since it is relying exclusively on sysfs access, it can never be faster than 80 kHz, but in practice it is a lot slower given the error checking, caching, and so forth.

From all of this performance hacking, we can draw some very interesting conclusions:

■ Pi4J raw-access performance is pretty good. Use it and your application will be faster than anything else out there that is not written in pure C.

■ Most applications don't really need that level of performance and will work fine with the high-level Pi4J and Device I/O libraries.

■ If you have made it through this entire performance testing section, you are a true embedded hacker. Welcome to the club!

CHAPTER
4

IoT Hat

This chapter shows you how to take advantage of your technical capabilities to build a magic prop that you can use to impress your friends. Well, they will probably be more impressed with your wearable Raspberry Pi hacking skills than your magic skills, but in either case it makes for a great conversation piece.

We are going to build a magic top hat that is capable of divining the values of seemingly ordinary playing cards. By simply brushing the playing cards over the top of the hat or dropping them in the hat one at a time, we will instantly know the value of whatever card in the deck was used. With a little clever scripting, this will allow us to trick the audience into believing that we can read the mind of our volunteers.

Bill of Materials

The IoT Hat is a great project to get started with to demonstrate wearable computing. You can build the entire project with a small set of components, and assembly doesn't even require sewing (although if you are handy with a needle and thread, feel free to make the installation more permanent).

Here is an itemized list of the components:

- **Raspberry Pi A+**   This is the mainstay of all the projects in this book. I chose the A+ model shown in Figure 4-1 because it is fairly compact, reduces power, and the project doesn't need USB and Ethernet ports. However, you can also do this project with any other Raspberry Pi model of your choice.

- **Wi-Fi adapter**   This allows us to remotely connect to the Raspberry Pi A+ since it has no Ethernet port. A common adapter with built-in support is the Edimax EW-7811Un Wi-Fi module.

- **Magician's top hat**   Any tall, black hat you have around the house will do. Costume supply or theatrical prop stores are a great source for this type of hat.

- **NFC/RFID card reader**   This project is designed for a card reader with the PN532 chipset, which supports reading Mifare Ultralight tags. A number of hardware vendors sell breakout boards using this chipset, but a couple I can recommend are the PN532 Breakout Board from Adafruit (https://www.adafruit.com/products/364) and the ITEAD PN532 NFC Module from ITEAD Studio (http://imall .iteadstudio.com/im130625002.html).

FIGURE 4-1.   *Raspberry Pi A+*

■ **Portable USB charger**   To make our project cordless, we are going
to slip in a small USB power supply meant for powering phones.
Any device that supplies 1A of charging power will work, but a nice
option is the Jackery Bar (www.jackery.com/jackery-bar/).

■ **Jumper cables**   These are mainly for connecting the NFC/RFID card
reader. Six female-to-female cables should do the trick. (I²C/UART
requires four and SPI requires six.)

■ **Tape** Tape is used to secure the components in the hat. Gaffer tape works great. Electrical tape is helpful to tidy up cables. Double-sided tape is handy as well.

■ **RFID cards or tags** To use the IoT Hat, the best option is to get a full pack of RFID playing cards, although you can stick your own tags on normal playing cards. Cartamundi (www.cartamundi.com) manufactures a variety of different cards for casinos, including cards with embedded Mifare Ultralight chips. The easiest way to buy them is from a video poker dealer such as Pokertronic in Germany (www.pokertronic.de) or VideoPokerTable in Australia (https:// videopokertable.net). The cards are virtually indistinguishable from a normal deck of playing cards, as you can see in Figure 4-2.

FIGURE 4-2. *RFID poker cards*

Since a full deck of RFID cards is not cheap (around $200 USD), another option is to simply get some small RFID tags and stick them to normal playing cards. For testing your project, this is definitely sufficient. These tags from Adafruit work well and are really easy to hide: https://www.adafruit.com/products/361.

Setting Up Your Raspberry Pi A+

Before getting started with this project, you will need to set up Raspbian on your Raspberry Pi A+ and connect it to a network via the Wi-Fi adapter. Chapter 1 has full details on how to go through the installation process to prepare your Raspberry Pi for programming. However, since the Raspberry Pi A+ has only one USB port, you have to choose between hooking up a keyboard or the Wi-Fi adapter. This makes doing the initial Wi-Fi adapter setup a little tricky since you can't scan for networks without the adapter present. Here are some ways to work around this limitation:

■ Use a powered USB hub to hook up your keyboard and Wi-Fi adapter simultaneously. Then, once you have established a remote SSH connection, you can remove the hub and use the Wi-Fi adapter exclusively.

■ Set up the SD card on a Raspberry Pi B, B+, or 2, and then transfer it over to the Raspberry Pi A+. This allows you to take advantage of Ethernet networking and multiple USB ports during the setup process. Once you have SSH access working, you can simply swap the SD card into your Raspberry Pi A+.

■ Manually add the wireless networks to your configuration. This is the most error prone option since a small typo in the configuration files can prevent the entire networking stack from loading. We will leave this in the category of possible, but not recommended options.

Once you are able to get a remote SSH connection to your Raspberry Pi A+, you are ready to continue building the IoT Hat project.

NFC/RFID Support on the Raspberry Pi

Hooking up an NFC/RFID card reader to your Raspberry Pi and accessing it from Java should be as easy as pie ... well, cake. Unfortunately, it is a little bit more complicated than either of those.

Java actually has had built-in support for reading NFC and RFID cards for quite a while. The original specification was defined by Java Specification Request (JSR) 268 and was called the Java Smart Card I/O API. It has been part of the Java SE releases on desktop since Java 1.6 was released on December 11, 2006, and it works exactly the same on the ARM port of Java SE, including the Raspberry Pi.

Being built originally for desktop platforms, the specification assumes that there are drivers installed for the target smart card reader and that these drivers expose the devices via the Personal Computer/Smart Card (PC/SC) specification. Microsoft first made this specification available on Windows XP, and a free implementation called PC/SC Lite is available on Linux and other Unix platforms.

However, rather than using a packaged device that communicates with the smart card reader chip, we can bypass this and directly communicate with the chip via the GPIO pins on the Raspberry Pi. This allows us to interface with the card reader chip on a much lower level, allowing us to cut out unnecessary hardware to create a more compact and energy-efficient design.

The chip we are using supports three different embedded protocols: I^2C, SPI, and UART (serial). I will show you how to use all three of these protocols along the way.

Configuring Your Raspberry Pi for I^2C, SPI, and UART

There are several different protocols that we can use to connect to the NFC/RFID card reader. However, by default Raspbian disables all the communication buses, including I^2C, SPI, and UART. Even though you will only need to choose one of these protocols to use for this project, I recommend enabling all of them. It will be helpful for other devices that require the communication buses, and give you more options in case you can't get one of the protocols to work.

To enable these buses, the easiest mechanism is to use the `raspi-config` command-line utility. It provides a console GUI with which to turn on and off each of the communication protocols.

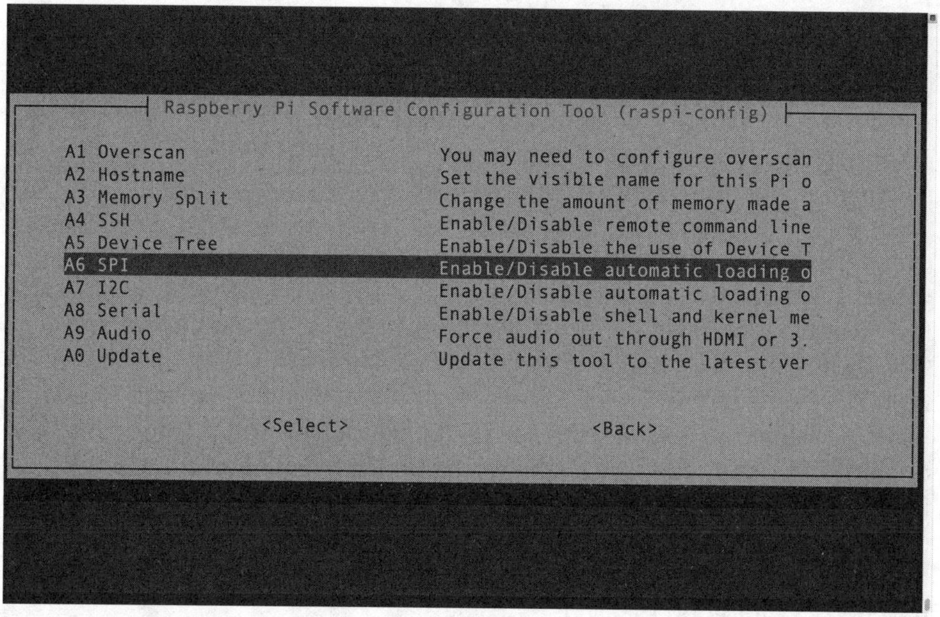

```
┌──────┤ Raspberry Pi Software Configuration Tool (raspi-config) ├──────┐
│                                                                       │
│   A1 Overscan              You may need to configure overscan         │
│   A2 Hostname              Set the visible name for this Pi o         │
│   A3 Memory Split          Change the amount of memory made a         │
│   A4 SSH                   Enable/Disable remote command line         │
│   A5 Device Tree           Enable/Disable the use of Device T         │
│   A6 SPI                   Enable/Disable automatic loading o         │
│   A7 I2C                   Enable/Disable automatic loading o         │
│   A8 Serial                Enable/Disable shell and kernel me         │
│   A9 Audio                 Force audio out through HDMI or 3.         │
│   A0 Update                Update this tool to the latest ver         │
│                                                                       │
│                                                                       │
│              <Select>                      <Back>                     │
│                                                                       │
└───────────────────────────────────────────────────────────────────────┘
```

FIGURE 4-3. *Advanced Options tab in* `raspi-config`

To open the `raspi-config` utility, you first need to get command-line access to your Raspberry Pi A+. Since it has no Ethernet port, the easiest way is to hook up a keyboard and HDMI screen. Once logged in to the console, you can then start the `raspi-config` utility by typing

```
sudo raspi-config
```

Navigate to the Advanced Options item (number 8) and enter that submenu. You will be given a list of new options as shown in Figure 4-3 (and described in Chapter 1).

On the Advanced Options tab, you need to enable SPI and I²C by choosing their respective menu items of A6 and A7. `Raspi-config` will first ask you if you want to enable the interface, to which you should respond Yes and confirm by choosing OK. Then the program will ask you if you want the kernel module loaded by default, to which you should respond Yes and confirm again with OK. Do this for both the SPI and I²C interfaces.

NOTE
On the latest version of Raspbian as of this writing,
`raspi-config` *doesn't properly enable the I²C*
kernel module. To enable it properly, you have to
edit /etc/modules by using the command `sudo`
`nano /etc/modules`*. In this file, add an extra*
line to the end that reads `i2c-dev`*.*

By default the serial port is used for console debugging access. However, we are going to disable this feature so we can use it to talk to the smart card reader or other peripherals. To do this, choose option A8 on the Advanced Options tab to modify serial access. Unlike SPI and I²C, we are disabling this feature rather than enabling it. When asked "Would you like a login shell to be available over serial?" choose No. It will now tell you that "Serial is disabled"; however, this is actually freeing up the serial port for other uses. Respond OK and you are all set to use the serial port to communicate with other devices.

Finally, choose Finish to exit `raspi-config`, and then reboot your Raspberry Pi for good measure by using

```
sudo shutdown -r now
```

Now you have successfully enabled I²C, SPI, and serial communication with devices over GPIO.

Connecting the Smart Card Reader

I am going to provide instructions for both the PN532 Breakout Board from Adafruit and the ITEAD PN532 NFC Module. Several other electronics vendors have similar breakout boards, and any of them that have a PN532 chip and allow you to hook up over I²C, SPI, or serial should work just fine.

The board from Adafruit comes without the headers attached, as shown in Figure 4-4. The blue circuit board has the PN532 chip and an antenna for reading smart cards from a reasonable distance. There are also status lights and mounting holes for several different common device connections. Along with the board you will get a strip of headers that you can solder on the board as needed, two jumpers to use for selecting the interface, and an RFID card that you can use to test and make sure your board is working fine.

The only pins we will need are the set of nine connectors on the right edge and the two jumper sets along the bottom, both in groups of three.

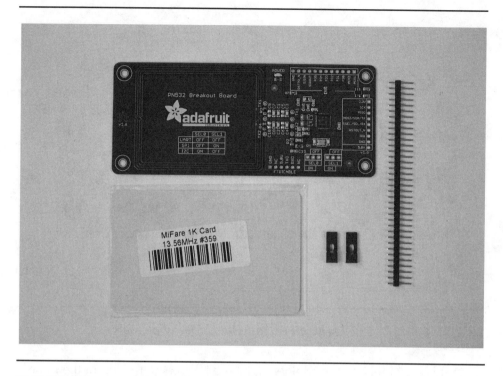

FIGURE 4-4. *PN532 Breakout Board from Adafruit*

You can leave the extra pins on the top and the FTDIC connector on the bottom disconnected. Soldering connectors onto the board is fairly straightforward, but if you have never done soldering before, here are a few tips:

- A soldering iron with a fine chisel tip will make it easier to work with small components. If your soldering iron is too large, you may damage nearby components.

- It is helpful to have a clamp or "helping hands" to secure the component you are trying to solder. Once the solder cools, your component will be stuck at whatever angle it was positioned, so your chance to align things is before you start soldering.

- Make sure the hole and pin are both fully heated before applying solder. If either is not sufficiently hot, you will get what is called a "cold solder joint," which may fail over time.

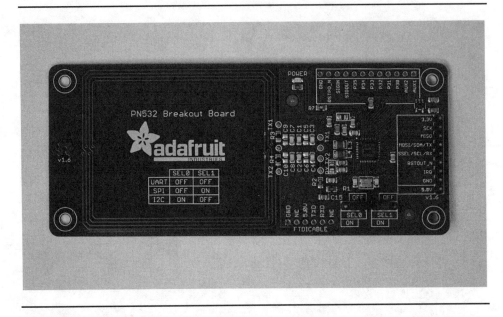

FIGURE 4-5. *PN532 Breakout Board with soldered headers*

In this case I recommend soldering all the headers to the top of the board so you can lay the smart card reader flat in the top of the hat. The antenna will pick up RFID playing cards that are near the top or the bottom of the breakout board, so this gives you the option of scanning cards either by dropping them in the hat or waving them over the top.

Figure 4-5 shows my fully soldered PN532 Breakout Board with the jumpers inserted into the position to enable SPI communication. Table 4-1 shows a list of all the different jumper positions and what communication protocol they enable.

	SEL0 (left jumper)	SEL1 (right jumper)
Serial (UART)	Off (right)	Off (right)
SPI	Off (right)	On (left)
I²C	On (left)	Off (right)

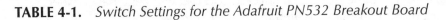

TABLE 4-1. *Switch Settings for the Adafruit PN532 Breakout Board*

	SET0 (left switch)	SET1 (right switch)
Serial (UART)	L (left)	L (left)
SPI	L (left)	H (right)
I²C	H (right)	L (left)

TABLE 4-2. *Switch Settings for the ITEAD PN532 NFC Module*

ITEAD Studio's board is a little bit simpler to set up in that all the headers and switches come preinstalled. Also, it has a convenient row of headers that matches the Raspberry Pi GPIO layout, so you can hook it up with a serial cable directly, although for this project I recommend using jumper cables to make it easier to hide the hardware in your hat.

Unfortunately, the switches are (you guessed it) backward from what the Adafruit board uses, so make sure that you set them correctly for your desired protocol. Table 4-2 shows the different switch positions for the ITEAD PN532 Breakout Board.

The final step is to hook the breakout board to your Raspberry Pi A+. I recommend trying the SPI protocol first since it is the highest-speed bus and is very reliable. I²C is another great option that allows you to easily hook up multiple devices. However, some of the Adafruit PN532 boards have a defect that prevents them from being accessible over I²C. And finally, serial is a pretty simple and easy-to-debug option even if it is not as fast as the previous two communication bus protocols.

To hook up via SPI you will need to connect the cables to the Raspberry Pi as shown in Figure 4-6 and enumerated in Table 4-3. Figure 4-6 shows a picture of an ITEAD PN532 Breakout Board; however, the pins on this Adafruit board happen to be ordered the same from left to right when both boards are oriented with the edge closest to the header facing down. You can safely ignore the ninth pin on the Adafruit board that doesn't exist on the ITEAD board. If you don't have the Raspberry Pi pin numbers handy, refer to Figure 3-2 in Chapter 3.

I²C is a little easier to connect, only requiring four cables total. The required connections are shown in Figure 4-7 and enumerated in Table 4-4. Again, refer to Figure 3-2 for the Raspberry Pi pin numbering.

FIGURE 4-6. *SPI connection diagram*

	Breakout Board	**Raspberry Pi**
5.0V	Pin 1	Pin 2
GND	Pin 2	Pin 6
SSEL	Pin 5	Pin 24
MOSI	Pin 6	Pin 19
MISO	Pin 7	Pin 21
SCK	Pin 8	Pin 23

TABLE 4-3. *SPI Pin Connections*

FIGURE 4-7. *I²C connection diagram*

	Breakout Board	**Raspberry Pi**
5.0V	Pin 1	Pin 2
GND	Pin 2	Pin 6
SCL	Pin 5	Pin 5
SDA	Pin 6	Pin 3

TABLE 4-4. *I²C Pin Connections*

FIGURE 4-8. *Serial connection diagram*

And finally, you can also hook up the PN532 Breakout Board via serial. When using serial connections rather than hooking up the pins to the identically labeled one on the Raspberry Pi, you need to cross the RX and TX pins. The required connections are shown in Figure 4-8 and enumerated in Table 4-5.

Figure 4-9 shows the basic smart card reader set up with the PN532 Breakout Board hooked up via SPI and the Raspberry Pi A+ powered by the Jackery Bar USB charger. The Raspberry Pi A+ also has an Edimax EW-7811Un Wi-Fi module hooked up so I can do remote SSH access and deploy new versions of the code easily.

	Breakout Board	Raspberry Pi
5.0V	Pin 1	Pin 2
GND	Pin 2	Pin 6
RX to TX on Pi	Pin 5	Pin 8
TX to RX on Pi	Pin 6	Pin 10

TABLE 4-5. *Serial Pin Connections*

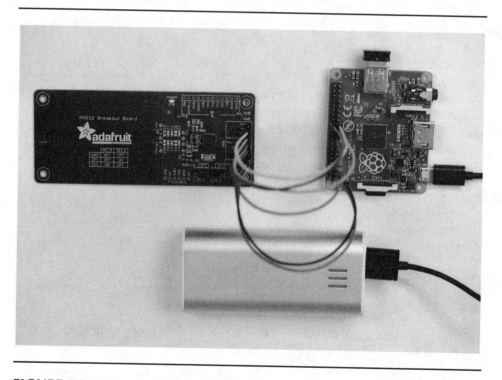

FIGURE 4-9. *PN532 Breakout Board hooked up to the Raspberry Pi A+*

Notice that the power light on the PN523 Breakout Board is on, indicating we have ground and 5V power hooked up correctly. In the next section we are going to test the breakout board using a native NFC library.

NFC Library Configuration

We are going to use libnfc to interface with the NFC reader. This supports low-level access to a bunch of different NFC chips. In addition we will use the PC/SC smart card interface, which Java requires. And to connect the two, we will use ifdnfc to see the libnfc devices as PC/SC devices in Java.

Compiling and Installing libnfc

Unfortunately, none of these libraries come prebuilt with the Raspbian distribution, so you have to build them from source. To start with, you should make sure your repository is up to date with the latest versions of Raspbian software available. To do this, run the following commands:

```
sudo apt-get update
sudo apt-get upgrade
```

The second command is optional and may take a long time depending on how out-of-date your Raspbian installation is. However, it will ensure your Raspberry Pi is on the latest version of all the installed software, which is a good thing to do when first setting it up.

The next step is to get libusb-dev, which you need to compile libnfc. You can obtain it by using the package manager like so:

```
sudo apt-get install libusb-dev
```

Then download and uncompress the libnfc source code to your home directory by using the following commands:

```
cd ~
wget http://dl.bintray.com/nfc-tools/sources/libnfc-1.7.1.tar.bz2
tar -xf libnfc-1.7.1.tar.bz2
```

This gives you the full source code for the libnfc project, which you can configure by doing the following:

```
cd libnfc-1.7.1
./configure --prefix=/usr --sysconfdir=/etc
```

You will know this is successful when it gives you a list of the drivers for which it will compile support, as shown in Listing 4-1.

Listing 4-1 *Selected drivers that libnfc is configured to build*

```
Selected drivers:
    acr122_pcsc...... no
    acr122_usb....... yes
    acr122s.......... yes
    arygon........... yes
    pn53x_usb........ yes
    pn532_uart....... yes
    pn532_spi....... yes
    pn532_i2c........ yes
```

The last three are the ones we care about: UART (serial), SPI, and I²C support for the PN532 chipset. To launch the actual compilation and install it on your Raspberry Pi, run the following commands:

```
make
sudo make install
```

The last step is to create a configuration file that tells libnfc which protocol to use. The configuration file must be located at /etc/nfc/libnfc.conf and support the following options:

- **allow_autoscan** The default value is true, allowing libnfc to automatically scan for devices. Unfortunately, this doesn't actually work, so you have to manually configure the reader.

- **allow_intrusive_scan** This is an even more aggressive scan, which is disabled by default. Enabling this option is not recommended.

- **log_level** The level of logging used by libnfc. The default is 1 (error), but it goes all the way up to 3 (debug) if you need more information.

- **device.name/device.connstring** These parameters let you manually specify the reader information, which is required on the Raspberry Pi version of libnfc.

Using a particular interface is as simple as configuring the right jumpers or switches on the smart card reader, hooking up wires according to the earlier diagrams, and enabling the right manual configuration for your device.

For example, if you are using SPI, you need to create a new libnfc.conf file by typing

```
sudo nano /etc/nfc/libnfc.conf
```

and then add the following contents to the newly created file:

```
device.name = "pn532_spi"
device.connstring = "pn532_spi:/dev/spidev0.0:500000"
```

Once you have saved the configuration, you can test libnfc by using the `nfc-scan-device` and `nfc-poll` commands. Listing 4-2 shows the output from running nfc-poll when you wave an RFID card across the reader successfully.

Listing 4-2 *Successful run of nfc-poll*

```
pi@iothat ~/libnfc-1.7.1 $ nfc-poll
nfc-poll uses libnfc 1.7.1
NFC reader: pn532_spi:/dev/spidev0.0 opened
NFC device will poll during 30000 ms (20 pollings of 300 ms for ↵
5 modulations)
ISO/IEC 14443A (106 kbps) target:
    ATQA (SENS_RES): 00  04
       UID (NFCID1): e0  dc  e6  16
       SAK (SEL_RES): 08
nfc_initiator_target_is_present: Target Released
Waiting for card removing...done.
```

You can also use the serial and I²C connections similarly. To enable serial, simply change the libnfc.conf file to read

```
device.name = "pn532_uart"
device.connstring = "pn532_uart:/dev/ttyAMA0"
```

To use the I²C protocol, you would use the following configuration:

```
device.name = "pn532_i2c"
device.connstring = "pn532_i2c:/dev/i2c-1"
```

I²C is probably the most challenging to troubleshoot since it is a multi-device protocol. To help with troubleshooting if your device does not immediately register with the I²C bus, you can install i2c-tools by running the following command:

```
sudo apt-get install i2c-tools
```

This gives you several additional commands, including `i2c-detect`, which you can run by typing the command `i2cdetect 1`, which should give you output similar to Listing 4-3 if your device is configured and working correctly.

Listing 4-3 *Output of running `i2cdetect 1`*

```
pi@iothat ~ $ i2cdetect 1
WARNING! This program can confuse your I2C bus, cause data loss and worse!
I will probe file /dev/i2c-1.
I will probe address range 0x03-0x77.
Continue? [Y/n]
     0  1  2  3  4  5  6  7  8  9  a  b  c  d  e  f
00:          -- -- -- -- -- -- -- -- -- -- -- -- --
10: -- -- -- -- -- -- -- -- -- -- -- -- -- -- -- --
20: -- -- -- -- 24 -- -- -- -- -- -- -- -- -- -- --
30: -- -- -- -- -- -- -- -- -- -- -- -- -- -- -- --
40: -- -- -- -- -- -- -- -- -- -- -- -- -- -- -- --
50: -- -- -- -- -- -- -- -- -- -- -- -- -- -- -- --
60: -- -- -- -- -- -- -- -- -- -- -- -- -- -- -- --
70: -- -- -- -- -- -- -- --
```

Compiling and Installing ifdnfc

Now you have the low-level library working, but you need to expose it as a PC/SC device so that Java can access it. For this you are going to use an open source library called ifdnfc that creates a wrapper for libnfc so that it looks like a generic PC/SC driver.

Again, ifdnfc does not come precompiled for the Raspberry Pi, so you have to build it from source. Unlike libnfc, there isn't even a stable release to point to, so you are simply going to build from the head of the public repository. While it should be fine, be prepared to deal with minor instabilities if there is development activity going on.

To start with, clone the GitHub repository by executing the following command:

```
git clone https://github.com/nfc-tools/ifdnfc.git
```

To build the code, you need a few libraries. The first one, `dh-autoreconf`, will allow you to configure the project for the right compiler settings on the Raspberry Pi's ARM v6/7 platform. The second one, `libpcsclite-dev`, is a required build dependency since this library is implementing a PC/SC driver. Finally, `pcscd` is the PC/SC daemon that Java will talk to and ifdnfc will interface with. You use the following command to install these libraries:

```
sudo apt-get install dh-autoreconf libpcsclite-dev pcscd
```

After installing all of these dependencies, you are ready to configure the code by running the following commands:

```
cd ifdnfc
autoreconf -vis
./configure
```

This will produce a lot of output as it inspects your platform to find the hardware specs and available compilers and libraries. Listing 4-4 shows the tail end of the output for a successful ifdnfc configuration.

Listing 4-4 *Configuration details for ifdnfc on a Raspberry Pi A+*

```
ifdnfc has been configured with following options:

Version:                0.1.4

Host:                   armv6l-unknown-linux-gnueabihf
Compiler:               gcc
Preprocessor flags:
Compiler flags:         -g -O2 -std=c99
Preprocessor flags:
Linker flags:
Libraries:
LIBNFC_CFLAGS:
LIBNFC_LIBS:            -lnfc -lusb
PCSC_CFLAGS:            -pthread -I/usr/include/PCSC
PCSC_LIBS:             -lpcsclite
BUNDLE_HOST:           Linux
DYN_LIB_EXT:           so

configure: creating ./config.status
config.status: creating Makefile
config.status: creating src/Info.plist
config.status: creating src/Makefile
config.status: creating config.h
config.status: executing depfiles commands
config.status: executing libtool commands
```

Once configuration is successful, you can build the project using the standard `make` command:

```
make
```

If compilation is successful, you can install it into your local distribution using the following command:

```
sudo make install
```

The last step is to set up the PC/SC driver file that points to ifdnfc. There is a template driver file that is installed into /usr/local/etc/reader.conf.d/ifdnfc. You can copy this file and edit it with the following commands:

```
sudo cp /usr/local/etc/reader.conf.d/ifdnfc /etc/reader.conf.d/
sudo nano /etc/reader.conf.d/ifdnfc
```

Within nano, all you need to do is uncomment the last four lines to make the file look similar to the editor shown in Figure 4-10. Then save the file and exit nano.

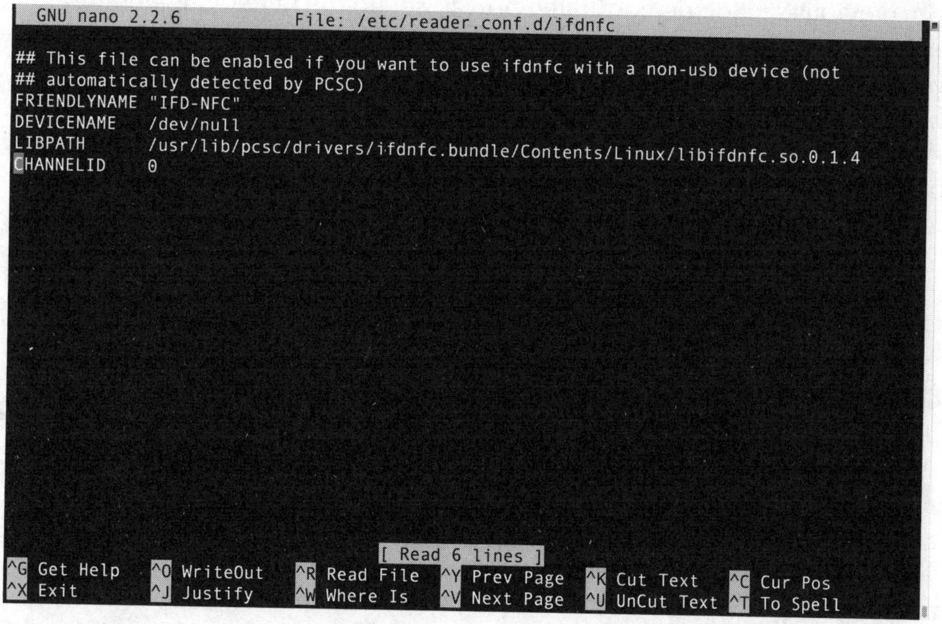

FIGURE 4-10.   *Configuration for ifdnfc in nano*

The last step is to restart the PC/SC daemon and activate the ifdnfc agent. The following two commands will do this:

```
sudo /etc/init.d/pcscd restart
ifdnfc-activate
```

NOTE
The ifdnfc agent does not automatically start on boot, so you will need to rerun this command each time you start up your IoT Hat. To make this more convenient, you may want to set up a launch agent to boot this on startup.

You now have prepared everything at the operating system level in order to enable smart card access directly from Java. The next section explains in detail how to use the smartcardio library to read RFID cards as they are scanned.

Reading Cards from Java

The previous section demonstrated how to set up the underlying libraries and infrastructure to interface with an NFC/RFID smart card reader. Now you are ready to create a Java application to read the card using the smartcardio API that is already a part of the JRE.

All the code in this section is available in the GitHub repository for the book. Feel free to follow along by downloading the code in the following repository:

https://github.com/RaspberryPiWithJava/IoTHat

The code fragments shown here assume that you are importing the correct classes from the `javax.smartcardio` package. Since this is a standard package on both desktop and embedded versions of Java SE, you don't need to download or link to any external JAR files in order to use the functionality.

To open a new connection to a smart card reader, you need to first open a `CardTerminal` to the specific smart card reader that you want to access. Since you are in control of the hardware, you can guarantee that you will always have exactly one smart card reader hooked up to the Raspberry Pi, so you can safely choose the first terminal in the list as shown in Listing 4-5.

Listing 4-5 *Initialization code for a smartcardio* `CardTerminal`

```
TerminalFactory factory = TerminalFactory.getDefault();
CardTerminals terminals = factory.terminals();
List<CardTerminal> list = terminals.list();
CardTerminal cardTerminal = list.get(0);
```

Once you have access to a `CardTerminal`, you can read cards that are passed over the reader. For this you can use a simple loop that continually checks for new cards and processes them by a helper function, as shown in Listing 4-6.

Listing 4-6 *Card processing loop*

```
while (true) {
    cardTerminal.waitForCardPresent(0);
    handleCard(cardTerminal);
    cardTerminal.waitForCardAbsent(0);
}
```

The parameter passed in to `waitForCardPresent` and `waitForCardAbsent` is a timeout in milliseconds. By passing in 0 we are telling the code to wait indefinitely.

And now you can query the `CardTerminal` to get the address of the card. Listing 4-7 shows a code snippet that will retrieve the address of the card and print it out in a human-readable format.

Listing 4-7 *Retrieve card address and print to System.out*

```
final byte[] readUID = new byte[]{(byte) 0xFF, (byte) 0xCA, 0, 0, 0};
Card card = cardTerminal.connect("*");
CardChannel channel = card.getBasicChannel();
CommandAPDU command = new CommandAPDU(readUID);
ResponseAPDU response = channel.transmit(command);
byte[] uidBytes = response.getData();
final String uid = bytesToString(uidBytes);
System.out.println(cardname);
```

By passing in * as the parameter to `connect`, you are telling the Java smartcardio library to use any available protocol. The byte array passed in to the transmit function on the channel is a specific instruction to retrieve the unique identifier (UID) of the smart card, which will let you identify which playing card has been used. To simplify reading the value returned, we have a helper function, shown in Listing 4-8, that converts the byte array into a human-readable string.

Listing 4-8 *Helper function to convert a byte array to a string*

```
private static String bytesToString(byte[] bytes) {
  StringBuilder result = new StringBuilder();
  for (byte b : bytes) {
    result.append(String.format("%02x", b));
  }
  return result.toString();
}
```

Now you are ready to try running this code on your Raspberry Pi. As usual, you need to set up a Remote Java SE platform and configure it in the run settings for your project so you can deploy and run code remotely.

There is additional configuration for using the smartcardio library, which is to specify the PC/SC native library on the target platform. To configure this, open the Project Properties dialog, click Run in the Categories pane on the left, and enter the following text in the VM Options field on the right:

```
-Dsun.security.smartcardio.library=/usr/lib/arm-linux-gnueabihf/
libpcsclite.so
```

Now you can run the application on your Raspberry Pi and will get back the UID of that card as a byte string each time you pass a card over it. Give it a try, and experiment to find out what UID is returned for each of the different tags that came with your card reader. This is pretty close to what you need to read the playing cards for the IoT Hat. However, there are a few features missing:

- It would be handy to have a mapping from UIDs to playing cards. I certainly would have trouble memorizing 52 UIDs in order to accurately recall the correct card.

- As you were playing with the card reader, you probably noticed that it is quite easy to double scan a card when passing it over. The last thing you need in a live performance is to get the card order wrong due to repeated scans.

For the first requirement, you can create a simple property file with the mapping. For the set of playing cards I am using, I did a quick one-to-one mapping and saved it in property key value format. Listing 4-9 shows the first ten entries in the file.

Listing 4-9   *Property file mapping from UIDs to cards*

```
049D7B7A831E80 = 2H
04EC8F7A831E80 = 3H
04B5A87A831E80 = 4H
04065B7A831E81 = 5H
04E2937A831E80 = 6H
04D8AB7A831E80 = 7H
04DE4672831E80 = 8H
04025D7A831E81 = 9H
0402467A831E81 = 10H
04EEFF7A831E80 = JH
...
```

Then in your code, you can load the properties file and look up entries as you scan by doing the following:

```
final Properties cardids = new Properties();
cardids.load(IoTHat.class.getResourceAsStream("cardid.properties"));
final String cardname = cardids.getProperty(uid);
```

For the second requirement, to prevent double scanning of cards, you can simply keep the last card value and ignore it for multiple scans. For example, the following is a very simple implementation:

```
private static String lastcard;
...
if (!cardname.equals(lastcard)) {
  lastcard = cardname;
  System.out.println(cardname);
}
```

That gives you all the pieces you need to assemble the full application to scan playing cards on your IoT Hat and list the card value. Again, the finished project for this chapter can be found at the following GitHub repo:

https://github.com/RaspberryPiWithJava/IoTHat

Physical Construction of the IoT Hat

Now that you have all the software working on your Raspberry Pi, it is time to do the physical assembly of the IoT Hat. In addition to the Raspberry Pi A+ and smart card reader that you have been using throughout this chapter, you will also need a USB power supply, a top hat, and some supplies such as gaffer tape. Refer to the section "Bill of Materials" at the beginning of the chapter to get the full list of parts.

The first thing to pull out is your trusty magic hat. Any deep hat with a wide brim will work fine for concealing your Raspberry Pi and associated hardware. The hat I chose, along with some playing cards added for visual trim, is shown in Figure 4-11.

Before pulling out your tape and adhesives, I would recommend laying out the components in the inside of the hat to see how they fit best. Ideally, you want the antennae at the end of the smart card reader to be centered in the middle of the hat to give you the widest contact area for scanning. Make sure it is facing with the flat side down so you don't crush your headers and wires,

FIGURE 4-11. *Magic top hat for assembly of design*

FIGURE 4-12. *Layout of components in the bottom of the IoT Hat*

and position the Raspberry Pi A+ and battery on the side. The planned layout
of my components is shown in Figure 4-12.

Once you are happy with the layout of the components, you can start
taping things to the inside of the hat. I chose to use one-inch-thick black gaffer
tape, because it comes off without residue and blends in with the color of
the material. However, you can use any sort of adhesive that will securely
mount the Raspberry Pi, smart card, and other components. Figure 4-13
shows the smart card reader securely taped down on the edges. Covering the
reader with tape won't affect the antennae range, so feel free to be even more
aggressive with the taping.

The next component to tape down is the Raspberry Pi A+. Tape it beside
the smart card reader in an orientation where the jumper cables will run

FIGURE 4-13. *Smart card reader taped to the bottom of the hat*

along the side of the hat. Then you can tape down the Raspberry Pi and the cables to secure them to the hat as shown in Figure 4-14.

NOTE
You may want to leave a gap over the Raspberry Pi processor for cooling purposes. I clearly didn't do this, but so far so good on the operation of the hat.

The last component to affix to the hat is the USB power supply. This is probably the trickiest component to safely fit in the hat, especially since you want to be able to remove it easily for charging. I created little "loops"

FIGURE 4-14. *Raspberry Pi taped to the bottom of the hat*

with the tape by taking a long strip and affixing a shorter one in the center to create a smooth part that touches the battery. Four of these little helper strips were enough to safely secure the battery in the hat, as shown in Figure 4-15.

And that completes the hardware build of the hat. If you are using the Jackery Bar battery I recommended in the build instructions, you have to press the power button on the battery to turn on the Raspberry Pi. Once it is powered, you can remotely connect to the hat via Wi-Fi and run the Java card-reading application.

FIGURE 4-15. *Battery held in place by a set of tape loops*

For scanning the cards, you have two options. The first is to drop cards in the hat, which will get them close enough to the sensor to be read. The other is to simply wave them over the top of the hat, which works since the smart card antennae doesn't care which side the card is scanned on. Figure 4-16 shows these two options juxtaposed.

FIGURE 4-16. *You can read the cards by either dropping them in the hat (left) or waving them over the top (right).*

Now you have successfully assembled the IoT Hat and are ready to put on a magic show! Who will you impress with your wearable card-reading hat?

CHAPTER
5

Line Runner

No discussion of embedded development would be complete without the creation of an autonomous robot. Having a robot that can utilize sensors to analyze its environment and that can move by itself brings your embedded projects to life.

We are going to build a simple tank that can follow a track and pause for obstacles. It will be able to accurately (and quickly) follow a black line on a white surface and identify if there are any blockages on the track. Also, we will use a simple infrared transmitter to issue commands to the robot.

Bill of Materials

For the project we are going to utilize the Makeblock robotic platform. This will allow us to build a modular robot that can be customized to add different motors and sensors easily.

Figure 5-1 is a photo showing all of the parts we need to build the robot (well, everything except the track).

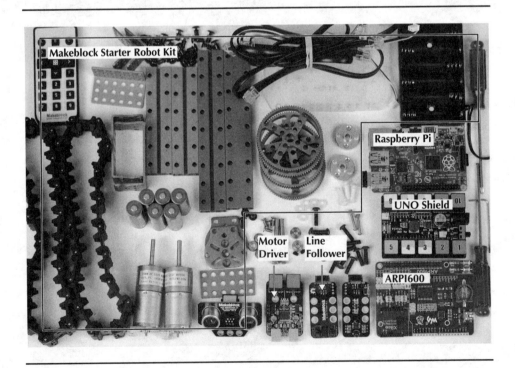

FIGURE 5-1. *Photo of the parts needed*

Here is an itemized list of the components:

- **Raspberry Pi B+ or 2**   For this project I recommend using a Raspberry Pi B+ or 2 so you can use the newer Arduino shields.

- **Waveshare Electronics ARPI600 Arduino shield**   This is the Arduino shield I recommend for this project. Any shield that adapts pins without being an Arduino microcontroller itself will work fine, but you might have trouble back-powering the Raspberry Pi.

- **Makeblock Starter Robot Kit (IR Version)**   This has most of the parts we need to build our line-follower robot. You can purchase it and the other Makeblock parts directly from www.makeblock.cc/.

- **Makeblock Me UNO Shield**   This will replace the Arduino microcontroller that comes with the Starter Robot Kit, allowing us to use a Raspberry Pi as the controller.

- **Makeblock Me Dual DC Motor Driver**   The UNO Shield doesn't have built-in motor drivers, so we need to get an extra external board for this. Fortunately it comes with two motor drivers, which is just enough for controlling the two motors of our robot's treads.

- **Makeblock Me Line Follower**   This is the line follower module that is compatible with the Makeblock platform.

- **White/black gaffer tape**   In order to have a clearly visible line for the robot to follow, it helps to lay down a tape track to follow. If your ground is light enough, you may be able to get away with just a strip of black. Otherwise, I recommend a 4-inch white tape strip with a 1-inch black tape strip down the center.

- **AA batteries**   You need six total to power the robot. It is easy to go through a lot of batteries, especially when you are debugging, so rechargeable NiMH batteries are a good idea.

- **USB battery**   To stabilize the Raspberry Pi power, you will need a USB battery in addition to the backpower from the Makeblock shield. The same Jackery Bar recommended for the IoT Hat project in the last chapter will work great.

This set of components provides everything you need to build the line runner robot using a Raspberry Pi B+ or 2.

NOTE
It is also possible to build a line follower using a Raspberry Pi board with fewer GPIO pins, such as the Model A and B, but you will need to use a different adapter board. The Raspberry Pi to Arduino Shields Connection Bridge (https://www .cooking-hacks.com/documentation/tutorials/ raspberry-pi-to-arduino-shields-connection-bridge) will work for this, although the pin assignments are different.

Robot Assembly

It is easier to assemble the robot first and then test it, so I will guide you through creating the line runner step by step. The parts you have may differ slightly based on which Makeblock set you are using, but you should have enough spare parts to adjust accordingly and get everything mounted.

NOTE
Due to variations in the kits, I recommend that you also look at the instructions provided with your Makeblock kit for the basic tank construction and adjust to accommodate the higher stacking of the ARPI600 and Raspberry Pi stack.

Start by assembling the base using a few of the aluminum rods. For this we are going to use the holes drilled in the side of the rod and the screw treads at the end of the rods to make a secure T connection. Since this is the frame of the vehicle, it needs to be sturdy, but don't overtighten the bolts or you can bend the aluminum. Figure 5-2 shows the completed body frame.

NOTE
Make sure that the side with the ridges is facing up. The reason for this will be clear in a few steps.

The next step is to attach the motors to the mounting brackets with a couple screws. Figure 5-3 shows what each of the assembled motors should look like. Also note the direction that the connector on the motor points. To keep your cables from dragging on the ground, you should mount the connectors facing the flat edge of the bracket.

FIGURE 5-2. *Body of the line runner*

After prepping both of the motors, you can then screw them on to the line runner base with two of the midsized bolts per motor as shown in Figure 5-4. They are mounted on opposing sides so that each can control one of the tire treads independently.

The free-moving wheels have a lot of pieces to assemble. Figure 5-5 shows all of the different pieces in the order in which you will need to mount them

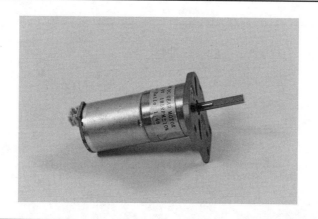

FIGURE 5-3. *Motor assembly*

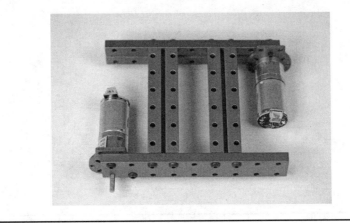

FIGURE 5-4. *Motors attached to the base*

on the rod. This includes a couple spacers, a miniature bearing, the geared wheel, another bearing, and an axle stop.

Make sure that you face the small end of the bearings toward the wheel so that they are centered on the rod. Also, the axle stop makes use of a small headless screw with a hex hole on one end, which should be tightened to prevent the wheel from coming off. Make two of the wheel assemblies as shown in Figure 5-6.

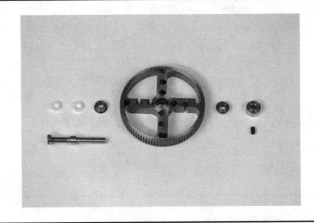

FIGURE 5-5. *Parts for the free-moving wheels*

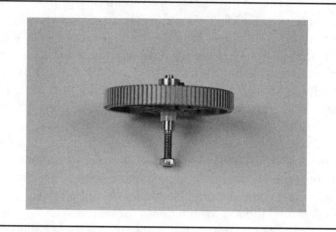

FIGURE 5-6.   *Completed wheel assembly*

Once you have assembled two wheels, you can attach them to the base by tightening the nut. To properly secure this, use a wrench and hold the geared wheel so that it doesn't spin.

The remaining two wheels are directly connected to the motor shafts. Attach the silver shaft connectors to the blue wheel rims with a couple screws and then connect that to the motor shaft using the small headless screw. Rotate the axle stop until the headless screw lines up with the flattened surface on the rod and tighten securely so that the wheel doesn't slip. The base with all four wheels attached is shown in Figure 5-7.

FIGURE 5-7.   *Base with wheels attached*

The next step is to add the battery holder and device platforms. You should have received a couple laser-cut plastic mounting boards with your kit. They come covered with a layer of brown paper on both sides that protect the acrylic plastic during etching. Remove this paper before you start assembly.

Before attaching these boards to the base, mount the battery holder on one of them. To do so, use a couple nuts and bolts or pop rivets as supplied with the Makeblock kit. If you have pop rivets, simply insert them into the hole and push down on the mushroomed end to secure it.

To attach the boards to the base, I took advantage of the ridged channel on the aluminum rods. This is a very clever design, because it allows you to screw in components perpendicularly at any point along the cutout, making it possible to attach things even when the predrilled holes do not precisely line up. With three screws (leave off the fourth so it doesn't short out your Raspberry Pi) and some of the longer bolts or pop rivets, you can attach the battery holder and device platform securely to the base as shown in Figure 5-8.

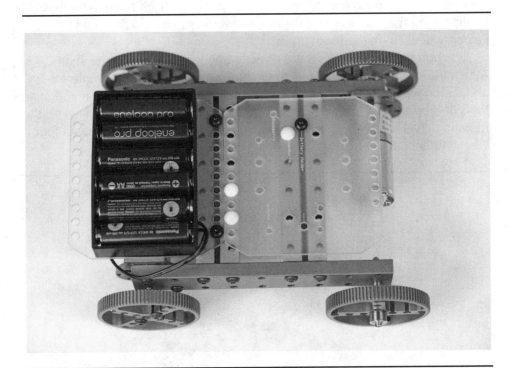

FIGURE 5-8. *Battery and device holders mounted on the base*

NOTE
The device platform can fit in a few different orientations; so make sure you have the mounting holes in the right position to attach a Raspberry Pi before you fully tighten the screws.

Now it is time to add a sensor and motor board to the bottom side of the line runner. We will be using the Makeblock Me Line Follower to detect white and black lines and using the Me Dual DC Motor Driver to control the two motors. The Line Follower needs to be mounted fairly close to the ground in order to accurately detect the lines, so you will need to add an extension as shown in Figure 5-9.

FIGURE 5-9.   *Makeblock Me Line Follower and Me Dual DC Motor Driver*

I used a couple L brackets, but you can also use the threaded rods to accomplish the same thing. The motor driver can be mounted directly on the bottom of the line runner. In both cases, pop rivets are the best way to attach the boards. The bottom side of the line runner with both boards mounted is shown in Figure 5-10.

There are a couple more sensor boards we need to attach to the top side of the line runner. This includes the Me Infrared Receiver Decode for remote control and the Makeblock Me Ultrasonic Sensor distance sensor so we can stop the robot when it gets near objects. For the Infrared sensor, I used some U brackets to raise it up, and for the ultrasonic sensor, I used an L bracket and a 6×3 flat board, as shown in Figure 5-11. You can use whatever spare parts you have left over to mount the sensors as you like.

The top side of the line follower with both sensor boards mounted is shown in Figure 5-12. Make sure to face the ultrasonic distance sensor

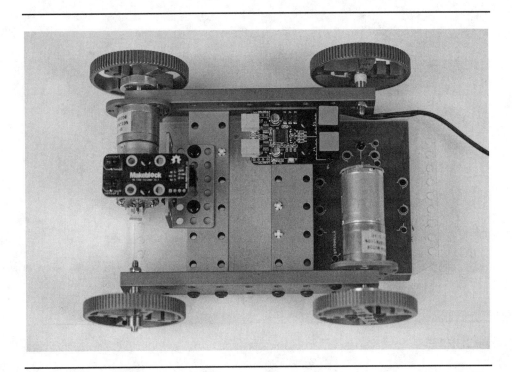

FIGURE 5-10. *Sensors attached to the bottom of the line runner*

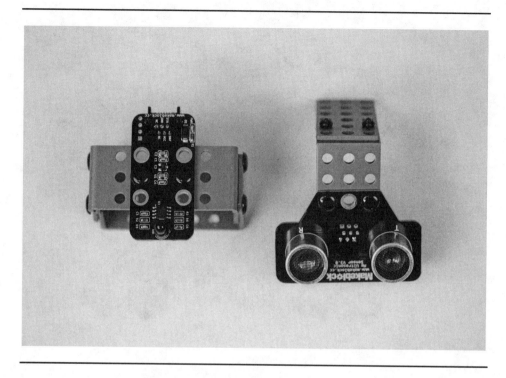

FIGURE 5-11.   *Infrared and ultrasonic sensors*

forward and raise it up enough so it won't drag on the ground. The infrared sensor just needs to be positioned so that it is easy to point the remote control at. Adjust as necessary to accommodate any variations in your kit version.

As you can see, I mounted the Raspberry Pi and ARPI600 Arduino boards at the same time. You will need two of the holes marked "Raspberry Pi" on the mounting board to secure the ARPI600. I recommend attaching the risers now while you have access to the bottom of the Raspberry Pi board. The other two holes marked "Raspberry Pi" can be used to attach the ARPI600 to the device platform as shown in Figure 5-12. For this I used a couple of the smaller screws that came in one of the Makeblock gripper kits, but you can use any available hardware you have that fits the holes marked "Raspberry Pi." The Makeblock spacers are a good size to provide a little distance from the platform so you can securely tighten the board down.

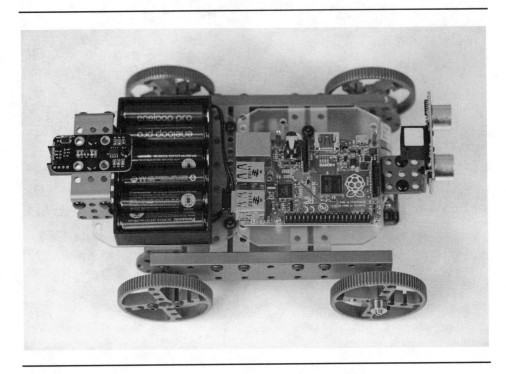

FIGURE 5-12. *The top side of the line follower with sensors and Raspberry Pi mounted*

The ARPI600 fits right on top of the Raspberry Pi and can be secured by screwing it onto the risers as shown in Figure 5-13.

The last board to add to the little device pancake is the Makeblock Me UNO Shield. This sits on top of the ARPI600 and stays securely in place just by the tight connection between the headers and the pins. However, before mounting this board, we need to make a little "adjustment.

"The Raspberry Pi uses 3.3V logic for GPIO, while the Arduino uses 5V logic for GPIO. Most of the time 3.3V is sufficient, since we really are interested in whether the digital pin is on or off. However, some circuits designed for 5V logic won't correctly identify the Raspberry Pi pins as being on. The Me Dual DC Motor Driver has this problem ... well, more accurately, the combination of the Me UNO Shield and the Me Dual DC Motor Driver has this problem.

FIGURE 5-13. *Line runner with ARPI600 attached*

The Motor Driver chip expects to see at least 2V to signal reversing the motor direction, but after we get through the logic circuit on the UNO Shield and Motor Driver, we end up with just under 2V from the starting Raspberry Pi voltage of 5V. The result is that the motors will go forward fine, but when you try to have them go backward, they will still go forward. To work around this, we can solder an 820Ω resistor in parallel with the 1kΩ resistor on the Me UNO Shield as shown in Figure 5-14.

Make sure that you connect the jumper between the correct mounting hole and connector pin. They are labeled on the board, so be sure to check the Arduino pin numbers on the top and the connector pin numbers on the bottom. To fix the direction for motor sockets 9 and 10, you would put a jumper on pins D4 and D7, respectively, as shown in Figure 5-14. To make a more secure join on the connector pin, you should remove the existing solder first using a solder wick or solder vacuum and then do a fresh solder joint with the connector and jumper cable.

FIGURE 5-14.   *Me UNO Shield with 820Ω resistors for motor direction*

After "adjusting" the board, you can now mount it on top of the ARPI600 as shown in Figure 5-15.

The line runner looks a little bare without any tire treads. To add the treads, simply connect the supplied rubber tread pieces together with the thin metal rods. A tighter fit is better since the treads will stretch over time and you want them to have a secure connection so they don't slip on the gears.

The last step is to attach wires to the line follower. Here is a list of connections you need to make:

- Port 3 to the line follower
- Port 4 to the ultrasonic sensor
- Port 5 to the infrared sensor
- Port 9/10 to the Motor Driver

In addition to these connections, you also need to hook up the motor board to the motors themselves. One end of the supplied cable needs to have jacks

FIGURE 5-15.   *Line follower with the Me UNO Shield attached*

screwed on to it, but other than that it is fairly easy to do. As a finishing touch, you may want to use some zip ties to keep the wires away from the tire treads.

This is also a good time to attach the USB battery to the Raspberry Pi. It can be mounted on top of the robot with some ties or tape and plugged into the Raspberry Pi's micro USB power jack.

NOTE

When powering on the robot, make sure to turn on both the USB battery pack and the MakeBlock Me UNO Shield. The robot will partially operate, but since the motors draw a lot of current, you may experience intermittent malfunctions and reboots with only one of the two power sources.

Congratulations on successfully assembling the line runner! Now you are ready to begin programming it so you can follow lines and stop for obstacles.

Programming the Line Runner

Now that you have finished assembling the line runner, you need to program it to do something interesting. All the sensor ports on the Makeblock shield are mapped to Raspberry Pi GPIO pins, so we can control it just like any other device hooked up to the Raspberry Pi.

We are going to use the Pi4J library since it has great support for pulse-width modulation (explained later in the chapter), and we will also need the performance of the low-level API in order to get accurate results from the distance sensor, which uses microsecond timings.

To prepare the Raspberry Pi for programming, set it up with a standard NOOBS image per the instructions in Chapter 1. You may also want to set up a Wi-Fi adapter, because attaching an Ethernet cable may be difficult once the Raspberry Pi board is mounted on the robot.

The Raspberry Pi can be powered directly off the six AA batteries that come with the Makeblock kit, so just insert your batteries and then flip the switch on the Me UNO Shield to turn on the Raspberry Pi. As noted earlier, you may want to invest in some rechargeable batteries, since running your robot will be an expensive proposition if you have to keep disposing of batteries after you accidentally leave it turned on.

This section will walk you through the coding and testing of the motors, infrared controller, line follower module, and distance sensor. To follow along, you can download the code from the following GitHub repo: https://github .com/RaspberryPiWithJava/LineRunner.

Makeblock/ARPI600 Pin Mappings

Before we start coding for the Raspberry Pi, it is helpful to know which pins on the Raspberry Pi GPIO header correspond to which of the ports on the Makeblock shield. Since we are going through two different adapter boards, it can be a bit tricky to figure this all out, but fortunately the wiring schematic of both boards is documented fairly well.

Table 5-1 shows the mapping of Arduino pins to Raspberry Pi pins using the Broadcom and Pi4J pin numbering schemes. In this project we are using the Pi4J library, so we only care about the first and third columns.

Note that the Arduino pins marked A0 through A3 are only hooked up to the Raspberry Pi GPIO directly if you change the jumpers on the ARPI600. By default they are hooked up to an onboard analog-to-digital converter, which

Arduino	Broadcom	Pi4J
D0	15	16
D1	14	15
D2	17	0
D3	18	1
D4	27	2
D5	22	3
D6	23	4
D7	24	5
D8	25	6
D9	4	7
D10	8	10
D11	10	12
D12	9	13
D13	11	14
A0	7	11
A1	5	21
A2	6	22
A3	13	23

TABLE 5-1. *ARPI600 Mapping from Arduino to Raspberry Pi Pins*

you can access via I²C. Since we aren't using any analog sensors from the Makeblock kit, we don't have to worry about this.

The second trick is figuring out which Arduino pins map to the pins on each of the Makeblock connectors. Fortunately, in the recent board revisions, they print them right on the PCB, but it is helpful to have a full list of them. Table 5-2 shows the mapping from Makeblock ports to the first and second pins. There are additional pins on each connector that supply ground and power, but the two data pins are the most important ones.

Makeblock Port	Pin 1	Pin 2
1	D10	D11
2	D12	D9
3	D8	D13
4	D3	
5	RX	TX
6	D2	
7	A3	A2
8	A1	A0
9	D4	D5
10	D7	D6

TABLE 5-2. *Mapping from Makeblock Ports to Data Pins*

Using Tables 5-1 and 5-2, you can figure out where any of the pins map to. To make it a little easier to figure out which of the GPIO pins are used for the devices connected in this chapter, Table 5-3 shows the mapping specific to our recommended wiring setup.

You will need to refer to this chart in the following sections as we start hooking up and testing sensors and devices.

Device	First Pi4J Pin	Second Pi4J Pin
Line follower	Left: 14	Right: 6
Distance sensor	1	
Infrared receiver	RX	TX
Left treads	Direction: 2	Pulse: 3
Right treads	Direction: 5	Pulse: 4

TABLE 5-3. *Mapping from Devices to GPIO*

Pulse-Width Modulation

DC motors are typically controlled using pulse-width modulation (PWM), where you give the motors a regular pulse to regulate their speed. By varying the width of the pulse, or the length of time current is being supplied, you can regulate the voltage and slow down the motors (vs. constant current). The advantage of using PWM to control motor speed is that it is more energy efficient when running at slow speeds.

The Raspberry Pi has hardware support for PWM on pin 1, but we need to use PWM on multiple pins to control both motors, so we need to simulate PWM using software on normal GPIO pins. Pi4J has support for this via the SoftPwm, which runs a process in the background that controls the pin timings to create a regular pulse. The timings are not guaranteed to be precise since it is done in software, but it is good enough for controlling LEDs and motors.

To initialize PWM on a pin, use the following method:

```
result = SoftPwm.softPwmCreate(MOTOR1_PWM, 0, 100);
```

The first parameter is the pin to use for PWM using the Pi4J pin numbering convention. The second parameter is the initial value of the motor, and the last parameter is the range of the value. The recommended default for the last parameter is 100. The result returned is 0 for success and –1 if there was an error.

> **TIP**
> *You might be wondering what the purpose of the range is and what happens if you change it. The way the SoftPWM implementation works is that it has a granularity of 100µs where it can set the pins to low or high. The range is the cycle time in 100µs units, so the default of 100 would give us a cycle of 10 ms. Then the value is how many of those units the signal stays high for, so if we used a value of 20, it would stay high for 2 ms and then be low for 8 ms. Changing the range to be higher gives you more control since you have more steps to control in the cycle, but the granularity doesn't go up—just your cycle time increases. To get a finer granularity than 100µs, you would need to do a software loop, which would tie up resources and make it difficult to control more than one pin.*

Once the pin is initialized, you can set the motor speed by using the `softPwmWrite` method:

```
SoftPwm.softPwmWrite(MOTOR1_PWM, 100);
```

This would set the speed of the motor to full power. The two parameters are the same as for the `softPwmCreate` method, the first being the pin and the second being the PWM value. To then stop the motor, you would use the following:

```
SoftPwm.softPwmWrite(MOTOR1_PWM, 0);
```

And, of course, you can adjust the speed by setting it to any value between 0 and 100. This is not a linear scale, because the power and speed of the motor drop off fairly quickly as you reduce the current and voltage, but it does give you a fair amount of control.

To change the direction of the motor, use the corresponding direction pin. Setting it to `PinState.LOW` goes forward and setting it to `PinState.HIGH` will reverse the direction of the motor. Here is an example of how to set up the GPIO pin and tell the motor to go backward:

```
GpioPinDigitalOutput motor1Dir = gpio.provisionDigitalOutputPin(MOTOR1_DIR, "Motor1Dir");
motor1Dir.setState(PinState.HIGH);
SoftPwm.softPwmWrite(MOTOR1_PWM, 100);
```

Putting this together, we can build out a little sample program that will make the robot go forward, backward, and turn in a circle. Listing 5-1 shows how to use PWM and the direction GPIO pins together to accomplish this.

Listing 5-1 *Motor test application*

```
public class MotorTest {
  private static final int MOTOR1_PWM = 3;
  private static final int MOTOR2_PWM = 4;
  private static final Pin MOTOR1_DIR = RaspiPin.GPIO_02;
  private static final Pin MOTOR2_DIR = RaspiPin.GPIO_05;

  public static void main(String args[]) {
    GpioController gpio = GpioFactory.getInstance();
    SoftPwm.softPwmCreate(MOTOR1_PWM, 0, 100);
    SoftPwm.softPwmCreate(MOTOR2_PWM, 0, 100);
    GpioPinDigitalOutput motor1Dir =
      gpio.provisionDigitalOutputPin(MOTOR1_DIR, "Motor1Dir", PinState.HIGH);
    GpioPinDigitalOutput motor2Dir =
      gpio.provisionDigitalOutputPin(MOTOR2_DIR, "Motor2Dir", PinState.HIGH);
    System.out.println("forward");
    motor1Dir.setState(PinState.LOW);
```

```
    motor2Dir.setState(PinState.HIGH);
    SoftPwm.softPwmWrite(MOTOR1_PWM, 100);
    SoftPwm.softPwmWrite(MOTOR2_PWM, 100);
    Gpio.delay(2000);
    System.out.println("back");
    motor1Dir.setState(PinState.HIGH);
    motor2Dir.setState(PinState.LOW);
    SoftPwm.softPwmWrite(MOTOR1_PWM, 100);
    SoftPwm.softPwmWrite(MOTOR2_PWM, 100);
    Gpio.delay(2000);
    System.out.println("spin");
    motor1Dir.setState(PinState.HIGH);
    motor2Dir.setState(PinState.HIGH);
    SoftPwm.softPwmWrite(MOTOR1_PWM, 100);
    SoftPwm.softPwmWrite(MOTOR2_PWM, 100);
    Gpio.delay(2000);
    System.out.println("stop");
    SoftPwm.softPwmWrite(MOTOR1_PWM, 0);
    SoftPwm.softPwmWrite(MOTOR2_PWM, 0);
    gpio.shutdown();
  }
}
```

Notice that we have defined constants to designate the two motor and direction control pins. These are taken from the pin numbers derived earlier in Table 5-3.

To run this application, set up a remote debugging session to your line follower in NetBeans and execute the application on the device. For more details on how to do this, see Chapter 2. This is also a great time to test out the wiring on your robot. If it goes forward when it should go backward and turns the wrong direction, you probably have the motors crossed. Just reverse the left and right motor cables and you should be fine.

Infrared Controller

To make it easier to control the robot, we are going to set up the infrared remote that comes with the Makeblock kit. It connects via an infrared receiver that provides commands over a serial interface to indicate what button is pressed. The serial pins are wired through to the Raspberry Pi's serial pins on both shields, so we can just use normal hardware serial to interface with the infrared receiver.

Here is how you set up serial in Pi4J:

```
Serial remote = SerialFactory.createInstance();
remote.open(Serial.DEFAULT_COM_PORT, 9600);
```

This creates a new serial factory on the predefined Raspberry Pi serial ports (15/16) and opens it for communication at 9600 baud, which is the correct speed for interfacing with the Makeblock serial module.

To receive data from the serial module, we have to add a listener to the serial object with a callback class. An easy way to implement this is to make use of a lambda expression that has a `switch` block for different return values, as shown in Listing 5-2.

 Listing 5-2 *Listener code to process serial remote data*

```
remote.addListener((SerialDataListener) (SerialDataEvent event) -> {
  String data = event.getData();
  byte command = (byte) data.charAt(2);
  switch (command) {
    case 69: // power/A
      System.out.println("Power/A pressed");
      gpio.shutdown();
      System.exit(0);
    default:
      System.out.println("Unrecognized Command: " + command);
  }
}
```

NOTE
While it would be nice to use the lambda shorthand syntax and leave off the type on this expression, it wouldn't compile because there are multiple types of callbacks that the addListener *method accepts, so you have to explicitly set the type.*

This code will print out a message with the value of the serial command pressed on the controller. It is very useful as a debugging aid to figure out the codes for all the buttons on the remote. Pressing the power button on the remote will cleanly terminate the Pi4J GPIO support and exit the Java process.

Now that we have a functioning remote and working motors, we can put this together to build a simple interface for manually controlling the robot.

I used the following key mappings in the sample (with two sets of key names separated by a slash based on different versions of the remote):

- **Play/Center**   Go forward or stop if already moving forward

- **Rewind/Left**   Turn left or stop turning if already turning left

- **Fast Forward/Right**   Turn right or stop turning if already turning right

- **Return/E**   Drive in reverse or stop if already driving in reverse

- **Plus/Up**   Speed up

- **Minus/Down**   Slow down

This allows you to control the robot by pressing a button once to do an action and a second time to cancel it. To implement the control logic, we need a couple extra abstractions. To handle driving we are using an enum that has the different possible states for the robot, as shown in Listing 5-3.

Listing 5-3   *enum to control the states for the robot*

```
public static enum Drive {
  reverse(PinState.HIGH, PinState.LOW),
  stop(PinState.LOW, PinState.LOW),
  forward(PinState.LOW, PinState.HIGH),
  left(PinState.LOW, PinState.LOW),
  right(PinState.HIGH, PinState.HIGH);
  private final PinState motor1;
  private final PinState motor2;

  Drive(PinState motor1, PinState motor2) {
    this.motor1 = motor1;
    this.motor2 = motor2;
  }
};
```

For each of the states, this enum defines the direction for motor 1 and motor 2. The only state that this doesn't matter for is when we are stopped, so we simply set both pins to PinState.LOW. To handle the speed, we have an enum that has different preset speed values as shown in Listing 5-4.

Listing 5-4 *enum for the speed of the line follower*

```java
public static enum Speed {
  slow(55), medium(65), fast(80), accelerate(100);
  private final int pulse;

  Speed(int pulse) {
    this.pulse = pulse;
  }

  public Speed speedup() {
    return this == accelerate ? accelerate : values()[ordinal() + 1];
  }

  public Speed slowdown() {
    return this == slow ? slow : values()[ordinal() - 1];
  }
};
```

Since the slowdown is not linear with pulse-width modulation, I have chosen some values that are weighted toward the upper end of the range. You may find through experimentation that you get better speed control by adjusting the values slightly. You can also add additional levels for more granularity.

After defining both of these enums with the values for the Motor Driver, the implementation of the doDrive method is relatively trivial. Simply set the direction for each of the motors and then the motor speed via PWM as shown in Listing 5-5.

Listing 5-5 *Implementation of doDrive to set the line runner speed and direction*

```java
private void doDrive(Drive drive) {
  motor1Dir.setState(drive.motor1);
  motor2Dir.setState(drive.motor2);
  SoftPwm.softPwmWrite(MOTOR1_PWM, drive == Drive.stop ? 0 : speed.pulse);
  SoftPwm.softPwmWrite(MOTOR2_PWM, drive == Drive.stop ? 0 : speed.pulse);
  this.drive = drive;
}
```

To connect this with the remote, we will add some additional case statements to the serial listener we implemented in Listing 5-2. The additional case statements for driving the car forward, backward, left, and right are shown in Listing 5-6.

Listing 5-6 *Case statements for driving the line follower manually*

```
case 21: // play/center
  doDrive(drive == Drive.forward ? Drive.stop : Drive.forward);
  break;
case 7: // rewind/left
  doDrive(drive == Drive.left ? Drive.stop : Drive.left);
  break;
case 9: // fast forward/right
  doDrive(drive == Drive.right ? Drive.stop : Drive.right);
  break;
case 64: // plus/up
  changeSpeed(speed.speedup());
  break;
case 25: // minus/down
  changeSpeed(speed.slowdown());
  break;
case 67: // return/E
  doDrive(drive == Drive.reverse ? Drive.stop : Drive.reverse);
  break;
```

With the updates to the code, we can now control the robot entirely from the remote. Since the turning speed is fairly quick, driving the robot accurately can be challenging, especially if we are trying to follow a precise path. However, with a little extra code, we are going to get the line runner to drive itself.

Line Following

The Makeblock Me Line Follower is a simple board that comes with two infrared LEDs and two IR photodiodes mounted in pairs to make two photo-couplers. When the infrared light bounces off the ground it will either be reflected if the surface is light or absorbed if the surface is dark. The photodiodes normally have a high resistance, but when they are exposed to infrared light the resistance decreases, allowing us to detect the presence of a reflective surface. For white and black surfaces the sensor is extremely reliable when used at a distance of 1–2 centimeters from the ground.

Using the two photo-couplers allows us to quickly follow a line without any "hunting." For a black line on a white surface, a single sensor would only tell us if we were on the line or off the line, but not the direction in which we went off the line. However, with two sensors mounted perpendicularly to the surface, we can tell the direction of the line by seeing which sensor goes off the line first. If the rightmost sensor goes off the line first, then the robot likely went off the right side of the line. If the leftmost sensor goes off the line first, then the robot likely went off the left side of the line.

The Makeblock board converts the analog data from the photodiodes into digital high/low signals on two separate GPIO pins. From Table 5-3 we know this is going to be pin 6 for the left sensor and pin 14 for the right sensor. You can initialize these pins as follows:

```
lineFollowA = gpio.provisionDigitalInputPin(LINE_FOLLOW_A, "LineFollowA");
lineFollowB = gpio.provisionDigitalInputPin(LINE_FOLLOW_B, "LineFollowB");
```

Listing 5-7 shows a simple run loop that will poll the infrared sensor approximately once per millisecond to adjust the direction of the robot. The most difficult case to handle is if both sensors leave the line simultaneously. Since we don't know where the line is, we just "keep calm and carry on" until we find the line again.

Listing 5-7   *Line-following loop that polls the infrared sensor*

```
public void run() {
  for (;;) {
    if (followLine) {
      boolean leftSensor = lineFollowA.getState().isHigh();
      boolean rightSensor = lineFollowB.getState().isHigh();
      if (leftSensor && rightSensor) { // we are lost
      } else if (!leftSensor && !rightSensor) { // on the line
        lineLocation = Drive.forward;
      } else if (!leftSensor && rightSensor) { // slipping off the right
        lineLocation = Drive.left;
      } else if (leftSensor && !rightSensor) { // slipping off the left
        lineLocation = Drive.right;
      }
      doDrive(lineLocation);
      Gpio.delay(1);
    } else {
      Gpio.delay(1000);
    }
  }
}
```

And finally, we can integrate the line-following functionality with the remote by tying it to the "D" button on the remote. Listing 5-8 has an additional case clause for our remote `switch` block that was originally defined in Listing 5-2.

Listing 5-8   *Case clause to turn on and off the line-following algorithm*

```
case 68: // D
  if (!followLine) { // initiate line following
    followLine = true;
    lineLocation = Drive.forward;
  } else { // terminate line following
    followLine = false;
    Gpio.delay(100);
    doDrive(Drive.stop);
  }
  break;
```

The reason for the delay on stopping is to avoid the line follower stop state being overridden by the line-following algorithm if it is in the middle of transitioning states.

Now you have a working line follower robot that you can test out on any level surface. If your floor is reflective enough you can get away with just taping a thin black line on the floor for the track. However, a good workaround for floors that are too dark or are of varying color is to put an outer track of white tape with an inner line to follow.

For the outer track, I recommend about 10cm total thickness, which can be done with multiple strips of tape if you don't have thick enough tape. For the black line, a strip about 3cm wide works well, although any thickness wider than the distance between the two photo-couplers should work. Figure 5-16 shows the line runner in action, happily racing around a taped track at a Java User Group event in Campinas, Brazil.

Obstacle Detection

The last trick for our line runner is to teach it how to stop and wait for obstacles that obstruct the track. To accomplish this, we are going to use the Makeblock Me Ultrasonic Sensor. This sensor uses high-pitched sounds to detect the presence of and distance to a solid object in front of the sensor. It is accurate from 3cm to 4m, although the effective range of the sensor is limited by the speed and precision with which we can read and write to the digital pins on the Raspberry Pi.

FIGURE 5-16. *Line runner in action (photo credit Bruno Borges)*

The protocol for the Makeblock Me Ultrasonic Sensor is as follows. First, initialize the sensor by performing these steps:

1. Write a low value to the GPIO pin.

2. Wait 2 microseconds.

3. Write a high value to the GPIO pin.

4. Wait 10 microseconds.

5. Write a low value to the GPIO pin.

Read the sensor as follows:

1. Wait for it to go high.

2. Start a timer.

3. Wait for it go low.

4. Capture the pulse width in microseconds.

Once we have the pulse width of the sensor, we can use this to calculate the distance of the object. The distance in centimeters is calculated by dividing the pulse width by 58 as shown in the following formula:

Distance (cm) = Pulse Width (uS) / 58

At the minimum distance of 3cm for the sensor, this would require timings as precise as 174µs or .174ms. Unfortunately, the Raspberry Pi GPIO libraries cannot handle this resolution, so at this distance you will miss the pulse entirely. Using the fastest GPIO interface available, Pi4J raw mode, we can measure distances starting at around 20cm and up, which gives us an effective range of 20cm to 4m for the sensor. This is reasonable for obstacle avoidance, and is the range we will focus on.

NOTE
You can achieve higher resolution on real-time chips such as the ATmega328 used in the Arduino, because they do not run a full operating system and therefore have no interrupts that interfere with timing. However, you are giving up on general-purpose computation power, so a good combination is to hook up an Arduino to the sensors and communicate with a Raspberry Pi that is doing more advanced processing via serial.

To measure the distance, Listing 5-9 provides a simple algorithm that follows the Makeblock Me Ultrasonic Sensor protocol to return the distance in centimeters.

Listing 5-9   *Algorithm to calculate distance using the Me Ultrasonic Sensor*

```
private int measureDistance() {
  Gpio.pinMode(ULTRASONIC, Gpio.OUTPUT);
  Gpio.digitalWrite(ULTRASONIC, 0);
  Gpio.delayMicroseconds(2);
  Gpio.digitalWrite(ULTRASONIC, 1);
  Gpio.delayMicroseconds(10);
  Gpio.digitalWrite(ULTRASONIC, 0);
  Gpio.pinMode(ULTRASONIC, Gpio.INPUT);
  long start = System.nanoTime();
  while (Gpio.digitalRead(ULTRASONIC) == 0 && System.nanoTime() - start < 23000000) {
  }
  long mid = System.nanoTime();
  if (mid - start >= 23000000)
    return -1;  // obstacle too close to detect distance
  while (Gpio.digitalRead(ULTRASONIC) == 1 && System.nanoTime() - mid < 23000000) {
  }
  long end = System.nanoTime();
  return (int) (end - mid) / 58000;
}
```

Using this method we can modify our line-following algorithm to stop if there are any obstacles detected ahead. The new lines are highlighted in bold in Listing 5-10.

Listing 5-10   *Modified run algorithm to stop when obstacles are detected*

```
public void run() {
  for (;;) {
    if (followLine) {
      if (measureDistance() < 20) {
        doDrive(Drive.stop);
      } else {
        boolean leftSensor = lineFollowA.getState().isHigh();
        boolean rightSensor = lineFollowB.getState().isHigh();
        if (leftSensor && rightSensor) { // we are lost
        } else if (!leftSensor && !rightSensor) { // on the line
          lineLocation = Drive.forward;
        } else if (!leftSensor && rightSensor) { // slipping off the right
          lineLocation = Drive.left;
        } else if (leftSensor && !rightSensor) { // slipping off the left
          lineLocation = Drive.right;
        }
        doDrive(lineLocation);
      }
```

```
        Gpio.delay(1);
    } else {
        Gpio.delay(1000);
    }
  }
}
```

And with that we have a line follower that is fast, intelligent, and safe!

Summary

In this chapter you learned how to interface with a variety of different Makeblock sensors and devices using GPIO and Pi4J to communicate over an Arduino bridge. This included driving motors using pulse-width modulation (PWM), communicating with a remote via serial, reading sensor data using GPIO pins, and simulating Arduino analog reads using tight timing loops.

The great thing about the Makeblock kits is that they are configurable and have a wide variety of additional sensors on convenient breakout boards. This gives you the opportunity to customize your line runner robot to accomplish all sorts of additional tasks, even taking advantage of Raspberry Pi–specific features like Wi-Fi support and high resolution cameras with streaming video.

CHAPTER

6

Tea Station

N ow that we have completed some larger projects that take advantage of GPIO, it is time to revisit the coffee brewing example from Chapter 2 to enhance it for use in brewing delicate tea leaves. While water temperature for brewing coffee is important, it is even more important for brewing tea because tea is more sensitive to temperature, requiring different temperatures based on the type of leaves you are brewing. Also, to brew the equivalent amount of tea and coffee, the weight of the dried tea leaves is much lighter than that of the coffee grounds, requiring more precise weight measurement of the tea leaves.

Some of the enhancements we are going to make to this example include

- **A high-precision serial scale** The USB scale you used earlier had two limitations. The first is that its accuracy is restricted to 2g. Also, the scale gives values but does not accept inputs. The serial scale I recommend using in this chapter allows you to programmatically "tare," eliminating a manual step in the recipe.

- **Accurate temperature measurement** Getting close to 100°C is fairly easy since the physical process of boiling limits the temperature. However, getting a precise temperature below 100°C is impossible without a thermometer. In this chapter you will utilize a high-temperature digital chip hooked up to the Raspberry Pi to accomplish this.

- **Touchscreen display** While it is possible to monitor terminal output to get instructions, most of us don't cook in the kitchen with our laptops open. By adding a touchscreen to the Raspberry Pi you will have the ability to monitor the tea-making process and select your variety of tea on-the-fly.

Bill of Materials

For this chapter you have several choices in the hardware you use. I will give some recommendations as well as some alternatives that are equally good at different price points.

Choosing a Scale

Most high-precision serial scales are designed for scientific use. They may also come with certifications and features that are handy in lab environments, such as adjustable legs, bubble levels, and hooks to hang weights. However, for this project, the only features that matter are

- **Weight range**   Choose a scale that can weigh the heaviest object you require. For this project you will need something that can hold at least one cup of tea, including the container. For this I recommend a scale with at least 600g capacity, which is just enough for a full one-cup glass tea infuser.

- **Accuracy**   Since tea is very light, a scale with precision to 0.1g is ideal. A scale any more precise than that is going to cost a lot more and you'll likely never need the additional accuracy.

- **Serial support**   You will need to interface the scale with the Raspberry Pi, so having a well-documented serial interface is important. Before buying a scale, make sure to read the serial protocol document to make sure that it can support standard 8/N/1 serial (8 data bits, no parity, 1 stop bit). It is possible to use other protocols, but in my experience the Java libraries do not support them very well.

The scale manufacturer I am going to recommend and code against for this chapter is Ohaus, which makes a wide variety of scientific and industrial scales and has a consistent serial protocol across its entire product line. Here are some of the models that I have tested and know to work well with the Raspberry Pi:

- **Scout Pro**   This is Ohaus's portable scientific scale line. It comes in a variety of different models, enabling you to choose the weight range and accuracy. As far as scientific scales go, it is also fairly inexpensive, with some educational discounts if you are a teacher or student (the Scout Pro is widely used in schools). The only downside is that you will have to purchase the serial interface kit separately, which is on the pricey side for what you get. The recommended scale models are the SP601 (least expensive), SP2001, SP4001, and SP6001.

- **Valor 7000**   This is designed as a food-grade scale, so it may be harder to find being sold used compared to the more ubiquitous Scout Pro. However, it has a pretty nice weight range, with one model capable of handling 3kg at 0.1g accuracy (V71P3T). Also, it comes with a built-in serial port, saving you the trouble and extra cost of buying a serial interface kit. This is sold as a "compact" scale, but it is pretty large, so make sure you have the available counter space.

Either of these scales will work fine with the Raspberry Pi. You get more scale for your money with the Valor, because the equivalent Scout Pro model plus the interface kit costs more at retail prices. However, because the Scout Pro is widely used in schools, you are more likely to find one that you can buy used for a discount (or one that you can borrow). Here are some links to the scales on Amazon:

- Scout Pro SP601: www.amazon.com/Ohaus-Portable-Electronic-Capacity-Readability/dp/B0051WAP8E/ or www.amazon.com/Ohaus-SP601-Portable-Balances-Readability/dp/B002SZEKJC

- Scout Pro Interface Kit: www.amazon.com/Ohaus-83032107-Balance-Interface-RS-232/dp/B007COOB5W/

- Valor 7000: www.amazon.com/Ohaus-V71P3T-Valor-Compact-Bench/dp/B00J3AWM2W/

In addition to the scales, you will need an RS232 to TTL (transistor–transistor logic) serial converter with a male connector. This is required because the serial logic on the Raspberry Pi's RX and TX ports operates from 0V to 3V, while standard serial signals are designed to work from –13V to 13V. There are a bunch of standard chips that do this conversion and plenty of companies that build packages compatible with both 3V and 5V logic that have the necessary DB9 connector. Here are a few recommended options (priced at around $10 on Amazon at the time of writing):

- **NulSom Inc. Ultra Compact RS232 to TTL Converter with Male DB9 (3V to 5.5V)** This converter is very tiny, so it is great for projects where space is tight.

- **NKC Electronics RS232 to TTL Converter Board DTE with Male DB9 3.3V to 5V** This converter has diagnostics lights for send/receive, which is handy for debugging.

Most RS232 to TTL converters will do fine and will use a MAX3232, ICL3232, SP3232E, or similar chipset.

Temperature Probe

For gauging the temperature of liquids, I recommend using the waterproof, high-temperature package sold by Adafruit that utilizes a DS18B20 sensor chip (https://www.adafruit.com/products/642). Since this is a digital chip, it is much easier to work with on the Raspberry Pi, which lacks any built-in support for analog inputs. The only trick is that it uses a 1-Wire serial protocol, which is not natively supported by the Raspberry Pi. However, there is Raspbian kernel support for software emulation of the 1-Wire protocol, which can be turned on using some boot flags.

The Adafruit package comes with a 4.7KΩ resistor as well, which is required to pull up the data pin for reliable transmission.

Touchscreen Displays

The Raspberry Pi supports a wide variety of different monitors and displays via the composite and HDMI outputs. However, it is notably missing any touchscreen displays that will work with the built-in DSI connector, which appears as shown in Figure 6-1.

FIGURE 6-1. *Raspberry Pi DSI connector*

The Raspberry Pi Foundation has stated that it is working on a display that utilizes the DSI connector, and this display may be available by the time you are reading this. However, you will likely have a lot more choice of display sizes and types if you utilize the HDMI output port.

NOTE
Shortly before this book's publication, the Raspberry Pi foundation came out with a screen that uses the DSI connector. As expected, it is only in one size (7"). The new screen should work with the project in this chapter, but has not been tested yet.

All of the touchscreens I recommend in this section utilize some additional circuitry to convert HDMI output from the Raspberry Pi to the native display signal and provide touch data back via the USB bus. This is identical to how touchscreen displays for desktops work, so you will find that many touchscreen displays marketed as Windows compatible will work just fine with the Raspberry Pi. However, the Java touch support can be a little finicky, so I recommend sticking with one of the following recommended displays:

- **Chalkboard Electronics displays (www.chalk-elec.com)**   All of its displays work really well with the JavaFX touch support. The 10-inch LCD LVDS bundle was the original display used to implement and test the code in this chapter, and the 7- and 14-inch models work equally well.

- **Hardkernel ODROID-VU (www.hardkernel.com)**   This is a nice universal touchscreen package that is designed for embedded use. The default cable that comes with it is micro HDMI, so you will want to pick up a full-size HDMI cable (or adapter) to allow it to work with the Raspberry Pi.

- **GeChic displays (www.gechic.com)**   If you want a really large, bright, high-resolution display, the GeChic 1502i is great. It is designed as a laptop display to work with touch computers, but works equally well with embedded devices like the Raspberry Pi. It can be powered off of USB, but don't expect to do this off the Raspberry Pi. Instead, use the power supply it ships with (and a second micro-HDMI cable for touch) or get a powered Raspberry Pi hub, such as Plugable's USB 2.0 7-Port Hub with a 60W Power Adapter (http://plugable.com/products/usb2-hub7bc), which is known to work well with the Raspberry Pi.

A wide variety of other touchscreens will likely work as well. Basically, anything that is recognized as a USB HID multi-touch display should work fine. However, due to the specialized touch support in JavaFX that directly implements multi-touch events, you may run across bugs or issues with other displays that need to be patched in the code to work correctly.

Tea Supplies

To brew premium tea, you will need a proper tea infusion pot plus some loose-leaf tea. If you don't have a local tea store that specializes in high-quality tea, you can order online. Teavana happens to have both a good selection of inexpensive teas and also a nice all-glass tea infuser that is close to the one I will be using in this chapter.

- **Joli Glass Mug with Infuser**   www.teavana.com/tea-products/tea-cups-mugs/glass-tea-cups/p/joli-glass-mug-with-infuser

- **Different varieties of loose-leaf tea**   www.teavana.com/the-teas

I have a preference for high mountain Oolong tea, and my favorite manufacturer is Hwa Gung (also spelled Hua Gang) tea from Li Shan mountain in Taiwan. Their tea plantation is at an altitude of 2450 meters, and makes use of traditional methods for tea harvesting and preparation as shown in Figure 6-2.

FIGURE 6-2.   *Workers picking tea leaves on the Hwa Gung plantation*

FIGURE 6-3. *Tea testing comparison at Hwa Gung*

Their tea is a little more expensive, but if you want to become a true tea connoisseur, getting high-quality tea helps you appreciate the flavors and aromas you are able to pull out by careful monitoring of the tea preparation process. They sell their teas worldwide, but if you can't find a retailer who has their tea in stock, feel free to e-mail them directly: hgtea1923@gmail.com. If you happen to be visiting Taiwan, stop by their new warehouse and showroom in Taichung and you can get a personal tea tasting comparison with Johnny as shown in Figure 6-3.

Miscellaneous Items

There are a couple extra items you may find helpful to have to complete this project. You likely have stock of these parts from earlier chapters, but here is the list:

- **Raspberry Pi**   Any Raspberry Pi will do for this project, although you may want to pick a Raspberry Pi B+ or two for the extra USB ports.

- **Breadboard**   A regular size breadboard or even a half-size one will work fine. This makes it easier to hook up all the wires for the temperature sensor and the RS232 to TTL adapter.

- **Pi Cobbler**   The Adafruit Pi Cobbler (introduced in Chapter 3) is a great way of connecting your Raspberry Pi to the breadboard along with labeled pins.

- **Jumper cables**   You will need a few jumper cables to hook things up on the breadboard. I ended up using nine total, but your mileage may vary.

Precise Measurement with a Serial Scale

The advantage of using a scale that communicates over a serial protocol is that scales designed for this purpose typically have much higher accuracy and allow for bidirectional communication. With a little bit of work we can get our Raspberry Pi to interface with scales like this.

To utilize a serial scale in our application we need to fix a few things first. Serial devices communicate using the RS232 standard, which operates on different voltages than the TTL that the Raspberry Pi uses. The Raspberry Pi Java libraries work better with 8-bit serial communication. And finally, we need to update our Raspberry Pi application to communicate using the serial protocol for our device.

The instructions in this section assume you are using one of the recommended Ohaus serial scales, but you can use any scale of your choice with some modifications for the serial protocol used by the manufacturer.

Connecting the Serial Scale

It is a good idea to test your scale in isolation first to make sure it is working correctly. Both the Scout Pro and Valor 7000 come with an A/C adapter, which is useful while testing so that you can leave the scale running without worrying about draining your batteries. If the scale came with a test weight, as shown in Figure 6-4, weigh that to test the calibration. If not, a good approximation is to use a measuring cup with milliliter markings. You can test different volumes of water to make sure the scale is reading values accurately.

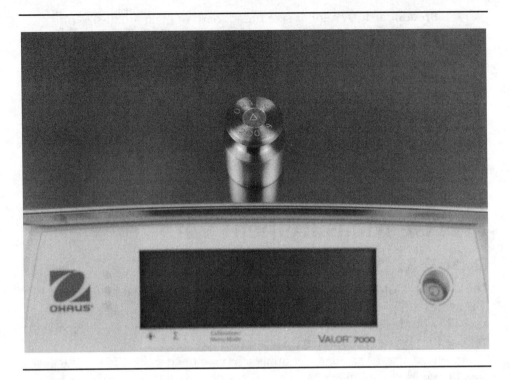

FIGURE 6-4. *Valor 7000 with a test weight*

Next, hook your scale up to the serial interface. If you have a Scout Pro, this is a small box that inserts on the bottom of the scale, as shown in Figure 6-5. For the Valor 7000 you can simply plug a normal straight-through serial cable into the connector on the bottom, as shown in Figure 6-6. In both cases you should end up with a regular DB9 female serial connector.

The serial connector attaches to the Raspberry Pi using an RS232 to TTL adapter. The adapter may come with separate headers that need to be soldered on. Only four of the pins are required to connect it to the Raspberry Pi with the following connections (all pin numbers are physical pin connections):

- **VCC** Connect this to 3V on your Raspberry Pi on Pin 1.

- **GND** Connect this to Ground on your Raspberry Pi on Pin 6.

- **TX** Connect this to TX on your Raspberry Pi on Pin 8.

- **RX** Connect this to RX on your Raspberry Pi on Pin 10.

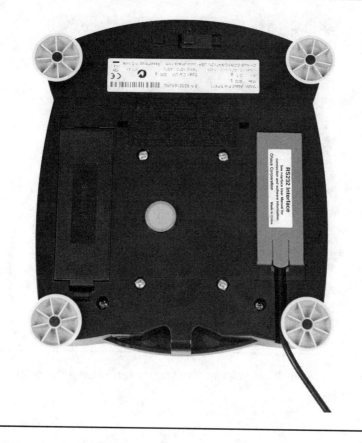

FIGURE 6-5.   *Scout Pro bottom with interface kit attached*

If your adapter has RTS and CTS pins, you can leave them disconnected since this project does not require flow control. Figure 6-7 shows a wiring diagram for connecting the RS232 to TTL adapter to the Raspberry Pi's GPIO pins using a Pi Cobbler. You can also connect them directly, but make sure to read the pin labels on your board, which may differ from the diagram. The diagram should match the order on the NKC Electronics board, which is clearly labeled. However, if you bought the NulSom board, the arrow pointing

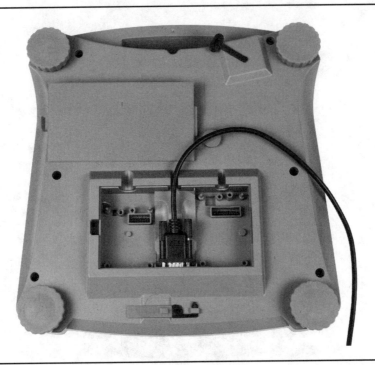

FIGURE 6-6. *Valor 7000 bottom with cover removed and serial cable attached*

toward the hole is RX and the arrow pointing away from the hole is TX, giving you a port order of Ground, RX, TX, and Power (from left to right when the DB9 connector is facing up).

The completed setup with the Raspberry Pi connected to GPIO for the Scout Pro is shown in Figure 6-8. In the next section we will test the connectivity between the Raspberry Pi and scale utilizing a terminal-emulation program.

Testing with Minicom

To make sure the serial interface on the scale is working and you have the RS232 adapter hooked up correctly, I recommend testing on the command line using a terminal-emulation program called Minicom.

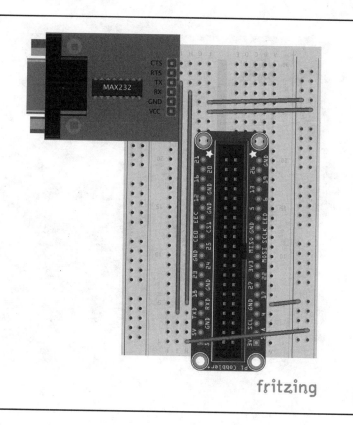

FIGURE 6-7.   *Wiring diagram for the RS232 to TTL adapter*

The very first step is to make sure that the serial port on the Raspberry Pi is freed from the console and available for programmatic use. For more details on using the `raspi-config` command-line tool to free the serial port, refer to the Chapter 4 section "Configuring Your Raspberry Pi for I²C, SPI, and UART."

Next, install the Minicom tool by using the following command:

```
sudo apt-get install minicom
```

If you have a network connection, via either a wired or Wi-Fi network, this will install the latest version of Minicom.

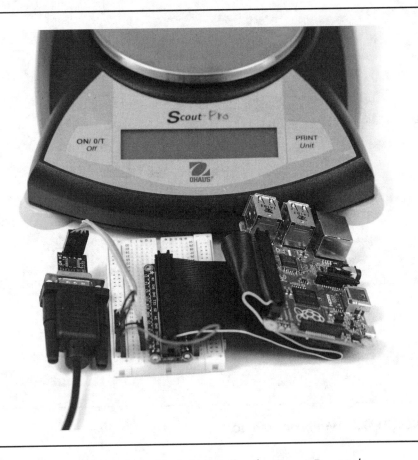

FIGURE 6-8. *Completed hardware setup for the Scout Pro scale*

If you are using a Valor 7000 scale, to launch Minicom, run the following command:

```
minicom -b 9600 -D /dev/ttyAMA0
```

This will start Minicom with the Valor's default communication settings of 9600 baud, 8 bits, no parity, and 1 stop bit.

If you have a Scout Pro, run this command instead:

```
minicom -b 2400 -D /dev/ttyAMA0
```

This will start Minicom at 2400 baud, which is the default baud rate of the Scout Pro. Unfortunately, the Scout Pro defaults to using 7-bit instead of 8-bit communication, which is required for communicating with the Java APIs. To modify the serial settings on the Scout Pro, refer to your owner's manual, but generally the steps should be similar to the following:

1. If the scale is on, turn it off. Then turn it on holding the power button (labeled "ON/ 0/T Off") until you get to the menus.

2. Press Print a few times (about four) to get to the RS232 prompt.

3. Press the power button to enter the RS232 menu.

4. Press Print a couple times (about two) to get to the parity prompt.

5. Press the power button to enter the parity menu.

6. Press Print until you get to the "8-none" item (about one time).

7. Press the power button to set the parity.

8. Turn off the scale and then turn it on normally.

In comparison, the Valor 7000 menus are much easier to enter and navigate. However, you won't need to change the default settings unless you accidentally changed them or purchased a used unit that was modified.

Once you have the correct scale settings and have launched Minicom, you can test connectivity by pressing the Print button on the scale. Figure 6-9 shows the return value for a properly configured Scout Pro scale. In contrast, if you don't have the right parity set, you will get garbled text as shown in Figure 6-10. The Valor output looks exactly the same except it has fewer leading spaces.

If you have trouble getting any output to show up, you may have misconfigured the Raspberry Pi serial or connected the cables incorrectly. The RX/TX lights on the NKC Electronics board are a handy debugging aid; they will light up when you press the Print button on the scale to let you know that data is being transmitted. The NulSom board has a smaller footprint, but unfortunately is missing any transmission indicator lights.

Here are some items to check when troubleshooting your serial connection:

■ *Are the GPIO cables connected to the correct ports?* You can use a multimeter to test continuity and safely swap the RX/TX pins for testing in case you connected them backward.

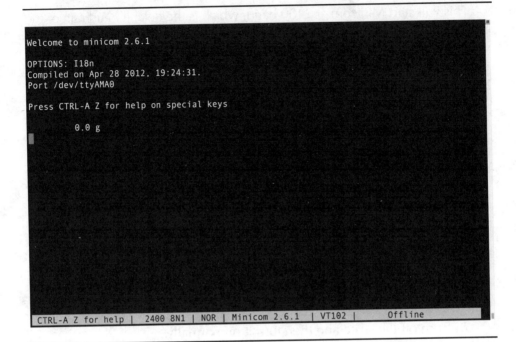

```
Welcome to minicom 2.6.1

OPTIONS: I18n
Compiled on Apr 28 2012, 19:24:31.
Port /dev/ttyAMA0

Press CTRL-A Z for help on special keys

        0.0 g
```

```
CTRL-A Z for help |  2400 8N1 | NOR | Minicom 2.6.1  | VT102 |      Offline
```

FIGURE 6-9.   *Minicom output for scale with correct parity*

■ *Did you choose the right terminal options?* At the bottom of Minicom, the legend should say 2400 8N1 for the Scout Pro and 9600 8N1 for the Valor.

■ *Is the Raspberry Pi serial console disabled?* You can always change this using `raspi-config`. See Chapter 4 for more details.

Once you have gotten Minicom to return scale data, you can try transmitting commands to the scale. The capability to programmatically control serial scales is what differentiates them from USB scales. To be able to see what you are typing, turn on echo in Minicom by pressing CTRL-A-E. The easiest command is to print the current weight by typing uppercase **P** and pressing ENTER. On the Valor you need to follow this with CTRL-J to type a line

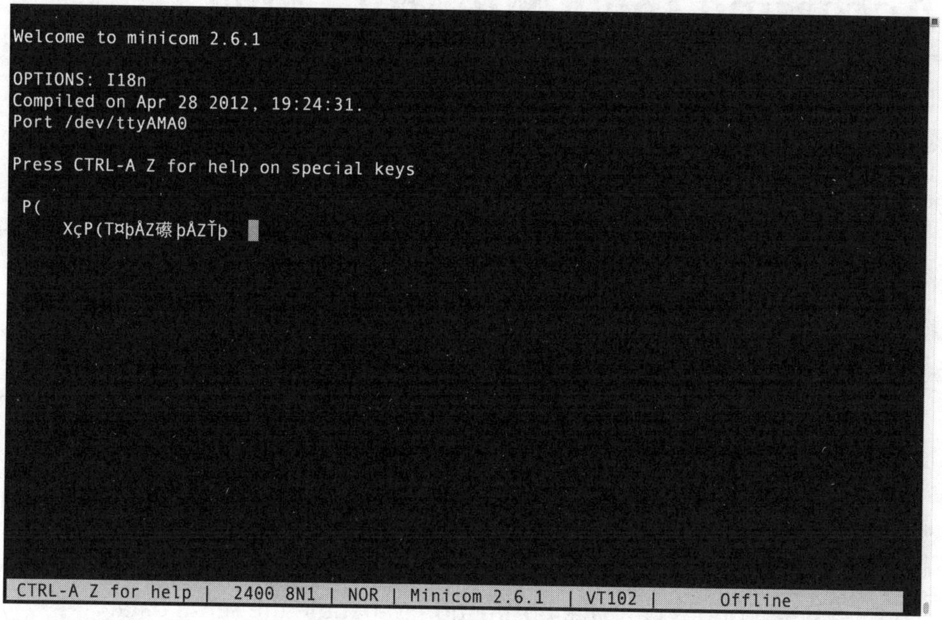

```
Welcome to minicom 2.6.1

OPTIONS: I18n
Compiled on Apr 28 2012, 19:24:31.
Port /dev/ttyAMA0

Press CTRL-A Z for help on special keys

 P(
     XçP(T¤þÅZ礅 þÅZŤþ  █




























CTRL-A Z for help  |  2400 8N1  |  NOR  |  Minicom 2.6.1  |  VT102  |      Offline
```

FIGURE 6-10. *Minicom output for scale with parity mismatch*

feed; otherwise it won't register the command. Both scales are case-sensitive, so make sure you use capital letters only!

Here is a list of commands to try out (remember to press ENTER and then CTRL-J for the Valor):

■ **Print** P

■ **Tare** T

■ **Continuous Autoprint** CA (Scout Pro), CP (Valor)

■ **Autoprint Off** 0A (Scout Pro), 0P (Valor)

Note the small differences in the commands between the scales. The functionality is pretty close, but Ohaus has made small updates to improve the Valor serial API, which is a more recent scale model.

Accessing the Scale from Java

To access serial scales from Java, you can use either the Pi4J library or the Device I/O library, which were introduced in Chapter 3. They both work great and provide similar functionality. Here is how the two libraries stack up against each other:

- **Serial protocol support** Pi4J only lets you set the baud rate, with future plans to add in more support for parity, stop bits, and other features in the future. The Device I/O library has flags for all of these settings, but they are unimplemented. So currently you have the same capabilities on both libraries.

- **Asynchronous processing** The Pi4J API supports synchronous writes and either synchronous or asynchronous reads via a `SerialHandler`. The Device I/O library routes are based on the Java non-blocking API (`java.nio`), which makes the processing implicitly asynchronous, although in practice you will have to create your own threaded asynchronous callback abstraction to handle the serial data.

- **Ease of use** For most applications the Pi4J API is a lot easier to use. It takes care of `byte` to `String` conversions, creates a simple callback handler for asynchronous processing, and lets you focus on your application logic rather than your non-blocking I/O jujutsu.

I am going to show examples using Pi4J in this chapter, which is a bit simpler and easier to use. However, if you want to integrate your code with some other Java libraries that take advantage of non-blocking I/O, it might be worthwhile to try out the Device I/O library, which takes a more standards-based approach.

To make it easier to follow along, all of the code for this chapter is available in the Raspberry Pi with Java GitHub repo at the following URL:

    https://github.com/RaspberryPiWithJava/TeaStation

Reading Scale Data with Pi4J

To get started with the Pi4J serial API, create a new project and add `pi4j-core.jar` to the class path. You will also need to configure a Remote Java Platform to connect to your Raspberry Pi with the correct IP address and root permissions by entering a value of `sudo` in the Exec Prefix field. In this

project, create a new class called `SerialScaleTest` with the code from
Listing 6-1 (shown for the Scout Pro scale).

Listing 6-1 *SerialScaleTest code version 1*

```java
public class SerialScaleTest {
  public static void main(String[] args) throws
  InterruptedException {
    Serial serial = SerialFactory.createInstance();
    serial.open(Serial.DEFAULT_COM_PORT, 2400);
    serial.addListener((sde) -> {
      System.out.println("sde.getData() = " + sde.getData());
    });
    serial.writeln("CA");
    TimeUnit.SECONDS.sleep(30);
    serial.shutdown();
  }
}
```

This code assumes you are using a Scout Pro scale at 2400 baud with
8 stop bits and no parity. If you are instead using the Valor 7000, adjust the
baud rate to 9600 and change the continuous print command to "CP" in
the argument passed to the `serial.writeln` method. Upon executing the
`SerialScaleTest` class with the Scout Pro scale, you will get output similar
to that shown in Listing 6-2.

Listing 6-2 *Output of SerialScaleTest code version 1*

```
sde.getData() =  g
         0.0 g
         0.0 g ?
         0.1 g ?
sde.getData() =           0.4 g ?
sde.getData() =
sde.getData() =           0.1 g ?
sde.getData() =
         0.0 g ?
sde.getData() =
sde.getData() =  0.0 g ?
sde.getData() =  0.0 g ?
sde.getData() =
         2.4 g ?
sde.getData() =
sde.getData() = 47.0 g ?
```

Notice that sometimes you get more than one result returned in a single callback, and other times you only get part of a line with results split across multiple calls. The reason for this is that the continuous autoprint rate of the scale and the default Pi4J buffering duration are not in perfect sync. To work around this you can use a `String` as a buffer to hold on to results until you have a full line of data. Listing 6-3 shows a modified version of the `SerialDataListener` that produces exactly one result per line.

Listing 6-3 *Modified version of the* `SerialDataListener`

```
static String data = ""; // this line goes outside the main method
...
serial.addListener((sde) -> {
  data = data.concat(sde.getData());
  String[] measurements = data.split("\r\n", -1);
  for (int i=0; i<measurements.length - 1; i++) {
    System.out.println("measurements[i] = " + measurements[i]);
  }
  data = measurements[measurements.length - 1];
});
```

This code takes advantage of the `split` method on `String`, which returns a `String` array based on splitting the `String` around the regular expression matches. By matching on the carriage return/linefeed characters (`"\r\n"`), we are able to split on whole lines. The second argument of −1 results in the `String` being evaluated (and split) as many times as necessary to process the entire `String`.

Running the `SerialScaleTest` class with the new code will clean up the output so that there is exactly one result per line, which makes it much easier to see what is going on. An example of what the output should look like is shown in Listing 6-4.

Listing 6-4 *Output from the new* `SerialDataListener`

```
measurements[i] =          0.0 g
measurements[i] =          0.0 g ?
measurements[i] =          0.0 g ?
measurements[i] =         35.1 g ?
measurements[i] =         93.1 g ?
measurements[i] =        109.8 g ?
measurements[i] =        111.7 g ?
measurements[i] =        111.9 g ?
measurements[i] =        111.9 g ?
measurements[i] =        111.9 g
```

From this new listing it is also very obvious what is going on. The return format of the scale output is as follows:

- 9–12 characters (depending on scale model) = weight on the scale; space padded and right justified

- 1 space

- 1–5 characters = unit of the result (no padding)

- 1 space

- 1 character = stability indicator; either a "?" character for unstable or a space for stable

Serial Implementation of Scale

Now that you are able to communicate with the scale from Java, it is time to augment the `JavaScale` application from Chapter 2 to add serial capabilities. You can make a copy of your own project from Chapter 2, or start with the previous solution from the GitHub repo here: https://github .com/RaspberryPiWithJava/JavaScale.

Rename the project to TeaStation so you can keep the two code bases separate. At the end of this chapter, you will have an application that is equally capable of brewing coffee, tea, or other recipes of your own invention.

Begin by creating a new implementation of the `Scale` interface called `SerialScale` in the `com.nighthacking.scales` package. This is also a good time to define some `String` constants for different operations you will need on the scale. I did a general-purpose implementation that will work on any of the Ohaus scales utilizing a factory pattern for class initialization, as shown in Listing 6-5.

Listing 6-5 *Initialization of the `SerialScale` class for either the Scout Pro or Valor 7000*

```
public class SerialScale implements Scale {

    private static final String CONTINUOUSAUTOPRINT_SCOUT = "CA";
    private static final String CONTINUOUSAUTOPRINT_VALOR = "CP";
    private static final String GRAMMODE_SCOUT = "0M";
    private static final String GRAMMODE_VALOR = "1U";
    private static final String TARE = "T";
```

```
private final int baudRate;
private final String continuousAutoprint;
private final String gramMode;


public static Scale createScoutPro() {
  return new SerialScale(2400, CONTINUOUSAUTOPRINT_SCOUT,
  GRAMMODE_SCOUT);
}

public static Scale createValor7000() {
  return new SerialScale(9600, CONTINUOUSAUTOPRINT_VALOR,
  GRAMMODE_VALOR);
}

private SerialScale(int baudRate, String continuousAutoprint,
String gramMode) {
  this.baudRate = baudRate;
  this.continuousAutoprint = continuousAutoprint;
  this.gramMode = gramMode;
}
```

After creating a `SerialScale` instance using either the `createScoutPro` method or `createValor7000` method, it will have all the commands you need set in variables. The class that initializes and calls methods on our `Scale` is called the `RecipeRunner` in package `com.nighthacking.recipe`. The very first operation that the `RecipeRunner` calls on your scale will be the `connect` method, which is where you should put the Pi4J initialization code.

If you haven't already done so, you will need to set up your project to work with Pi4J. Just like in the last section, include `pi4j-core.jar` as a library and make sure that the remote Java runtime you are using has a `sudo exec` prefix (which it should already have if you use the same project that supports USB scales).

The `connect` method should have almost the same code that you used in the previous section to connect to the serial scale. The only difference is that you are going to want to leave Pi4J running, so don't call `shutdown` at the end of the method, as shown in Listing 6-6.

Listing 6-6 *connect method of the `SerialScale` class*

```
private Serial serial;
private String data = "";
public void connect() {
  serial = SerialFactory.createInstance();
```

```
serial.open(Serial.DEFAULT_COM_PORT, baudRate);
serial.addListener((sde) -> {
  data = data.concat(sde.getData());
  String[] measurements = data.split("\r\n", -1);
  for (int i=0; i<measurements.length - 1; i++) {
    processMeasurement(measurements[i]);
  }
  data = measurements[measurements.length - 1];
});
serial.writeln(continuousAutoprint);
}
```

Instead, call shutdown from the close method as shown in Listing 6-7.

Listing 6-7 *close method of the SerialScale class*

```
public void close() {
  serial.shutdown();
}
```

Since we need to extract the weight, units, and stability from the String returned by the scale, each line is passed in to a processMeasurement method that will extract the values, as shown in Listing 6-8.

Listing 6-8 *ProcessMeasurement implementation*

```
private volatile double weight;
private volatile boolean stable;
private void processMeasurement(String measurement) {
  try {
    String[] components = measurement.split("[ ]+");
    if (!components[2].equals("g")) {
      serial.writeln(gramMode);
      return;
    }
    weight = Double.parseDouble(components[1]);
    stable = components.length <= 3 || !components[3].equals("?");
    scalePhaser.arrive();
  } catch (Throwable e) {
    Logger.getLogger(SerialScale.class.getName()).log(Level.FINER,
    "Can't process measurement " + measurement, e);
  }
}
```

From the earlier analysis of the data returned by the scale, you know that the scale will return three different pieces of information separated by spaces: the weight, unit of measurement, and stability indicator (either a "?" or a space). Use a regular expression to split the `String` and extract these values regardless of the exact amount of whitespace used (which varies in different scale models). Some points to highlight about this implementation include

- Rather than getting the value and converting it to grams (my preferred unit of measurement), I simply check the unit returned and issue a command to change the scale unit.

- Sometimes the scale returns odd values, either due to stale data upon initialization or transmission errors on the serial line. This could result in a number of exceptions from `ArrayIndexOutOfBounds` to `NumberFormatException`, so checking for a `Throwable` (and logging it) is a good catch-all.

- Since you are running in continuous print mode, skipping readings due to incorrect units or occasional exceptions is not a big deal … in a fraction of a second you will have another (hopefully valid) reading.

This implementation also uses the `Phaser` class, which was also used in the `UsbScale` implementation from Chapter 2. This makes synchronizing on new data coming from the scale on the serial bus simple and reliable, as shown in Listing 6-9 where the methods to wait for specific conditions on the scale weight are implemented.

Listing 6-9 *Implementation of the `waitFor` and `waitForStable` methods*

```
@Override
public void waitFor(DoublePredicate condition) {
  while (!condition.test(weight)) {
    scalePhaser.awaitAdvance(scalePhaser.getPhase());
  }
}
@Override
public void waitForStable(DoublePredicate condition) {
  while (!stable || !condition.test(weight)) {
    scalePhaser.awaitAdvance(scalePhaser.getPhase());
  }
}
```

These methods will block until the given condition passes, waiting for stability in the latter method before doing the comparison. Using the awaitAdvance method on scalePhaser provides a reliable way of blocking until the next reading from the scale is ready to check.

The remaining methods in the Scale interface are getWeight, isStable, and tare. The implementation of all of these methods is straightforward, as shown in Listing 6-10.

Listing 6-10 *Implementation of remaining methods from the Scale interface*

```
public double getWeight() {
  return weight;
}
public boolean isStable() {
  return stable;
}
public void tare() throws UnsupportedOperationException {
  serial.writeln(TARE);
}
```

Now you have a working SerialScale implementation that can be used with the existing coffee demo example. To plug in the new SerialScale implementation, modify the constructor of the RecipeRunner class to create a new SerialScale instead of a USBScale. Or better yet, add a setScale method and move Scale initialization to the main application creation by making the changes shown in Listings 6-11 and 6-12.

Listing 6-11 *New RecipeRunner method to allow setting a scale after creation*

```
public void setScale(Scale scale) {
  this.scale = scale;
  scale.connect();
}
```

Listing 6-12 *Creation of SerialScale in main method*

```
public static void main(String[] args) throws InterruptedException {
  RecipeRunner runner = new CommandLineRecipeRunner();
  runner.setScale(SerialScale.createScoutPro());
  runner.runRecipe(new PourOverCoffeeJavaOne(CoffeeCalculator.STRONG));
  runner.close();
}
```

Make sure to also delete the constructor that previously was creating a USBScale in RecipeRunner. You can also push the setScale method up into the RecipeEnvironment interface by creating a method with the same name and signature, but no implementation.

Now the TeaStation project should behave identically to the Chapter 2 example, but with one big difference: you no longer need to stop and press the tare button on the scale since your application can transmit data to the scale. While it may not seem like a big deal, a simple change like this has a huge impact on the usability of the project by others in your household or workplace who may use it to make coffee and/or tea.

Accurate Temperature Sensing

The secret to bringing out the best flavor in tea is careful control of the steeping process. Besides time, the most important factor in this process is the temperature of the water. Tea should never be exposed to boiling water or it will develop a bitter taste. However, water that is too tepid won't extract the full flavor. To complicate things further, there are many varieties of tea, as shown in Figure 6-11, and each reacts differently to water temperature.

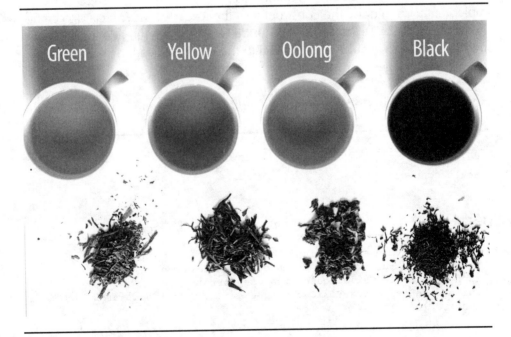

FIGURE 6-11. *Different types of tea (original photo by Hermann Hammer, public domain)*

Variety of Tea	Temperature	Steep Time	Quantity
White	71–77°C	2–3m	2–3g/120ml
Green	77–83°C	2–3m	2–3g/120ml
Oolong	82–94°C	1.5–2m	2–3g/120ml
Black	88–94°C	2–3m	2–3g/120ml
Pu-erh	94–100°C	3–4m	2–3g/120ml

TABLE 6-1. *Temperature, Steep Time, and Quantity by Variety of Tea*

While you will have to experiment a bit to find the right temperature and steep time for your favorite tea, Table 6-1 shows some common ranges for different varieties.

NOTE
Notice that all the quantities are identical! Variation in amount of tea is a side effect of different densities by style of preparation. In this chapter we will use the ISO 3103 standard of 2 grams per 100ml of water.

As you can see, the temperature used for different varieties of tea is an extremely important part of brewing tea, and an essential part of our tea station setup.

1-Wire Serial Interface

The temperature sensor for this section is a DS18B20 digital sensor. It uses the Dallas 1-Wire serial protocol for device communication that was developed by Dallas Semiconductor Corporation and is used by a wide range of different sensors and devices. The Dallas 1-Wire protocol is similar to the serial communication we used in the previous section, but trades off communication speed for a few unique advantages that are helpful for sensors. Some of the unique aspects of 1-Wire include

- Devices can be connected with only two wires. One wire is used for communication and intermittent power and the other is used for ground return. (The temperature sensor we are using in this chapter has a third wire for dedicated power.)

■ Multiple devices can be hooked up to the same pin, sharing the same communication wire and controlled by a single master.

■ It can be used over fairly long distances. With dedicated master hardware and fast lines, this can be up to 200 meters (see www .maximintegrated.com/en/app-notes/index.mvp/id/148). However, when using the Raspberry Pi's software implementation (known as *bit banging*, which refers to serial communications using software instead of dedicated hardware), you should keep the distance to under 1 meter for reliable communication.

I recommend getting the Adafruit high-temperature, waterproof packaging for the sensor that comes with a half-meter cable. This will give you an easy way to monitor an electric kettle near your setup (but far enough away that it is not a water hazard) and allow you to fully immerse the sensor without damaging it.

Testing the DS18B20

The DS18B20 sensor can be sampled from the Raspberry Pi by utilizing a kernel module that emulates the Dallas 1-Wire protocol in software. Doing bit banging in software is unreliable, but the protocol is forgiving enough that it works over short distances.

To enable the kernel module, add the following comment and line to the /boot/config.txt file on your Raspberry Pi:

```
# Turn on 1-Wire support
dtoverlay=w1-gpio
```

After editing this file, reboot your Raspberry Pi. This should also automatically load the correct kernel modules for 1-Wire support. You can check for this after booting by running the `lsmod` command, which should show the items `wire`, `w1_therm`, and `w1_gpio` (among other modules) as shown in Listing 6-13.

Listing 6-13 *Partial output of `lsmod` showing 1-Wire modules*

```
w1_therm                3325  0
w1_gpio                 4287  0
wire                   31248  2 w1_gpio,w1_therm
```

By default, these modules will create some extra files that get updated whenever a new 1-Wire device is connected to the bus. The default GPIO pin used for 1-Wire is Broadcom GPIO 4 (which in the Pi4J library would be pin 7). The DS18B20 sensor comes with a 4.7KΩ pull-up resistor and is easy to wire up, as shown in Figure 6-12.

The chip in the diagram is the "raw" DS18B20 sensor without extra packaging. The high-temperature packaging from Adafruit puts the sensor inside a metal cap with polytetrafluoroethylene (PTFE, a commercial brand of which is Teflon) wire wrap and heat shrinking, as shown in Figure 6-13, making it suitable for immersion in boiling water.

The three leads on this packaging are color coded as follows:

- **White**   Ground (leftmost pin in Figure 6-12)

- **Striped blue**   Data (center pin of diagram)

- **Striped orange**   Power (right pin of diagram)

NOTE
Be careful not to get the power and ground pins flipped or the sensor will heat up to dangerous levels and may cause permanent damage.

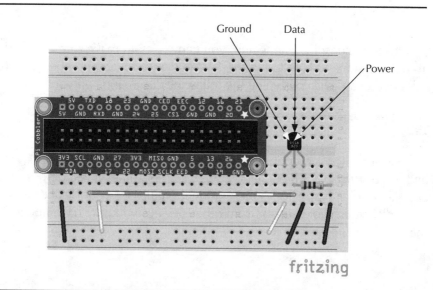

FIGURE 6-12. *DS18B20 wiring diagram*

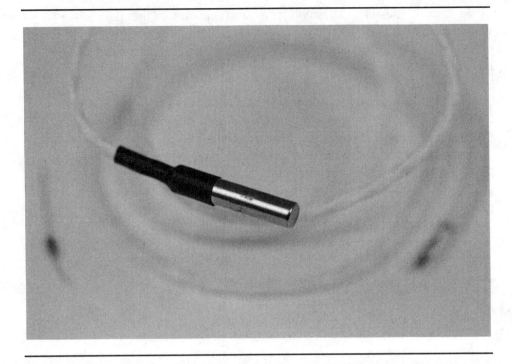

FIGURE 6-13. *Waterproof, high-temperature DS18B20 packaging*

Once the sensor is connected, you can check to make sure it is working from the command line. Go to the 1-Wire device folder and check for the existence of a device by typing the following commands on your Raspberry Pi:

```
cd /sys/bus/w1/devices
ls
```

If your device is recognized, you should have a folder that starts with "28-" and has a string of 13 hex digits. The 28 code signifies it is a DS18B20 chip and the 13-digit hex string is the unique identifier for your device. Together these distinguish your sensor from other devices you may have hooked up to the same 1-Wire bus.

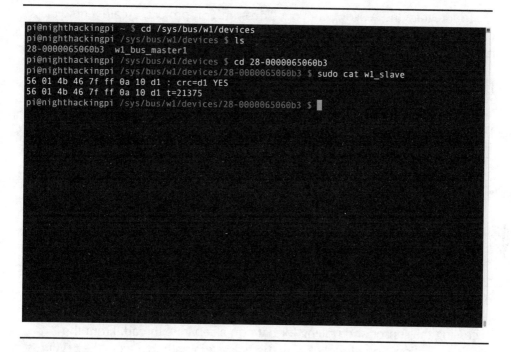

FIGURE 6-14. *Command-line results from the temperature sensor*

To communicate with the device, simply switch to the device directory and list the contents of the w1_slave file with root privileges. For my device identifier, I used the following commands:

```
cd 28-0000065060b3
sudo cat w1_slave
```

The thermometer returned a current temperature reading of 21375, as shown in Figure 6-14. The data returned by the kernel module is in 1/1000 of a degree, so to convert to Celsius, simply divide by 1000, giving you about 21.4°C.

Accessing the Temperature Sensor from Java

To get temperature readings from your Java application, you need to access the same files that you did from the command line in order to read the data. Since the temperature sensor data format is simple and consistent, you can easily read the sensor data and parse out the temperature in a few lines of code.

To integrate the sensor with your `TeaStation` project, create a new class called `TemperatureSensor` in a `com.nighthacking.temperature` package. Similar to the `Scale` interface, this class will have a few methods that allow you to wait for a specific reading on the sensor before proceeding. Listing 6-14 shows the interface methods you will need for tea brewing.

Listing 6-14 *Temperature sensor interface methods*

```
public interface TemperatureSensor {
  void connect() throws IllegalStateException;
  double getTemperature();
  void waitFor(DoublePredicate condition);
  void close();
}
```

Now create a class called `OneWireTempSensor` that implements the `TemperatureSensor` interface, so that you can implement these methods by grabbing the 1-Wire sensor data from the filesystem.

The `connect` method is where I did most of the heavy lifting to start accessing the sensor and polling for data on a separate thread. From the previous section, you already know the filesystem path to access the 1-Wire data file, which can be navigated to by using the new `Paths` and `Files` classes in Java 8, as shown in Listing 6-15.

Listing 6-15 *Lambda-style access to the 1-Wire file path*

```
private Path sensorFile;
private Thread tempListener;
private volatile boolean running = true;
public void connect() throws IllegalStateException {
  Path w1Folder = Paths.get("/sys/bus/w1/devices");
  try {
    Optional<Path> deviceFolder = Files.list(w1Folder).filter(
        f -> f.getFileName().toString().startsWith("28")).
findFirst();
    if (!deviceFolder.isPresent()) {
      throw new IllegalStateException("No 1-Wire device found");
    }
    sensorFile = deviceFolder.get().resolve("w1_slave");
  } catch (IOException ex) {
    throw new IllegalStateException(ex);
  }
```

```
    tempListener = new Thread(this::pollForTemperature);
    tempListener.start();
}
```

This code also creates and starts up a new thread that will poll for temperature by calling the `pollForTemperature` method, as shown in Listing 6-16.

Listing 6-16 *Implementation of temperature polling*

```
private double temperature;
private final Phaser tempPhaser = new Phaser(1);
public void pollForTemperature() {
  while (running) {
    try (Stream<String> lines = Files.lines(sensorFile)) {
      Optional<String> temp = lines.filter(l -> l.contains("t=")).
findAny();
      if (temp.isPresent()) {
        temperature = Integer.parseInt(temp.get().substring(
            temp.get().indexOf("t=") + 2)) / 1000d;
        tempPhaser.arrive();
      }
    } catch (IOException ex) {
      Logger.getLogger(OneWireTempSensor.class.getName()).log(
          Level.SEVERE, "Error reading from sensor", ex);
    }
    try {
      TimeUnit.MILLISECONDS.sleep(100);
    } catch (InterruptedException ex) { /* continue on */ }
  }
}
```

This will check for a new temperature reading ten times per second by reading the device file and looking for a substring that starts with "t=" and updating the temperature variable, which can be returned to implement `getTemperature` as shown in Listing 6-17.

Listing 6-17 *Implementation of* `getTemperature`

```
public double getTemperature() {
  return temperature;
}
```

It also uses a `Phaser` instance, which makes it very efficient to wait on results from other threads, such as the implementation of `waitFor` in Listing 6-18, which should look very familiar.

Listing 6-18 *Implementation of `waitFor`*

```
public void waitFor(DoublePredicate condition) {
  while (!condition.test(temperature)) {
    tempPhaser.awaitAdvance(tempPhaser.getPhase());
  }
}
```

The last method to implement to finish the class is the `close` method, which lets the thread polling the 1-Wire interface know that we are done with the recipe, as shown in Listing 6-19.

Listing 6-19 *Implementation of `close`*

```
@Override
public void close() {
  running = false;
}
```

To make the temperature sensor visible to recipes, we need to make some modifications to `RecipeRunner` and `RecipeEnvironment` to allow getting and setting the sensor, as shown in Listing 6-20. Make sure to pull the methods up into the `RecipeEnvironment` interface as well.

Listing 6-20 *Getter and setter for adding a temperature sensor in* `RecipeRunner`

```
TemperatureSensor tempSensor;
public TemperatureSensor getTemperatureSensor() {
  return tempSensor;
}
public void setTemperatureSensor(TemperatureSensor tempSensor) {
  this.tempSensor = tempSensor;
  tempSensor.connect();
}
```

Next, you can access the `getTemperatureSensor` method from the `Step` class to add in a few new recipe actions that you will need for brewing tea, as shown in Listing 6-21.

Listing 6-21   *New methods in the `Step` class*

```
public static Step waitForTemp(double temp) {
  return waitForTemp(temp, 5);
}
public static Step waitForTemp(double temp, double margin) {
  return new Step(e -> e.getTemperatureSensor().waitFor(w -> Math.
abs(w - temp) < margin));
}
```

The infrastructure is in place for reading the device temperature, so all you need now is a recipe that can take advantage of it.

Tea Recipe

With the new high-precision serial scale, temperature probe, and timing capabilities of our Java recipe application in place, we can now create a precise tea brewing recipe. If you haven't already bought some tea, make sure to purchase good-quality loose-leaf tea of your preferred type. Also, I highly recommend using an all-glass teacup and strainer like the Joli Glass Mug mentioned in the "Bill of Materials" section so you can quickly and precisely remove the tea leaves when the timer goes off. My tea setup is all ready to go, as you can see in Figure 6-15.

To start with, create a new tea recipe in the `com.nighthacking` `.recipes` package. For the tea recipe, I took advantage of Table 6-1 from earlier in this chapter to create an enumeration of different tea types to choose from, as shown in Listing 6-22.

Listing 6-22   *Tea type enumeration*

```
public static enum TeaType {
  WHITE(74, 3, 120),
  GREEN(80, 3, 120),
  OOLONG(88, 6, 90),
  BLACK(91, 3, 120),
  PUER(97, 3, 180);
```

```
private final double temperature;
private final double margin;
private final int time;
private TeaType(double temperature, double margin, int time) {
  this.temperature = temperature;
  this.margin = margin;
  this.time = time;
}
}
```

This creates customized tea profiles for different types of tea that you may want to brew, complete with temperature ranges and steeping time. For the tea to water ratio, I recommend sticking to the ISO 3103 tea standard of 2g per 100ml, as set up in the tea constructor of Listing 6-23.

FIGURE 6-15. *Tea hardware and consumables*

Listing 6-23 *Tea constructor*

```
private final TeaType type;
private static final double CUP_SIZE = 200; // grams
private final Ingredient tea;
private final Ingredient water;
public Tea(TeaType type) {
  tea = Ingredient.byWeight(2 * CUP_SIZE/100, "Tea"); // ISO 3103
Tea Standard
  water = Ingredient.byWeight(CUP_SIZE, "Water");
  this.type = type;
}
```

Similarly, you can set up the name, description, and ingredients to describe your tea recipe similar to Listing 6-24.

Listing 6-24 *Metadata information about the tea recipe*

```
public String name() {
  return "Tea Station";
}
public String description() {
  return "Precisely steeps 1 cup of tea using a scale and
temperature sensor.";
}
public Ingredient[] ingredients() {
  return new Ingredient[]{tea, water};
}
```

But the most important part is the recipe itself, where you can make full use of the new methods available with the temperature sensor as well as the higher-precision scale. The tea recipe that I used is shown in Listing 6-25.

Listing 6-25 *Steps that make up the tea recipe*

```
public Step[] steps() {
  return new Step[]{
    Step.say("Boil water to " + type.temperature + "C"),
    Step.waitForTemp(type.temperature, type.margin),
    Step.say("Add " + tea),
    Step.waitFor(tea),
    Step.tare(),
    Step.say("Now pour " + water),
    Step.waitFor(water),
```

```
    Step.countdown(type.time),
    Step.say("Tea time!  Remove your leaves from the tea and
enjoy!")
  };
}
```

To execute this new recipe, edit your main class and pass your recipe and tea type into the `RecipeRunner`. Also, make sure your scale and temperature sensors are initialized properly, as shown in Listing 6-26.

Listing 6-26   *main method with device and recipe initialization for tea*

```
public static void main(String[] args) throws InterruptedException
{
  RecipeRunner runner = new CommandLineRecipeRunner();
  runner.setScale(SerialScale.createValor7000());
  runner.setTemperatureSensor(new OneWireTempSensor());
  runner.runRecipe(new Tea(Tea.TeaType.OOLONG));
  runner.close();
}
```

Give your new tea recipe a try and see how the recipe comes out. I did a brew of fresh tea, and you can see the program output in Listing 6-27 and the results in Figure 6-16.

Listing 6-27   *Tea brew program output*

```
Precisely steeps 1 cup of tea using a scale and temperature sensor.
Boil water to 88.0C
Add 4.0g of Tea
Now pour 200.0g of Water
90 seconds left
89 seconds left
88 seconds left
...
1 second left
Remove your leaves from the tea and enjoy!
```

Based on how your tea came out, you can adjust the recipe. Some of the variables to play with include

- If the tea is too weak, try increasing the brew time (I chose the shortest recommended time to start).

FIGURE 6-16. *Fresh tea brewed using Java*

- If you find that your tea is bitter, the water might be too hot. Try adjusting the temperature down.

- Different types of tea can be reused for multiple brewings. Try experimenting with successive brewing and see how the taste changes.

JavaFX UI

The last step in our journey to tea nirvana is to create a simple user interface for controlling our tea brewing process. The Raspberry Pi has great graphics capabilities, which you can fully take advantage of by building a user interface using JavaFX. There is even full touchscreen support, allowing you to build a kitchen-friendly user interface that will work when you only have one hand free.

I recommended several touchscreens in the "Bill of Materials" section that will work great for this project. Figure 6-17 shows the GeChic 1502i, Hardkernel ODROID-VU, and a selection of Chalkboard Electronics screens side by side. They all hook up to the Raspberry Pi via HDMI and need to be externally powered by a wall adapter. Also, they have a USB connector for touch that will work with the latest version of JavaFX.

However, you can design and build the UI without a touchscreen, simply using a spare HDMI monitor or TV and an input device, such as a mouse. JavaFX is extremely portable, so the same UI code will work on a touchscreen exactly the same way.

Your Raspberry Pi comes with Java preinstalled and may also have JavaFX on it. As of the time of writing, JavaFX was still available as part of the NOOBS Java distribution, but the version was slightly outdated. I recommend grabbing the latest version of JavaFX Embedded from its new home at Gluon: http://gluonhq.com/open-source/javafxports/downloads/.

FIGURE 6-17. *Assortment of touchscreens that will work for this project*

While you are there, you should also pick up a copy of Scene Builder, which is a visual UI creation program. We will use Scene Builder to build a quick user interface that provides feedback on our tea brewing process and accepts some simple inputs. You can download the latest version of Scene Builder from http://gluonhq.com/open-source/scene-builder/.

To install JavaFX on your Raspberry Pi, follow the instructions on the Gluon website, which should give you the most up-to-date information. However, just as a high-level guide, here are the steps I followed to install JavaFX:

1. I grabbed a compatible JDK for ARM image from the JDK 8 download page: www.oracle.com/technetwork/java/javase/downloads/jdk8-downloads-2133151.html.

2. I copied both the JDK and JavaFX bundles over to the Raspberry Pi using an SFTP client.

3. On the Raspberry Pi, I extracted both bundles to separate folders.

4. Finally, I merged the JavaFX directory structure into the JDK folders, being careful to line up the directory names.

NOTE

These instructions are likely to have changed by the time you read this, so please make sure to follow the Gluon JavaFX installation instructions on the website.

Once you have JavaFX installed on your Raspberry Pi, it is time to create the JavaFX UI for your tea station. Go back to NetBeans and create a new FXML file for the UI layout using the New File wizard as shown in Figure 6-18.

The FXML file format is XML-based, so you can edit it directly, but it is much easier to do this task visually in Scene Builder. After installing Scene Builder from the Gluon website, it will automatically associate with FXML files, allowing you to double-click the new empty FXML file you created to open it in Scene Builder for editing.

Creating professional-looking UIs in Scene Builder is extremely easy. Simply drag and drop the components from the left tree navigation into the center area. There is a wide selection of layouts, controls, and charts that you can take advantage of in building your UI. Also, each component has a large

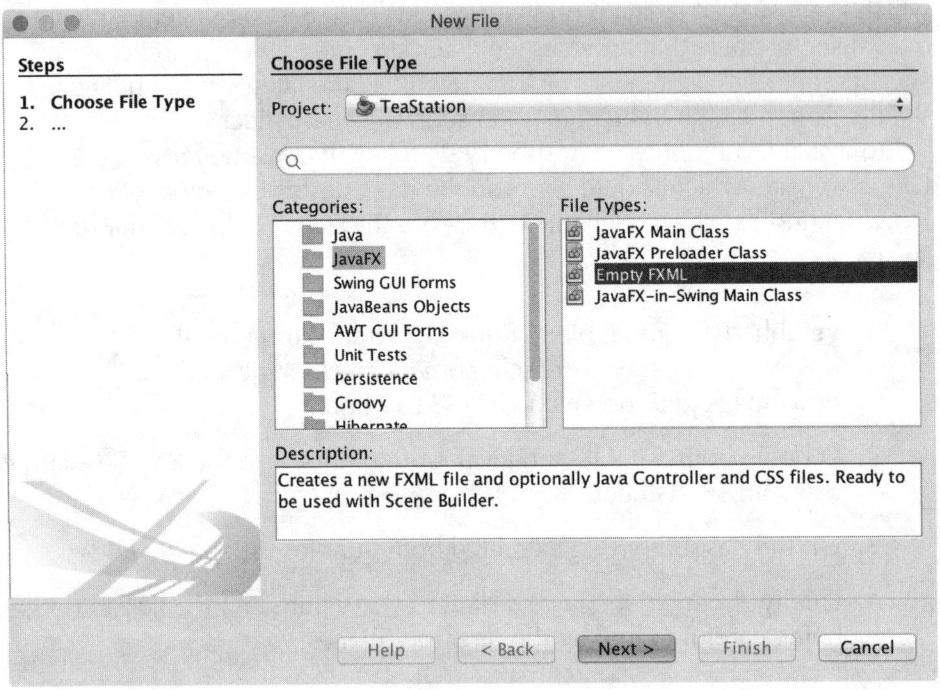

FIGURE 6-18. *New File wizard for creating an empty FXML file*

set of properties you can configure by entering in values in the right pane. The Scene Builder UI I created for tea brewing is shown in Figure 6-19.

I used the following elements in the user interface:

■ A text area (via a `TextArea` control) at the bottom to display the current message for the recipe

■ Two arrow buttons on the lower-left and right corners to go forward and backward in steps and a Quit button in the upper-right corner

■ A progress bar in the center to show temperature/weight/time

■ Some labels showing the current recipe information and detailed weight/temperature status

■ A background image to give the application a little flair

FIGURE 6-19. *Scene Builder user interface for tea brewing*

You can design your own UI slightly differently and it will be equally functional. Save your design and go back to NetBeans to launch and test the UI. The code in Listing 6-28 is standard boilerplate for launching a JavaFX FXML GUI that you can put in a new main class.

Listing 6-28 *Code to launch a JavaFX FXML UI*

```
public class JavaFXTest extends Application {
  @Override
  public void start(Stage stage) throws Exception {
    Parent root = FXMLLoader.load(getClass().getResource("ui/CoffeeUI.fxml"));
    Scene scene = new Scene(root, 1280, 800);
    stage.setScene(scene);
    stage.show();
  }
  public static void main(String[] args) {
    launch(args);
  }
}
```

Upon running this main class, you will see a user interface appear on your touchscreen. Make sure you are on the command line and not in the X Window System, because JavaFX takes over the entire screen and writes directly to the frame buffer. Since there is no code backing the UI yet, it won't do much, but you can test touch events by clicking in the text area and moving the cursor. If you can't get touch functionality working on your panel, check for error messages on the console output of your program, and it will point to one of the following problems:

- If you have no messages at all, then your touchscreen is likely not giving events over USB. Try the display in the X Window System, and if it still doesn't work, contact the manufacturer.

- The application needs to be running as root to receive touch events, so if you got a message about this on startup, double-check to make sure you have an exec prefix of sudo set on your remote Java runtime.

- If you get errors on multi-touch events every time you click the screen, but they are not registering as clicks, then you are likely running an outdated version of JavaFX. Make sure that the version of Java you actually launched your application with is the one that you have installed the Gluon JavaFX embedded release into.

Once you have the basic UI coming up on the Raspberry Pi, the next important step is to wire it to your application code using a controller class. The JavaFX controller class is simply a regular Java class that is referenced in the FXML file and has resources injected into it and can get callbacks from UI controls, such as buttons.

Listing 6-29 shows a controller class that implements the `Display` interface so we get callbacks on recipe messages, and sets up a recipe runner, our scales and temperature sensor, and a recipe to brew Oolong tea.

Listing 6-29 *UIController class to interface with FXML*

```
public class UIController implements Display {
  public TextArea message;
  public Label name;
  public Label description;
  public void initialize() throws InterruptedException {
```

```
    runner = new UIRecipeRunner(this);
    runner.setScale(SerialScale.createValor7000());
    runner.setTemperatureSensor(new OneWireTempSensor());
    final Tea recipe = new Tea(Tea.TeaType.OOLONG);
    runner.runRecipe(recipe);
    name.setText(recipe.name());
    description.setText(recipe.description());
  }
  private UIRecipeRunner runner;
  @Override
  public void say(String message, Object... args) {
    setText(new Formatter().format(message, args).toString());
  }
  public void quit() {
    runner.close();
    Platform.exit();
  }
}
}
```

In order to have this controller interface with the FXML file you defined previously, you need to specify the fully qualified class name of your controller. You can do this either in the Scene Builder tool or by directly editing the XML file by right-clicking it in NetBeans and choosing Edit. The tag for setting a controller is on the root element similar to the following:

```
<StackPane fx:controller="com.nighthacking.ui.UIController" …>
```

NOTE
The ellipses signify other required tags that were previously populated by Scene Builder.

To have the UI components be injected into the variables in your controller class, you need to specify an fx:id that matches the variable name. Again, you can do this either in Scene Builder or by editing the XML file directly and adding attributes like the following:

```
<Button fx:id="previous" …
<TextArea fx:id="message" …
<Button fx:id="next" …
```

TIP
The FXML controller will only see UI components that have an id set with the fx namespace (which resolves via xmlns:fx="http://javafx .com/fxml/1"). If you use an id tag without a prefix, then your UI components won't get properly injected.

The last FXML trick is to set a method that gets called when a control action is triggered, such as a button press. You can do this via the Scene Builder UI in the Code tab, or by entering it directly in the XML using an onAction attribute with the method name prefixed by a # character:

```
<Button fx:id="quit" mnemonicParsing="false" onAction="#quit"
opacity="0.75" text="Quit">
```

To finish your first recipe UI test, you also need the UIRecipeRunner class that was referenced in the controller initialize method. The code for that is shown in Listing 6-30.

Listing 6-30 *UIRecipeRunner implementation*

```
public class UIRecipeRunner extends RecipeRunner {
  private final UIController controller;
  public UIRecipeRunner(UIController controller) {
    this.controller = controller;
  }
  @Override
  public void runRecipe(Recipe recipe)
      throws InterruptedException {
    new Thread(() -> {
      initRecipe(recipe);
      for (Step step : recipe.steps()) {
        step.execute(this);
      }
    }).start();
  }
}
```

```
@Override
public Display getDisplay() {
  return controller;
}
}
```

Now you can run the `TeaStation` application on your Raspberry Pi and see the results conveniently on a small touchscreen. The functionality is the same as the command-line runner, but this setup is a lot more portable and has the opportunity to have additional user interaction via the touchscreen.

The full `TeaStation` code is available on GitHub at the following location:

https://github.com/RaspberryPiWithJava/TeaStation

Here are some additional enhancements that I made in the `TeaStation` version that is available in the GitHub repo:

■ **Screen scaling** It is helpful to have the application scale cleanly to different display sizes. There are a couple options for this in JavaFX since it supports both dynamic layouts and clean vector scaling of UIs. I chose the latter so that on high-resolution displays the buttons are not too small to interact with.

■ **Moving back and forward between steps** This is possible since steps are passed back as an array and all the processing happens via a lambda expression on demand. Just make sure that all the steps honor thread interrupts so you can switch steps without waiting for execution to finish.

■ **Progress indicators for weight/temperature/time** There is a built-in control in JavaFX for doing progress indicators, so this is simply an exercise in exposing that information to the control. As an another benefit, I added a Status text field under the progress bar with detailed information.

A screen capture of the fully decked-out version of the application is shown in Figure 6-20.

In this chapter you learned how to interface directly with RS232 serial devices and 1-Wire serial, and you were even able to build a touchscreen UI using JavaFX technology. With all of the different devices and interfaces you have learned how to use up to this point in the book, the sky is the limit with the sort of devices you can build. In the next chapter we will literally take to the skies with an autonomous drone that is powered by the Raspberry Pi and Java!

FIGURE 6-20. *Finished* `TeaStation` *application shown displaying temperature*

CHAPTER
7

Autonomous Drone

I n this chapter we are going to utilize a Raspberry Pi and some Java applications as a brain for a quadcopter. Quadcopters are often referred to more generally as drones, and we'll use that term in this chapter. Usually drones made for recreational purposes are flown with a remote control, often in the form of an application that exists on a smartphone or tablet. The person flying the drone influences its flight by interacting with the user interface controls in these applications. The mobile device typically connects to the drone using a wireless access point that is onboard the drone. This is similar to the idea of connecting to a wireless router at home with a client such as a computer or mobile device.

In this chapter we are going to take a step into more advanced capabilities by enabling the drone to fly without a remote control—the control will be onboard the drone. This will enable the drone to fly with a very basic level of autonomy, which is why the name of this chapter is "Autonomous Drone." There are more advanced levels of autonomy possible for drone flight, and at the end of this chapter I'll discuss ideas for achieving one of them.

CAUTION
Because the drone created in this project actually flies in the air, it is a lot of fun to build and test, but its flight is often unpredictable. Given this unpredictability, and the fact that there are multiple spinning blades, minors should be allowed to use this drone only with adult supervision. Assuming that you're fine with that caveat, then let's get started!

Hardware Bill of Materials

The main component in this project is a quadcopter, specifically the Parrot AR Drone 2.0, shown in Figure 7-1, which is a very capable quadcopter that is well suited for this project.

Some of the standard features of the AR Drone that make it very capable include

- Inertial Measurement Unit (IMU) consisting of a gyroscope, accelerometer, and a magnetometer, all with three degrees of freedom

- Ultrasound height sensor for measuring low flight

- Pressure sensor for measuring high flight

- Front camera with 720p resolution

- Downward-facing camera with 360p resolution

- Lithium polymer battery, 1000mAh

- Onboard wireless access point

- Indoor shell/outdoor shell

- Four brushless motors for the spinning blades

Naturally, the hardware of the brain that we're giving the drone in this project is a Raspberry Pi. This inexpensive computer is very well suited for this role for several reasons: it is small, lightweight, and consumes relatively low power. In addition, the Linux operating system may be loaded on it, which allows various modifications that would typically be more difficult to do on other platforms.

Here's a full list of components that you'll need to build the project. Because the drone will be flying with most of this equipment mounted to it, please choose smaller and lighter components when those options are available. Some of these components are shown in Figure 7-2. For reference I've included Amazon.com links to most of the parts, but you are welcome to find other suppliers, of course.

FIGURE 7-1. *Parrot AR Drone 2.0*

TIP
The Amazon.com links are valid at the time of writing. If any of them do not work by the time you are reading this, trying searching by product name.

- **AR Drone 2.0**   Other AR Drone 2.0 models should work for this project as well, but I chose the Elite Edition: www.amazon.com/Parrot-Drone-Quadricopter-Elite-720p/dp/B00FS7SV1U

- **Raspberry Pi**   Shown encased in Figure 7-2, I used the Model B, but any model of Raspberry Pi that has two USB ports will do.

- **Raspberry Pi case**   The smaller and lighter the better. Shown in Figure 7-2, the SB Raspberry Pi Case by SB Components is one option, and you can even get it in raspberry red: www.amazon.com/gp/product/B008TD1FSQ/

- **SD card, Class 10, minimum 8GB**   I chose the PNY Elite Performance card because it has 32GB for plenty of room for growth: www.amazon.com/gp/product/B00DX5D9I4/

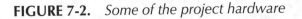

FIGURE 7-2.   *Some of the project hardware*

- **Two Edimax EW-7811Un Wi-Fi adapters**   Shown in Figure 7-2, these plug into the Raspberry Pi's two USB ports. Here's a link: www.amazon.com/Edimax-EW-7811Un-Adapter-Raspberry-Supports/dp/B003MTTJOY/

- **Raspberry Pi power adapter**   You can get one here: www.amazon.com/gp/product/B00GWDLJGS/

- **dodocool portable "lipstick" cell phone charger**   Shown in Figure 7-2, this powers the Raspberry Pi. It is available at this link: www.amazon.com/gp/product/B00H7TR9WY/

- **CableJive microStubz extra short USB to micro USB cable**   Shown in Figure 7-2, this connects the "lipstick" charger to the Raspberry Pi. Here's a link: www.amazon.com/CableJive-microStubz-Compatible-including-Blackberry/dp/B00578KYZG

- **Ethernet cable for initial configuration steps**   This is a standard Ethernet cable, available most anywhere that electronics or computers are sold. The length of the cable doesn't matter, as it won't be onboard the drone during flight.

- **Velcro**   Available in most hardware and fabric stores, this is used to fasten the cell phone charger to the Raspberry Pi case, and the Raspberry Pi case to the drone.

Required Software
In addition to the hardware specified in the previous section, this project requires software running onboard the Raspberry Pi brain to make it smart enough to control the drone:

- One component of this software is an API library named parroteer that provides an abstraction for controlling a Parrot AR Drone in Java. This API library, located at https://github.com/parrotsonjava/parroteer, is written in Java by Thomas Endres and Martin Förtsch of ParrotsOnJava.com.

- Another component of this software is an API library named autonomous4j that utilizes the parroteer library to provide an even higher-level abstraction for controlling the AR Drone in Java. This library, located at https://github.com/RaspberryPiWithJava/Autonomous4j, is written in Java by Mark A. Heckler.

The autonomous4j library enables you to write Java code such as shown in Listing 7-1 to make the drone fly in a rectangular pattern.

Listing 7-1 *Java code for flying in a rectangular pattern*

```java
private static void doDemoFlightBox(A4jBrain brain) {
    brain.takeoff().hold(5000); // ms duration
    brain.goRight(20).doFor(8000); // % speed, ms duration
    brain.stay().hold(5000);
    brain.backward(20).doFor(7000);
    brain.stay().hold(5000);
    brain.goLeft(20).doFor(8000);
    brain.stay().hold(5000);
    brain.forward(20).doFor(7000);
    brain.stay().hold(5000);
    brain.land();
}
```

The code in Listing 7-1 causes the drone to take off and hold its position for five seconds. It will then fly to the right at 20 percent speed for eight seconds, backward at 20 percent speed for seven seconds, to the left at 20 percent speed for eight seconds, and forward at 20 percent speed for seven seconds. It will then land, theoretically in the same position at which it took off. Because we're implementing a very basic level of autonomy, factors such as wind can cause the drone to land in a different position. As mentioned earlier, more advanced levels of autonomy than implemented in this project are certainly possible.

Figure 7-3 is a stop-action shot of the drone with its Raspberry Pi brain and USB charger flying in a rectangular pattern in Mark Heckler's living room.

FIGURE 7-3. *Drone and onboard brain assembly flying*

Building an Autonomous Drone

Now that you are familiar with the hardware and software component of this project, let's discuss how you can build an Autonomous Drone. Here is a list of the overall steps that you'll need to perform, which are covered in detail in the following sections:

1. Set up your Raspberry Pi.

2. Establish a wireless network connection between the Raspberry Pi and the drone. This uses one of the Edimax Wi-Fi adapters.

3. Configure the Raspberry Pi as a wireless access point (WAP). This uses the remaining Edimax Wi-Fi adapter.

4. Assemble and fasten the hardware to the drone.

5. Write a Java method that contains flight instructions similar to the example in Listing 7-1, using the parroteer and autonomous4j libraries.

6. Connect to the Raspberry Pi via NetBeans to remotely deploy the Java application and supporting libraries.

7. Fly the drone by invoking the Java application.

Setting Up Your Raspberry Pi

The first thing you need to do is set up Raspbian on your Raspberry Pi. Chapter 1 has full details on how to go through the installation process to prepare your Raspberry Pi for programming.

Establishing a Network Connection Between the Pi and Drone, and Configuring the Raspberry Pi as a WAP

We'll tackle these steps together, as they involve several steps to be performed "manually" on the Pi itself.

At this point, you should have your Pi up and running, connected to your network via Ethernet cable or one of the Wi-Fi adapters. If you haven't already (and with power to the Pi off), plug in the two Edimax Wi-Fi adapters. As previously shown in Figure 7-2, they both plug into the Raspberry Pi USB ports.

■ One of these Edimax adapters enables the Raspberry Pi to act as a client to the drone, just like your mobile phone or tablet would.

■ The other Edimax adapter enables a laptop to communicate with the Raspberry Pi. This facilitates pushing software to the Raspberry Pi, debugging and profiling it live, and even taking control if required.

If it's possible to connect your Pi to your network via Ethernet cable again, please do so now, as it simplifies things considerably when updating Wi-Fi adapter settings. I'll assume your connection is wired until indicated otherwise in the following instructions.

Once you're at your Pi's shell prompt, we'll first update Raspbian and install a couple essential packages by executing the following commands:

```
sudo apt-get update
sudo apt-get install hostapd isc-dhcp-server
```

The `hostapd` application enables you to configure the Pi as an access point, and `isc-dhcp-server` provides the ability to assign IP addresses to connected devices dynamically.

Next, we set up the DHCP server by opening the dhcpd.conf file in an editor and making a few changes. We'll use `vi` here, but if you have a different favorite editor on the Pi, please use it instead. Here are the steps to follow.

Edit the dhcpd.conf File

Edit the dhcpd.conf file as follows:

1. Enter **sudo vi /etc/dhcp/dhcpd.conf**.

2. Find the lines that say

   ```
   option domain-name "example.org";
   option domain-name-servers ns1.example.org, ns2.example.org;
   ```

   and add a # at the beginning of each line to comment them out:

   ```
   #option domain-name "example.org";
   #option domain-name-servers ns1.example.org, ns2.example.org;
   ```

3. Find the lines that say

   ```
   # If this DHCP server is the official DHCP server for the
   local
   # network, the authoritative directive should be
   uncommented.
   #authoritative;
   ```

   and remove the #, uncommenting the line:

   ```
   authoritative;
   ```

4. Scroll to the bottom of the dhcpd.conf file and add the following lines:

```
subnet 192.168.42.0 netmask 255.255.255.0 {
range 192.168.42.10 192.168.42.50;
option broadcast-address 192.168.42.255;
option routers 192.168.42.1;
default-lease-time 600;
max-lease-time 7200;
option domain-name "local";
option domain-name-servers 8.8.8.8, 8.8.4.4;
}
```

5. Save the file and exit your editor (press ESC, then enter **ZZ** in vi).

Edit the isc-dhcp-server File

Edit the isc-dhcp-server file as follows:

1. Enter **sudo vi /etc/default/isc-dhcp-server**.

2. Scroll down to the line
   ```
   INTERFACES=""
   ```
   and change it to

   ```
   INTERFACES="wlan0"
   ```

3. Save the file and exit your editor (press ESC, then enter **ZZ** in vi).

Edit the /etc/network/interfaces File

At this point, we configure wlan0 for the WAP functionality (assigning it a static IP), while the wlan1 interface acts as a DHCP client to the drone's onboard WAP.

To configure these network interfaces, we'll edit the /etc/network/interfaces configuration file:

1. Enter **sudo vi /etc/network/interfaces**.

2. Edit the file to look like this (the eth0 section may be different, depending upon your wired connection; this is fine):

   ```
   auto lo
   iface lo inet loopback
   ```

```
iface eth0 inet static
address 192.168.1.149
netmask 255.255.255.0
network 192.168.1.0
broadcast 192.168.1.255
gateway 192.168.1.1

#auto wlan0
allow hotplug wlan0
iface wlan0 inet static
address 192.168.42.1
netmask 255.255.255.0
gateway 192.168.42.1

#auto wlan1
allow hotplug wlan1
iface wlan1 inet dhcp
wireless-essid ardrone2_wap  (NOTE: This is your drone's named WAP)
```

3. Save the file and exit the editor (press ESC, then enter **ZZ** in vi).

Edit the /etc/hostapd/hostapd.conf File

Next, we provide configuration details to the WAP daemon by creating a hostapd.conf file:

1. Enter **sudo vi /etc/hostapd/hostapd.conf** (this creates an empty file).

2. Enter the following details to configure the wlan0 interface:

```
interface=wlan0
driver=rtl871xdrv
ssid=Positronic
hw_mode=g
channel=6
macaddr_acl=0
auth_algs=1
ignore_broadcast_ssid=0
wpa=2
wpa_passphrase=Raspberry
wpa_key_mgmt=WPA-PSK
wpa_pairwise=TKIP
rsn_pairwise=CCMP
```

3. Verify that no line has extra spaces or tabs at the beginning or end, then save the file and exit the editor (press ESC, then enter **ZZ** in vi).

Now we must tell the Pi where to find the hostapd.config file we just created. To do so, we'll edit another configuration file to point to it:

1. Enter **sudo vi /etc/default/hostapd**.

2. Find the line
   ```
   #DAEMON_CONF=""
   ```
   and change it to read as follows (be sure to remove the # at the beginning of the line!):
   ```
   DAEMON_CONF="/etc/hostapd/hostapd.conf"
   ```

3. Save the file and exit the editor (press ESC, and then enter **ZZ**).

Make Those Daemons Run

The last step to configure our Raspberry Pi as a drone communications mastermind *should* be simply to configure the `hostapd` and `isc-dhcp-server` applications to run as services, and for the most part, that is true. However, running two network interfaces that do two very different things—while coordinating with each other—can make for no small amount of conflict. So we'll configure the services "ideally" in this step, then add a bit of insurance to boost reliability. After all, we want to ensure we can connect at any time to our very brainy drone!

To configure these two apps as services (*daemons,* pronounced "demons" in UNIX/Linux parlance), simply issue these commands from your Raspberry Pi command prompt:

```
sudo update-rc.d hostapd enable
sudo update-rc.d isc-dhcp-server enable
```

And now, the "insurance step." To address the conflicts that arise when two network interfaces fight for control, here are the steps you'll need to take to make your Pi reliably responsive.

Edit the ifplugd Configuration File The `ifplugd` daemon allows you to "hotplug" a network interface to your Pi and have it recognized, which is normally a good thing: after all, plugging in a network cable shouldn't require a reboot just to connect to a network. But this causes issues when dealing with multiple Wi-Fi adapters simultaneously, causing one to be "ejected" when another is loaded. Here are the steps to eliminate this issue, while retaining hotplug capabilities for the (wired) eth0 interface:

1. Enter **sudo vi /etc/default/ifplugd**.

2. Change these two lines:

   ```
   INTERFACES="auto"
   HOTPLUG_INTERFACES="all"
   ```

   to read:

   ```
   INTERFACES="eth0"
   HOTPLUG_INTERFACES="eth0"
   ```

3. Save the updated file and exit the editor (press ESC, then enter **ZZ**).

Edit the rc.local File   Per its header, this script is run at the "end of each multiuser runlevel," executing each included command as the system boots. We'll use it for two purposes: to force both Wi-Fi adapters online (using the `ifup`, or "interface up," utility), and to ensure the DHCP server is loaded. Doing so is simple:

1. Enter **sudo vi /etc/rc.local**.

2. Anywhere before the "exit 0" statement, add the following lines:

   ```
   ifup wlan0
   /etc/init.d/isc-dhcp-server start
   ifup wlan1
   ```

NOTE
Adding these lines before the section "#Print the IP address" retains the clean reminder of the destination's IP address just above the boot prompt for those times when you connect via `ssh`.

3. Save the file and exit the editor (press ESC, then enter **ZZ**).

Throw the Switch, Igor!

Now, we reboot the Pi to enable all changes and bring our drone's new "Positronic brain" online! Issuing **sudo reboot** from the shell prompt does the magic, and once the Pi is fully booted again, you can connect to it just like your current WAP, but in this case by going to your laptop's network settings, choosing the Pi's WAP identifier ("Positronic" in the settings provided previously), and providing the key ("Raspberry"). Congratulations! To borrow a phrase, "It … is … alive!"

With this in place, you shouldn't experience any connectivity issues … but when you do, it's nearly always the connection from Pi to the drone that fails. On those exceedingly rare occasions, here is how to get back on track quickly:

1. Log in to the Pi via ssh.

2. Execute the following commands from the shell:

```
sudo su
ifdown -force wlan1
ifup wlan1
ifconfig -a (to verify connections - but give the previous
several seconds to connect)
exit (from su connection)
exit (from ssh connection)
```

3. At this point, both connections should (again) be active!

Please refer to https://bitbucket.org/autonomous4j/autonomous4jga/wiki/PiConfiguration for additional or updated information.

Assembling and Fastening the Hardware to the Drone

Now it's time to assemble the hardware and fasten it to the drone. We've already configured the Wi-Fi adapters; next, we turn our attention to making the Pi "transportable" by removing its land-based power tether and powering it on the drone during flight.

The stock AR Drone 2.0 doesn't have the capability of supplying power to the Raspberry Pi, which is why we're using the portable "lipstick" charger. The dodocool charger in this project provides 2600 milliamp hours, so it's got a good time range. It puts out one amp of current, and since we're using

FIGURE 7-4. *Assembling some of the hardware*

Wi-Fi plugs that don't draw a lot of current, we can run the Pi, the two plugs, and everything else we need off of the USB charger. First, use Velcro to fasten the USB charger to the Pi case. As shown in Figure 7-4, plug the short USB cable to the power source and the Pi, and then turn it on. That boots the Raspberry Pi "brain."

Then, using Velcro, fasten the Raspberry Pi to the drone. As shown in Figure 7-5, we now have the makings of an intelligent drone.

Now that we've assembled the hardware components and attached them to the drone, let's examine how we give the drone's new brain some flight instructions.

FIGURE 7-5. *Hardware assembly attached to the drone*

Writing a Java Method that Contains Flight Instructions

The `org.autonomous4j.control` package of the autonomous4j library contains a Java file named A4jMain.java that consists mainly of a few methods with flight instructions. These methods demonstrate various capabilities of the autonomous4j library. For example, Listing 7-2 shows a method that demonstrates the ability to automatically navigate to the drone's takeoff location. This is achieved via the use of the `A4jBrainA goHome()` method near the end of the listing.

Listing 7-2 *Java code for demonstrating goHome() functionality*

```
private static void doDemoFlightHome(A4jBrain brain) {
    brain.takeoff().hold(6000);
    brain.forward(20).doFor(400);
    brain.stay().hold(2000);
    brain.goRight(20).doFor(400);
    brain.stay().hold(2000);
    brain.forward(20).doFor(400);
    brain.stay().hold(2000);
    brain.goRight(20).doFor(400);
```

```
    brain.stay().hold(2000);
    brain.backward(20).doFor(400);
    brain.stay().hold(2000);
    brain.goHome();
    brain.stay().hold(2000);
    brain.land();
}
```

   You may create additional methods with your own flight instructions as well. Table 7-1 contains some commonly used flight control–related methods available to you in the autonomous4j library. Methods may be chained together in a fluent API pattern as demonstrated in Listing 7-2.

Method	Description
takeoff()	Causes drone to start and take off.
stay()	Causes drone to stay in one place.
forward(int speed)	Causes drone to fly forward at a given percent of speed.
backward(int speed)	Causes drone to fly backward at a given percent of speed.
goLeft(int speed)	Causes drone to fly left at a given percent of speed.
goRight(int speed)	Causes drone to fly right at a given percent of speed.
up(int speed)	Causes drone to fly up at a given percent of speed.
down(int speed)	Causes drone to fly down at a given percent of speed.
doFor(long ms)	Modifier for how long an operation should occur.
hold(long ms)	Synonymous with the doFor() method.
goHome()	Causes drone to navigate to its takeoff point and stop.
playLedAnimation()	Blinks a specified LED color for given number of times and duration in seconds.
replay()	Causes drone to repeat the previous flight. Flights are automatically recorded in the A4jBlackBox object.
land()	Causes drone to land and stop.

TABLE 7-1. *Commonly Used Flight Control Methods in autonomous4j*

Connecting to the Raspberry Pi via NetBeans to Remotely Deploy the Java Application and Supporting Libraries

You already should have a connection established from NetBeans to your Pi, but if not, please review the steps provided in previous chapters to configure the JDK on your Pi as a remote JDK. Once this is in place, simply running (or debugging) your application from within NetBeans (with the Pi's remote JDK selected) will deploy the application and all supporting libraries to the Pi.

Flying the Drone by Invoking the Java Application

For our inaugural flight, let's use the A4JMain.java file as it appears in the code distribution available with this book. The flight behavior is programmed to take off, hover, blink some LEDs, and land.

The simplest way to do this is to run the application from within NetBeans, allowing it to deploy and execute the app remotely. This allows you to remain connected during the program's execution, even remotely debugging or profiling it "live," while the program executes fully on the Pi itself. Of course, you can also choose to execute it directly on the Pi—external to NetBeans— by connecting to the Pi via ssh, navigating to the deployment directory (usually /home/pi/NetBeansProjects/<program_name>/dist), and running the usual `java -jar` command.

After you've flown a couple of successful missions, go ahead and experiment by editing A4JMain.java to modify the flight behavior. Following the previous instructions, download the modified code into the Raspberry Pi, and invoke the application. Have fun!

Achieving Greater Degrees of Autonomy

Now that you've successfully built and tested the project, let's discuss a potential enhancement that you could make to the autonomous4j library to make the drone smarter. As you've seen in this project, many of the flight control methods cause the drone to fly in a given direction, at a given percentage of power, for a given period of time. This demonstrates a very basic level of autonomy, but you may have noticed that the drone doesn't always fly and land exactly where instructed. For example, air currents in the room can cause the drone to drift off course. A good next step for improving this would be to implement a way for the drone to know its position in three-dimensional space so it can make course corrections.

Orienting the Drone in 3D Space

The Parrot AR Drone 2.0 comes with a cardboard "oriented roundel," shown in Figure 7-6.

The purpose of the oriented roundel is for the drone to recognize it in its downward-facing camera. The AR Drone can report information about what portion of the camera lens contains the oriented roundel. Given that information, the client (in our case the Raspberry Pi brain) could calculate its position in 3D space relative to the oriented roundel.

Implementing a Control Loop

If the drone knows where it is in 3D space, then it can know when it is off course. A control loop, such as the one represented in Figure 7-7, could be implemented to keep the drone on course. This loop would iteratively:

1. Estimate its position in space

2. Compare that position with the desired position

3. Calculate and apply control with the goal of arriving at the desired position

FIGURE 7-6. *Oriented roundel*

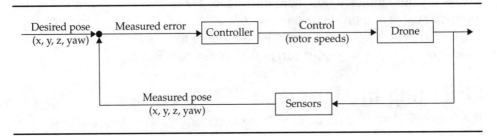

FIGURE 7-7. *State estimation and position control*

Consequently, instead of supplying flight instructions that specify direction, speed, and time, we could give instructions that specify positions in space (see Figure 7-8).

Have fun building and testing the project. I hope you've enjoyed this chapter on creating an autonomous drone, employing a Raspberry Pi as its brain!

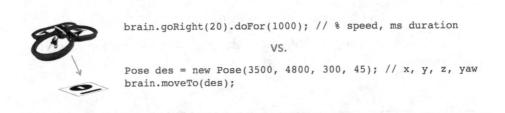

```
brain.goRight(20).doFor(1000); // % speed, ms duration

                             VS.

Pose des = new Pose(3500, 4800, 300, 45); // x, y, z, yaw
brain.moveTo(des);
```

FIGURE 7-8. *Potential instructions when drone knows its position in space*

CHAPTER
8

Retro Video Game Emulator

There has been a resurgence of interest in retro video games from the 1980s and 1990s on 8-bit gaming platforms. Games back then had relatively limited graphics capabilities, so instead they focused on mechanics, level design, and most of all challenge. Compared to modern video games, many of the early classics were difficult and unforgiving, making completing them a real achievement. The Nintendo Entertainment System (NES), shown in Figure 8-1, was the most successful 8-bit console in history, with 61.9 million units sold worldwide.*

Since these early systems used dedicated chips, doing a perfect job of emulating the system (and its quirks) in software requires a reasonably fast processor. The Raspberry Pi is a great choice for this since it has decent processing capabilities and really great graphics performance, making it an excellent platform for emulating classic video games.

In this chapter and in Chapter 9, we will develop a portable gaming system with a pure Java NES emulator and custom 3D printed case as a revival of the early handheld gaming systems. However, if you are only interested in the game emulation and do not want to build the handheld version, by the end of this chapter you will have a fully functional game emulator and GPIO controller.

FIGURE 8-1. *Nintendo Entertainment System (public domain by Evan-Amos)*

---

*Nintendo Co., Ltd., "Consolidated Sales Transition by Region": www.nintendo.co.jp/ir/library/historical_data/pdf/consolidated_sales_e1506.pdf

NOTE
This project is the most difficult project in this book. It requires specific hardware that you need to order in advance and a bit of patience working through soldering and delicate assembly. Unless you are very experienced with hardware, I recommend trying some of the other projects in the book first before tackling this one.

Bill of Materials

The set of materials for this project is oriented toward the creation and prototyping of the internal components that we need in the handheld system that is assembled in Chapter 9. If you plan on putting together the 3D handheld system, make sure to get exactly the same items listed here so that they will fit in the custom enclosure without modification.

Raspberry Pi

You will, of course, need a Raspberry Pi. I recommend the Raspberry Pi 2, because the extra performance from the ARM7 quad-core chip is extremely helpful in doing accurate emulation of the NES in Java. Also, don't forget the SD card and power adapter to go along with your Raspberry Pi.

NOTE
You can also use a Raspberry Pi B+, although you may see some slowdowns in emulation. The Raspberry Pi A+ also works, but will require a case redesign. Older Raspberry Pis without the 40-pin connector will not work for this project because they do not support the Kippah display hat described in the following section.

Display and Adapter

The Adafruit Kippah is a very cool touchscreen adapter board that utilizes the GPIO pins to directly communicate with an LCD display. Compared to the HDMI touchscreen displays recommended in Chapter 6, the Kippah is more compact and power efficient since it does not require extra circuitry to convert from an HDMI signal. It also is unique in that it exposes the full graphics capabilities of the Pi, including 3D acceleration and fast refresh rates, unlike some of the SPI-based displays.

The technology behind the Kippah is reconfiguration of the GPIO ports using a device tree overlay. By reconfiguring the GPIO ports to instead carry display interface information, you can directly integrate native LCD displays that are commonly used in small portable electronics. It is even possible to support touch through a USB connection.

Of course, all of this power comes at a price. The Kippah sits on top of the Raspberry Pi like a hat, and it takes over almost all of the GPIO pins, including all the buses, I²C, SPI, and Serial. You are left with six standard GPIO pins for program usage, which is why we could not use it for the Tea Station.

Fortunately, with some clever wiring, six pins are enough to implement our controller gamepad. Also, the graphics performance and low power consumption is much more important than additional GPIO pins for expansion, so it is perfect for this project.

Here is what you need:

- **Adafruit DPI TFT Kippah for Raspberry Pi with Touch Support**   https://www.adafruit.com/products/2453

- **Two 40-pin FPC Extension Board + 200mm Cable**   https://www.adafruit.com/products/2098

- **4.3" 40-pin TFT Display - 480×272 with Touchscreen**   https://www.adafruit.com/products/1591

NOTE
Even though I recommend getting the Kippah with touch support, you technically do not need it for this project. Similarly, the 4.3" screen has touch support that we will not use. However, feel free to hook up the touchscreen and test it out on your own.

I recommend getting two of the 40-pin extension cables in case you break one during assembly. These ribbon cables are very sensitive and can easily get damaged from a sharp kink or rough handling during insertion in a socket. You may want to get two touchscreens for the same reason, although I have designed the case so that the extension cable gets all of the flexing and load to remove stress on the more expensive LCD connector.

Speaker and Audio

Classic gaming is not complete without a retro soundtrack to go along with it. The NES game developers cranked out some amazingly catchy tunes given the simplistic hardware they had available. For both music and sound effects, NES games were limited to only five audio tracks total, each of which had a special purpose.

Here's what you need for the audio component of your gaming experience:

- **Two Mini Metal Speaker w/ Wires - 8 ohm 0.5W**   https://www.adafruit.com/products/1890

- **Stereo 2.8W Class D Audio Amplifier - TS2012**   https://www.adafruit.com/products/1552

- **Right-Angle 3.5mm Stereo Plug to Pigtail Cable**   https://www.adafruit.com/products/1700

Since NES audio is definitely mono, having two speakers is not necessary. However, I recommend picking up a couple since they are easy to damage if you are not careful with handling the tiny speaker driver. Also, plugging up a second speaker is a great way to boost the sound.

The stereo plug cable will be used for testing audio in this chapter, but it will be dropped in the final 3D case assembly (in Chapter 9) to free up space.

Navigation and Buttons

You will also need several different types of buttons and a joystick controller to create an authentic gamepad controller for your device:

- **Two Thru-Hole 5-Way Navigation Switch (Alps Model SKQUCAA010)**   https://www.adafruit.com/products/504

- **Tactile Switch Buttons (12mm square, 6mm tall) × 10 pack**   https://www.adafruit.com/products/1119

- **Four C&K Components D6F90 F1 LFS switch**   www.digikey.com/product-detail/en/D6F90%20F1%20LFS/401-1970-ND/1466327

- **Half-Size Breadboard** The perfect size for putting together a small test controller with buttons: https://www.adafruit.com/products/64

- **1N4148 Signal Diode - 10 pack** https://www.adafruit.com/products/1641

The five-way navigation switch supports standard up/down/left/right D-pad movement and also a fifth click if you press directly down. For NES emulation, which has no concept of analog movement, this is perfect and provides a nice, precise, tactile feedback when you are moving in a specific direction. The fifth click is not necessary, although the longer control arm makes it easy to mount our 3D printed D-pad.

I have recommended at least twice as many buttons as needed to cover breakage and wear-and-tear. The case design in the next chapter is specifically tailored to these buttons, so make sure you get exactly the same models listed. The 12mm tactile button switches are nice, inexpensive buttons with a high actuation force, which makes them perfect for the Select and Start buttons. (You don't want to accidentally press these while in a heated battle!) In contrast, the C&K D6 buttons have a nice tactile feel with a very low actuation force and relatively long travel distance. Therefore, these are great for the heavily used A and B buttons on the gamepad.

For the C&K D6F90 F1 LFS buttons, here is the breakdown of the lettering code:

- **D6** Model number

- **F** Flat button (any of the other types will protrude from the case)

- **90** Black color (they also come in white with code 00)

- **F1** 1.3N actuation force

- **LFS** Lead-Free Status under the Restriction of Hazardous Substances (RoHS) directive

The only variation that will work in this project is to choose a different color. Black is a good choice because it matches the caps on the 12mm buttons, but if you prefer white you can go for that color. Since these are fairly specialized, your best bet is to order them online from Digi-Key Electronics or Mouser Electronics.

You will also need a breadboard to connect the buttons and do wiring to the Kippah board. I recommend using a half-size one, because you won't need a lot of room for wiring the buttons and it is a better size to hold as a controller.

We will use the final item in the list, some standard 1N4148 small diodes, to creatively "share" GPIO pins between buttons. You only need four of them, but you will probably find that it is a much better deal to purchase them in bulk since they are so inexpensive.

Wiring and Tools

Finally, you will need some wiring and tools to assemble this project. All of this stuff is pretty standard electronics gear that you may have used in previous chapters as well, but the following list includes some additional items that will be helpful with surface-mount soldering on the Kippah board. All the products are available from Adafruit, so I have included URLs here to help you easily locate each item. You can also save on shipping costs by ordering multiple items at one time from the same vendor.

- **Soldering iron**   Preferably one with a fine tip on it since the soldering pads on the Kippah are very small. I recommend the Digital Genuine Hakko FX-888D soldering iron (https://www .adafruit.com/products/1204) and Hakko Soldering Tip: T18-S4 Fine SMD (https://www.adafruit.com/products/1249).

- **Solder wire**   You won't need much for this project, but it never hurts to have extra good-quality solder on hand (https://www.adafruit.com/ products/1886).

- **Solder sucker/wick**   In case you accidentally solder two pads together, having a solder sucker and some desoldering wick is very handy (https://www.adafruit.com/products/148 and https://www .adafruit.com/products/149).

- **Helping hands**   This is an inexpensive and very useful device with a couple alligator clips mounted on adjustable arms. This will make the task of soldering multiple wires to a single pad much easier. I recommend the Helping Third Hand Magnifier w/ Magnifying Glass Tool (https://www.adafruit.com/products/291).

- **Board holder**   Keeps your Raspberry Pi or Kippah elevated at a nice height for the helping hands device. The Panavise Jr. is good choice: https://www.adafruit.com/products/151.

- **Hook-up wire spool**   Having good quality wire in multiple colors handy will be extremely helpful (https://www.adafruit.com/products/1311).

- **Wire cutters/strippers**   Very handy for quickly stripping wire ends (https://www.adafruit.com/products/527).

- **Heat shrink wrap**   This will help ensure that you don't have exposed wires touching and shorting out your project (https://www.adafruit.com/products/344).

- **Multimeter**   Having a good multimeter is handy, and will help you diagnose whether your circuit is working or not without frying your delicate hardware. I recommend the Extech EX330 12-function autoranging multimeter (https://www.adafruit.com/products/308).

As you can see from the extensive list of materials, this project is a little trickier than the ones in previous chapters. I recommend you go full out and invest in a fine-tip soldering iron, helping hands, and proper wire strippers to make completing this project successfully much more feasible. And for the occasional mistake, having a multimeter to check and solder sucker/wick to fix it is really helpful. All of this hardware will come in handy with your future electronics projects and is a great investment that will last a long time.

Creating a GPIO Controller

Probably the most important aspect of a portable gaming system is the comfort of the controller for ergonomics and long-term playing. If the controller buttons are too stiff or feel mushy when you press them, you are unlikely to pick it up again.

Most controllers use rubber dome switches that are layered on top of a custom circuit board. This is actually the technology used in most computer keyboards and works well if you can print your own circuit board and manufacture rubber domes in the right type of material. However, I am a big fan of mechanical key switches for the nice, sharp, tactile feedback and precise control they afford.

FIGURE 8-2.   *NES Controller (public domain by Evan-Amos)*

A photo of the NES controller is shown in Figure 8-2. This is actually one of the most basic controller designs with only four buttons and a directional pad capable of four angles, but it is very functional.

Wiring the Controller

Here is the mapping of hardware to the controller buttons:

- **D-pad**   For this we will use the Alps 5-way navigational switch.

- **Start/Select**   We will use the 12mm tactile switches with a sharp press.

- **A/B**   For the "active" switches on the controller, we reserve the nice C&K buttons with a light touch and smooth mechanical click.

To create your controller pad, lay out these buttons on the half-size breadboard, being careful to keep the electrical connections separate. The layout I show in Figure 8-3 keeps all of the button contacts on separate rails

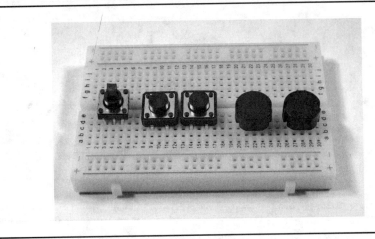

FIGURE 8-3. *Button layout on the breadboard*

and spreads the navigation contacts on both sides of the breadboard. Here are the constraints you should keep in mind when laying out the buttons:

- Each of the navigational switch legs needs to be separated, so straddle the switch across the center of the breadboard. It is not a perfect fit for the breadboard hole spacing, so you will need to bend the pins slightly. I oriented mine with the wider-spaced pins on the left. You should be able to find a good position where the switch stays in place by itself but does not put enough stress on the pins to break them off.

- The 12mm switches have four leads, but they are connected together in pairs. They fit nicely across the center of the breadboard as well, and in that orientation the leads that cross the internal switch are both accessible from the same half.

- The C&K D6 switches are also sized nicely for the breadboard, but are not wide enough to span the center. They also have four leads, so make sure the flat edge of the round switch is facing the long edge of the breadboard, which will keep the electrically connected leads on the same rail.

A Fritzing diagram with my button layout and the connections to the Kippah is shown in Figure 8-4. In this figure, the navigational switch is positioned with the leads spaced farther apart on the left-hand side. Also, the switches don't look visibly different, but the 12mm Select/Start switches are in the center and the C&K A/B switches are on the right, the same as the NES controller order.

Using more of the rails on the breadboard would optimize the wiring, but I chose instead to connect multiple leads to the Kippah directly. This will be important later when we move the design to the 3D printed case, because we won't have room for a circuit board. Keeping all the connections directly wired to components (including ground) will allow for a seamless migration to the case.

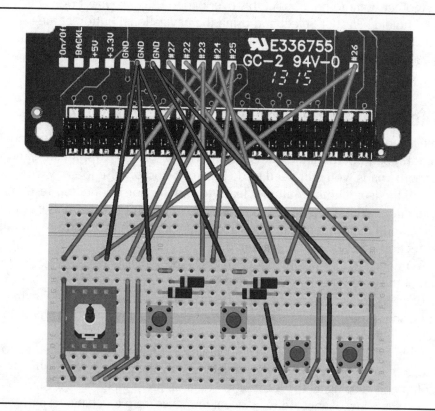

FIGURE 8-4. *Fritzing layout of the buttons and Kippah*

I left the first ground connection unsoldered for later use. Also, note the use of diodes to connect the Start and Select buttons. Since there are only six usable GPIO pins, it is necessary to "overload" some of the other GPIO pins by connecting multiple buttons. Since it is physically impossible to press left and right or up and down at the same time, you can overload those operations by having the Select button press left/right and having the Start button press up/down simultaneously. However, if you were to hook a straight wire from the Start or Select button to two GPIO pins simultaneously, it would create an electric coupling with those two GPIO pins such that pressing one would trigger the other. By using a diode, the electrical flow is limited to one direction, preventing the current from leaking when one direction is pressed but still allowing the Start and Select buttons to trigger both GPIO pins simultaneously. For this to work, the diodes need to be oriented such that the cathode (black ring) is facing the switch.

Another point to note about this overloaded usage is that it prevents the use of holding Start or Select and using the navigational button at the same time. This would produce a problem for the A or B button, but since Start and Select are used exclusively for mode selection, pausing, and so forth, this is not a problem.

Soldering the Kippah

Time to pull out the soldering iron and hook the breadboard connections up to the Kippah board. Since the GPIO connectors on the Kippah are simply electronic pads, you will need to do a careful and precise job of wiring each of the (sometimes multiple) leads to exactly one connector. Testing the connections with a multimeter afterward is important to ensure there are no shorts, and I recommend adding some heat shrink tubing to ensure that the connections stay electrically isolated.

To understand the wiring connections, Table 8-1 lists which Kippah lead each of the components is connected to.

This should also match the breadboard wiring shown earlier in Figure 8-4, but having a second reference handy from the Kippah standpoint will help make sure that you don't make any mistakes while wiring.

Table 8-1 also gives you a good idea of how many wire leads need to go to each of the Kippah's terminals. For later use by the portable enclosure, I recommend keeping all the leads at least 4in or 10cm long. Also, it is important to keep the wires connected to adjacent terminals from touching, so leave enough space when soldering and use heat shrink tubing to seal the wires.

Kippah Lead	Connection 1	Connection 2	Connection 3
Ground 2	Navigation –	Select button –	Start button –
Ground 3	B button –	A button –	
GPIO 27	B button +		
GPIO 22	A button +		
GPIO 23	Navigation left	Select diode 1	
GPIO 24	Navigation down	Start diode 1	
GPIO 25	Navigation right	Select diode 2	
GPIO 26	Navigation up	Start diode 2	

TABLE 8-1. *Kippah Wiring Connections*

Figure 8-5 shows the first set of connections soldered successfully to one of the ground connections.

The easiest process for doing this is as follows:

1. Put the Kippah in the board holder to keep it elevated and at a convenient angle for working.

2. Tin the connection by dropping a solder ball on the Kippah's exposed plate.

3. Position the wires you want to solder above the connection and hold them in place with the helping hands.

4. Use the soldering iron to simultaneously heat the wires and push them into the solder ball.

5. After the solder cools, you should have a firm connection. Test this by gently pulling on the wires. If they come loose, clean up the solder using the sucker/wick and go back to step 2.

Repeat this process for all of the wires that you need to connect to the Kippah board. Probably the most difficult part is making sure that none of the

FIGURE 8-5. *Surface-mount solder connection to the Kippah board*

solder balls or wires from adjacent terminals cross. Even if you think that you have sufficient distance, it is good to take a run through all the wires with a multimeter to check for electrical connectivity. Wires hooked up to the same terminal should have no resistance and wires hooked up to adjacent terminals should have near infinite resistance. A complete set of connected wires is shown in Figure 8-6.

A good precaution to take once you have tested all the connections is to use some heat shrink tubing to surround the wire bundles connected to each terminal. This way they won't accidentally touch and short out the Raspberry Pi (for example, crossing a GPIO pin and Ground would not be good).

After connecting all the leads to the breadboard and adding in the diodes and bridge wires, your completed Kippah and breadboard controller should look similar to Figure 8-7.

FIGURE 8-6. *All of the wires connected to the Kippah*

FIGURE 8-7. *Kippah hooked up to the breadboard*

Donning the Kippah

Before hooking up the Kippah to the Raspberry Pi, we need to do a little work to prepare it. We need to reroute the GPIO ports to control the LCD screen via a device tree overlay, and we need to disable other functions that utilize the GPIO ports, such as I²C and SPI. Also, we need to tweak the 4.3-inch touchscreen we are using to fix the overscan. Finally, we are going to flip the screen upside down to better fit the connectors inside the case.

To install the device tree overlay, grab the latest version off of Adafruit's share:

```
wget http://adafruit-download.s3.amazonaws.com/dt-blob.bin
```

Then, copy it to the /boot folder using root privileges:

```
sudo cp dt-blob.bin /boot/
```

In the same folder, edit config.txt using the nano text editor:

```
sudo nano /boot/config.txt
```

To the end of this file, add the additional configuration options shown in Listing 8-1.

Listing 8-1   *Configuration for the Kippah screen*

```
# Disable spi and i2c, we need these pins.
dtparam=spi=off
dtparam=i2c_arm=off
# enable the DPI display
enable_dpi_lcd=1
display_default_lcd=1
# For 4.3in displays
hdmi_ignore_edid=0xa5000080
hdmi_ignore_edid_audio=1
framebuffer_width=480
framebuffer_height=272
dpi_output_format=520197
# Flip the screen
display_rotate=2
# And adjust overscan as necessary
disable_overscan=0
overscan_top=150
overscan_left=160
overscan_right=0
overscan_bottom=-59
```

This configuration handles enabling the display and setting configuration to work with the 4.3-inch screen, including overscan. Based on your particular display you may need to tweak the overscan parameters slightly, but it should be pretty close to perfect. Also note that the display rotation flips the overscan edges, so if you later decide to remove the rotation, you will need to swap the left/right and top/bottom overscan values.

To physically hook up the hardware, I recommend connecting the touchscreen to the Kippah first. Rather than directly connecting the 40-pin ribbon cable to the Kippah, use the 20cm extender cable recommended in the "Bill of Materials" section earlier in the chapter. This makes it easier to position the display relative to the Raspberry Pi and also reduces strain on the very delicate connectors hooked up to the LCD screen.

When connecting the ribbon cable and adapter board, be careful not to force the cable or you could damage it. The connectors on the adapter board have little plastic locks that pivot upward to open and allow insertion of a cable. Carefully slide the 20cm cable in with the metal connectors facing downward. Once the cable hits the end of the slot, flip the lock back down to secure the cable in place. Repeat this for the cable attached to the LCD screen, completing both connectors on the adapter board.

The other end of the 20cm cable connects to the Kippah, but unlike the adapter board, for the Kippah you want to insert the cable with the metal connectors facing up. Also, the cable lock on the Kippah pulls straight out to release it, and then goes back in the locked position by pushing it straight back in. Keeping the different locking mechanism and opposite pin orientation in mind, unlock the connector, slide the cable in, and carefully press the lock back in to secure it.

Now you can hook the Kippah up to the Raspberry Pi by putting it over the Raspberry Pi like a little hat. Make sure the GPIO headers are lined up perfectly and press down firmly, but be careful not to pinch the wires connected to the breadboard. The completed setup with the Kippah, LCD, and fully wired breadboard is shown in Figure 8-8.

Now it is time to turn on your Raspberry Pi. The LCD should receive power through the GPIO ports on the Raspberry Pi and display a white screen. After a few seconds this will change to the familiar Raspberry Pi boot screen and then a login prompt. Connect a keyboard to the Raspberry Pi so you can log in on console, and you have a complete portable Raspberry Pi setup.

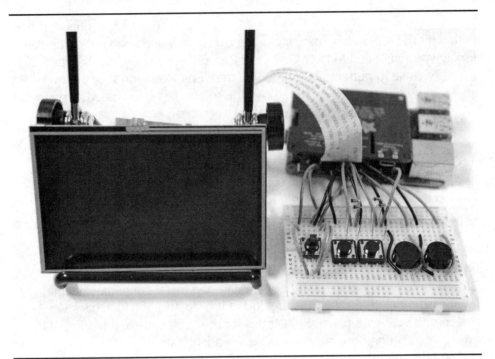

FIGURE 8-8. *4.3-inch display connected to the Kippah*

Hooking Up Speakers

The Raspberry Pi has a special four-pole TRRS jack that combines both audio and composite video signals in a single 3.5mm connector. We are interested in just the audio portion, so a standard stereo audio plug will work just fine.

To make this a truly portable setup, we are going to use a TS2012 powered mini amplifier that is powered off the Raspberry Pi, as well as some small speakers that will accurately reproduce quality retro music from the game emulator. The Adafruit breakout board for the TS2012 amp has all of the connections clearly labeled for the speakers and left/right audio jacks. We will also need to hook up the holes labeled VDD and GND to the amp to power it off the Raspberry Pi.

To make it easier to fit in the 3D printed case, I recommend skipping the headers and jacks and simply soldering directly on the board. Here are the connections you will need to make:

- **VDD**   Connect this to the Raspberry Pi's 5V line via the Kippah.

- **GND**   Connect this to the Raspberry Pi's Ground via the Kippah.

- **R+**   This goes to the red lead from the audio cable.

- **R–**   This goes to the bronze lead (ground) from the audio cable.

- **SDL**   Connect this to the Raspberry Pi's Ground line as well.

- **Right speaker +/–**   Connect these leads to the mini .5W speaker.

For this soldering job I recommend using the board holder and helping hands to keep the TS2012 breakout board and cables lined up nicely. The speaker is easy to hook up, and the order of the +/– connectors doesn't matter since we are connecting only one speaker. The only tricky part with this is that the cables are a little thin and flimsy, so be prepared to desolder them and replace them with regular hookup wire if they break.

Make sure to keep the stereo ground and Raspberry Pi ground distinct. The stereo ground comes from the 3.5mm cable pigtail end and should go to the R– jack. The Raspberry Pi ground comes from the third ground pad on the Kippah board that we left open and should go to the pins labeled GND and SDL. The reason for tying SDL to ground is to disable the left speaker and save power.

You can see my soldered board in Figure 8-9. Notice that I used a short piece of hookup wire to carry the ground over to the SDL pin. Saving on wires between the Kippah and the TS2012 board will make it easier to fit everything inside the case later.

You might be wondering what the jumpers on the bottom of the board are for. They let you control the audio volume in rough increments from 6db to 24db. Table 8-2 lists the different jumper settings and what volume they correspond to. I recommend starting at 6db and incrementing it up until it is loud without any noticeable humming or clipping.

FIGURE 8-9. *Fully wired TS2012 audio amplifier*

Earlier, in the config file, we already set the audio to come out of the 3.5mm jack with the following command:

```
hdmi_ignore_edid_audio=1
```

And to do a quick test of the audio, you can try one of the audio files that come with the Raspbian distribution:

```
aplay /usr/share/scratch/Media/Sounds/Animal/Kitten.wav
```

G0 Jumper	G1 Jumper	Sound Level
On	On	6db
Off	On	12db
On	Off	18db
Off	Off	24db

TABLE 8-2. *TS2012 Audio Volume Settings*

Emulating the NES

To do the actual NES emulation, I started with the great Java-based NES emulation library called halfNES, written by Andrew Hoffman. Andrew did a great job building an emulator from the ground up with a particular focus on accurate emulation. Most of the emulators that are known for their high performance achieve results by implementing per-game hacks instead of focusing on correctness of the emulator implementation. With over 800 games available, this makes the emulator codebases complex and unapproachable since you are not sure which game depends on various little hacks.

In contrast, Hoffman's halfNES codebase is relatively short and simple to understand—and, of course, a little bit on the slow side. It is not slow for modern desktops, but on a 900-MHz ARM chip, even four cores don't seem like enough. Fortunately, with a little bit of tuning, his codebase works great on the Raspberry Pi 2 (and runs acceptably on the older Raspberry Pi B+).

Running the Emulator

Start by grabbing the forked emulator code from here:

https://github.com/RaspberryPiWithJava/halfnes

This codebase is derived from Hoffman's mainline code development, with a particular focus on performance and features that make it playable on the Raspberry Pi. Just as with previous examples, open the codebase in NetBeans to compile and run it.

There are two main classes that you can choose to run:

- `com.grapeshot.halfnes.halfNES` is the original Swing UI that needs to be run in X-Windows.

- `com.grapeshot.halfnes.JavaFXNES` is a JavaFX-based version that runs in a direct framebuffer.

They both work and have been aggressively tuned for the Raspberry Pi, but the JavaFX version turns out to be faster, so I will provide instructions for that specifically.

Since the JavaFX version is fairly minimalistic on the UI right now, you will need to pass in the game you want to open on the command line. The configuration for doing this when launching from NetBeans is shown in Figure 8-10.

You can enter your game of choice into the Arguments field as a path to a file you have already copied to the Raspberry Pi. While I can't recommend playing game images copied from read-only memory (ROMs) cartridges that you do not legally own, there are some really great examples of homebrew NES games that are free to run, such as the 2014 winner of the NES Coding Competition, Love Story, a screenshot from which is shown in Figure 8-11.

You can download Love Story and other free NES games from the NES Coding Competition website here: http://nesdevcompo.nintendoage.com (click the links under NES Competitions and scroll down).

Since we are using the Pi4J library for GPIO access, you will need to acquire root permissions for the Remote Java Platform that you choose

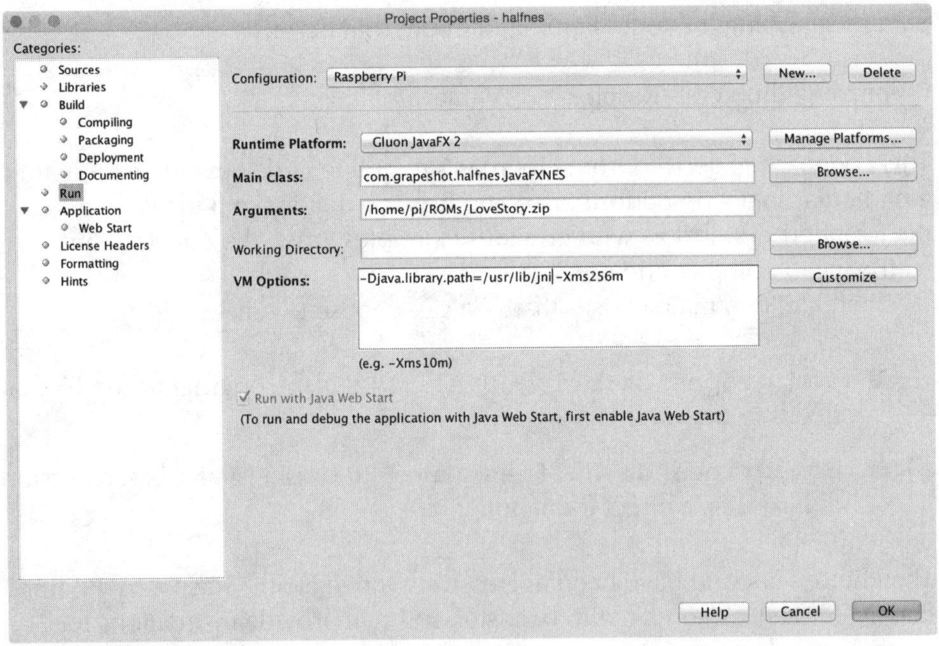

FIGURE 8-10. *Launching JavaFXNES from NetBeans*

FIGURE 8-11.   *Love Story, winner of the 2014 NES Coding Competition*

by picking a runtime platform that has an exec prefix of "sudo" set in its properties. Also, there are two recommended virtual machine options to pass in, as shown here:

```
-Djava.library.path=/usr/lib/jni -Xms256m
```

Setting the `java.library.path` allows you to use native libraries installed on the Raspberry Pi. This is particularly important if you want to use USB game controllers to play on the Pi via the JInput library. The second argument increases the minimum heap size, which is helpful to reduce the amount of garbage collection and heap resizing on startup.

To finish the installation of JInput, you will need to run the following commands from the Raspberry Pi:

```
sudo apt-get install libjinput-jni libjinput-java
sudo ln -s /usr/lib/jni/libjinput.so /usr/lib/jni/libjinput-
linux64.so
```

These commands install the JInput library from the Raspbian repository and create a symbolic link for a 64-bit version, which is what Java tries to access.

You are almost ready to run the emulator. However, there are a few tweaks needed on the Raspberry Pi to get the best resolution and performance.

JavaFX ignores the overscan specified in the configuration and doesn't provide an alternate mechanism to do overscan directly. However, we can hack this by modifying the framebuffer width and height to account for the overscan needed. Edit /boot/config.txt to change the framebuffer width and height to the following:

```
framebuffer_width=640
framebuffer_height=472
```

NOTE
This assumes a top overscan of 150 and a left overscan of 160. If you have different overscan values, simply add them to the original framebuffer width and height to get the correct values.

Also, the overscan Insets in the JavaFXNES main class should match the overscan values in your config.txt file. Feel free to modify this member variable to match your display:

```
Insets overscan = new Insets(-59, 160, 150, 0);
```

I recommend a few other simple changes to the /boot/config.txt file:

```
framebuffer_depth=32
framebuffer_ignore_alpha=1
gpu_mem=128
```

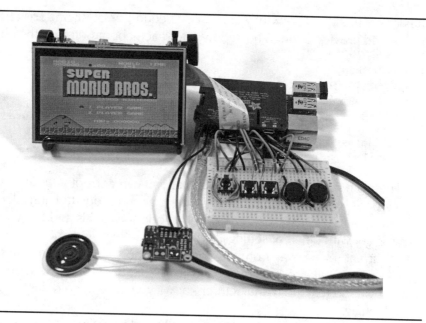

FIGURE 8-12.   *Fully operational Raspberry Pi emulator*

Setting the framebuffer depth to 32 is important for the Swing halfNES version's performance, because it eliminates a very expensive copy from 32- to 16-bit graphics. For JavaFX there is no performance difference either way, since it sits on top of an accelerated graphics pipeline. However, JavaFX greatly benefits from the additional GPU memory, so setting this to 128 makes a difference in performance.

You are now ready to run the halfNES emulator on the Raspberry Pi. Click the Run Project button in NetBeans, which will remotely execute the halfNES codebase on your Raspberry Pi. With any luck you will see (and hear) your favorite NES game come to life, as shown in Figure 8-12.

Overclocking Your Raspberry Pi

I also recommend overclocking your Raspberry Pi a bit. As long as you stay in a reasonable range, small amounts of overclocking will not void the warranty on your Raspberry Pi but can have a big impact on performance. For my

Raspberry Pi 2, the following values specified in `/boot/config.txt` are stable and provide enough horsepower to reach about 60fps on the emulator:

```
#overclocking
arm_freq=1050
over_voltage=4
core_freq=525
gpu_freq=350
sdram_freq=480
over_voltage_sdram=2
```

The main risk with overclocking is that you can corrupt your SD card during boot if it fails to load. Either having a backup copy to fall back on or setting the SD card to be in read-only mode solves this and lets you experiment with different settings. Also, if you are worried about voiding your warranty, stay away from the `force_turbo` setting. When paired with certain settings, like high `over_voltage` values, it will set a warranty bit on your device so that the manufacturer knows you have been doing aggressive overclocking.

One other essential tweak that you will need to make to see any benefit from overclocking on the Raspberry Pi is to change the governor settings. Since the halfNES emulator is largely single-threaded, the default power-saving governor sees low CPU utilization and will refuse to increase the speed. To work around this, set the governor to `"performance"` and it will more aggressively raise the CPU speed. The command for doing this is as follows:

```
echo "performance" | sudo tee
/sys/devices/system/cpu/cpu0/cpufreq/scaling_governor
```

NOTE
This command is specific to the Raspberry Pi 2 and only changes the first CPU's governor. On the Raspberry Pi B+ or A+, you would omit cpu0 to do the same function.

Automatic NES Startup

The last tweak you may want to make to your Raspberry Pi software is to configure it to automatically boot the gaming emulator on startup. The easiest way to do this is to edit `rc.local` and add in a command to launch your emulator right after the startup sequence.

To do this, first open `rc.local` in nano:

```
sudo nano /etc/rc.local
```

Then go to the bottom and add a couple lines before the call to `exit`:

```
echo "performance" | sudo tee
/sys/devices/system/cpu/cpu0/cpufreq/scaling_governor
su -s /bin/bash -c "/home/pi/jdk1.8.0_51/jre/bin/java  -Dfile.
encoding=UTF-8
-Djava.library.path=/usr/lib/jni -Xms256m  -jar /home/pi/
NetBeansProjects/halfnes/dist/halfnes.jar /home/pi/ROMs/LoveStory.zip"
```

NOTE
*Your path for the Java executable may be slightly
different based on which runtime you are using.*

The first line fixes the governor to improve performance, and the second
line launches the JavaFX front end for halfNES right after launch. Now your
software is ready for stand-alone usage as a gaming platform; all you need is
a stylish case to hold it in. Fortunately, we describe how to do this in the final
chapter of *Raspberry Pi with Java*.

CHAPTER
9

NightHacking RetroPi

In Chapter 8 you built a fully functional Nintendo Entertainment System emulator utilizing GPIO to create a custom controller. In this chapter you can continue the project by adding rechargeable power circuitry and encasing it in a custom 3D printed enclosure that is reminiscent of classic portable gaming systems.

Before starting this chapter, you should assemble and test all the components in the Chapter 8 project, which will serve as the foundation of your portable gaming system. You will also need some additional hardware and access to a 3D printer in order to print the case. However, this will be worth the investment in time and tooling to create a portable system that you can call your own and customize to show off your creativity.

Bill of Materials

You will need all of the recommended hardware from Chapter 8. Since the case is fairly specialized, you should ensure that you have chosen the same models of components that were specified. Any substitutions of parts will require a substantial redesign of the case.

Power Supply

For the power source, we are going to use the PowerBoost 1000 Charger from Adafruit. This is a clever little device that packs a voltage converter and lithium-ion (li-ion) battery charging circuit into a very small form factor. It is capable of providing a steady 5V 1000+mA power signal off of a 3.7V rechargeable li-ion battery.

You will need to purchase the following components:

- **PowerBoost 1000 Charger - Rechargeable 5V Lipo USB Boost @ 1A** https://www.adafruit.com/products/2465

- **Lithium Ion Battery Pack - 3.7V 4400mAh** https://www.adafruit .com/products/354

- **Two Breadboard-Friendly SPDT Slide Switch** https://www.adafruit .com/products/805

Similar to my advice in Chapter 8, I recommend getting a couple of the switches in case one breaks from wear and tear or you accidentally damage it while soldering. They are inexpensive, and it would be a shame to have everything else working and installed but no power button to fire it up.

You will also need the soldering iron, multimeter, board holder, and helping hands from Chapter 8 to finish assembly. Having plenty of hookup wire, solder, desoldering wick, and heat shrink tubing will ensure you don't run out while in the middle of the project.

3D Printer

You will also need access to a fused deposition modeling (FDM) 3D printer to create the enclosure for this project. FDM printing extrudes a thin layer of plastic from a heated nozzle, building up a 3D form one layer at a time. 3D printers used to be reserved for industrial use, but recently some of the key patents have expired, and now there is a growing open source development community focused on building DIY printers, such as the RepRap project: http://reprap.org.

As a result, the price of 3D printers has dropped significantly, making it affordable to purchase a fully assembled hobbyist printer. You can also find 3D printers available for use at makerspaces and universities across the world. To find a makerspace near you, check out this convenient centralized directory: http://spaces.makerspace.com/makerspace-directory.

Typically, the printed material is either polylactic acid (PLA) or acrylonitrile butadiene styrene (ABS). Either PLA or ABS will work for this project, although I recommend starting with PLA if you are new to 3D printing. There are also a variety of different new materials that are growing in popularity for printing, such as thermoplastic elastomers (TPEs, a popular brand of which is NinjaFlex) and nylon, both of which give you a flexible print and may be handy for small parts like the directional pad cover in this project (although this is optional).

If you are interested in purchasing a 3D printer, I recommend looking for a company that has an open source design and an active community. 3D printing technology is far from perfected, so keeping a printer in good working condition requires a lot of attention to detail and occasional replacement of parts. Having an open design means you can swap and replace parts as needed, often printing the replacement part right on your printer (or a friend's). And an active community means that when you encounter issues with print quality, you have a source of folks with the same model to submit questions to.

Also, there are some minimum specifications that you will need to print this model successfully:

- **100-micron layer height** The case is designed and tested to print at 100 microns. If you print at a larger layer height, you will run into issues with tolerances on the parts and reliably printing the overhangs. Printing at lower layer heights is fine and may result in higher quality.

- **.4mm nozzle (or finer)** This is standard on most printers, but a larger diameter nozzle will lose detail and be unable to print some of the features.

- **Cooling fans** There are several overhangs and bridges that will only print successfully if you have cooling fans to quickly solidify the filament.

- **Print volume** The case can be printed on a very small printer, requiring only a 10mm×12mm build plate. Getting a larger printer is nice since you can do multiple parts at once, but is not required.

One feature that is nice to have, but it is possible to print without, is a heated bed. This handy feature allows you to keep the large, flat surfaces of the model from peeling up, while providing a clean, glossy surface. However, there are other solutions to keep the print from peeling, such as glue or painter's tape, so follow your printer manufacturer's instructions for this.

And finally, the following are some gimmicks that you can do without. If you are buying a printer because it has one of these features, then you are making a mistake.

- **Auto bed leveling** In practice this doesn't actually work on most printers, so you will end up manually leveling. It's better to get a printer with a refined manual leveling system that works.

- **Multiple color printing** This is another feature that sounds great but doesn't actually work. FDM printers are quite happy printing in a single color. Switching colors during a print is guaranteed to result in blending of colors, offset layers, or a failed print. The enclosure in this chapter is designed to print in a single color.

■ **Cameras, networking, bling**   It is tempting to get a printer chock-full of features such as the ability to print remotely or take movies of your print. However, there are some nice open source options like OctoPrint (http://octoprint.org) that are based on the Raspberry Pi and give you all these features and more.

The 3D printer that I will be using in this chapter is the Ultimaker 2, shown in Figure 9-1. It is a bowden tube–style FDM printer that is known for producing very high quality prints. Bowden tube printers have the extruder motor that pushes the filament mounted on the back, and utilize a teflon

FIGURE 9-1. *Ultimaker 2 Printer*

coated tube to guide the filament to the print head. Since there is no motor on the print head, this lightens the assembly and allows the printer to operate at higher speeds without any degredation in quality.

The Ultimaker 2 also fits the open source and community criteria with a design that is 100 percent open source, which means not only that you can download the schematics and build files for the entire printer and software, but also that there is a very active community that has produced some very detailed and helpful guides to solving common printer quality issues. You can buy the Ultimaker 2 directly from the manufacturer (https://ultimaker.com) or from Adafruit, which recently started stocking it (https://www.adafruit.com/products/2673).

If you want to save some money and don't mind getting your elbows greasy, the Ultimaker Original+ is a great deal. It is similar in design to the Ultimaker 2, but is instead sold as a do-it-yourself kit that you put together. In some aspects the Ultimaker 1 is superior to the Ultimaker 2, such as the stronger extruder, and you can upgrade it to have even better specifications than the Ultimaker 2 with a second nozzle and other community modifications. However, be prepared to lose lots of weekends and evenings tweaking and tuning a printer that you plan to put together yourself.

Construction of the RetroPi Case

3D printers are a lot of fun because of all the flexibility they give you as a designer to build whatever you can imagine. As long as you understand the limitations of the machine, you can print some pretty complex and amazing structures, some of which cannot be fabricated by any other type of production.

My goal for the NightHacking RetroPi case was to create a minimal-sized enclosure for the Raspberry Pi and Kippah screen that is reminiscent of the Game Boy Advance SP, shown in Figure 9-2. The Game Boy Advance SP was the first Nintendo handheld console to sport a hinged design, which has been a popular feature of all Nintendo handheld consoles since then. That also turned out to be the trickiest part of this design, as you will see shortly.

Some specific design goals that I had related to the 3D model included

- **Capable of being printed without supports** One of the limitations of FDM printers is that they can only print on top of existing material, so printing hanging stalactites is impossible and many

FIGURE 9-2. *Game Boy Advance SP portable console*

overhangs or steep angles will simply not print. To make this easy to print, I designed it so the model is fully self-supporting (except in two small areas where I have built break-away supports into the model to improve printability).

- **No screws/nuts needed for assembly**   Printing a project only to realize that you are missing a nut or screw of a very specific dimension is frustrating, and depending upon whether your country is on the metric or imperial standard can be a showstopper on finishing a project. The hardware stores in the U.S. rarely stock small metric fasteners, and I imagine finding parts in inch measurements requires a special order if you live in a fully metrified country.

- **Kid friendly**   If you have children, or nieces and nephews visiting, they are going to pick up your RetroPi and start playing. They will mash on buttons, drop it, play with the power button, and otherwise abuse it, so it needs to be fairly robust or all the hard work you put into re-creating it will be destroyed in an afternoon. I enlisted my daughter to test (and destroy) multiple versions so that you don't have to suffer the same frustration!

3D Modeling in Autodesk Fusion 360

For the case design I chose to use Autodesk Fusion 360. This is a commercial, solid modeling program that is very similar to the industrial standard, SolidWorks. It also is a successor in a lot of ways to Autodesk Inventor, which is a popular choice for solid modeling.

One of the reasons I chose Autodesk Fusion 360 is that Autodesk, Inc., is very friendly to students and hobbyists. During the beta period, Autodesk gave hobbyists free use of Fusion 360, and after commercial launch, it added a special tier for startups and enthusiasts that enables you to get a free license for use until you have a commercial product. This is perfect for tinkerers like me who are going to build cool stuff and then share it for free to see how others can improve it.

I have made the full case design available for you to explore at http://a360.co/1NKpg7U. This page gives you a 3D view of the model and lets you download the file to edit it yourself. The completed model loaded up in Fusion 360 is shown in Figure 9-3. This figure also shows the basic UI, which

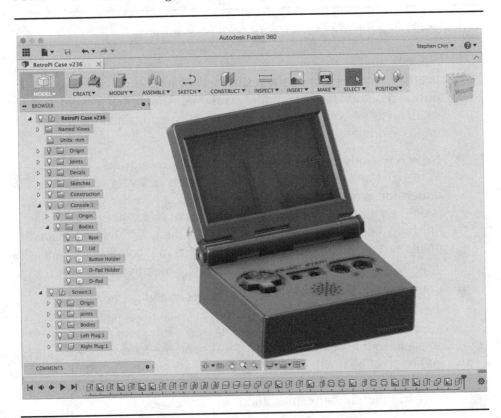

FIGURE 9-3. *Fusion 360 UI showing the RetroPi model*

has solid modeling operations on the top, an object browser on the left, and a navigable history list across the bottom of the screen.

By hiding individual components, such as the case lid, you can see the inside of the RetroPi, as shown in Figure 9-4. Here you can see the D-pad and removable button holder inserts. By printing these inserts as separate models, it is possible to leave a large gap below them for other components without worrying about support structures. Also, it makes assembling the case easier since you have lots of room to insert components in the bottom layer.

As I mentioned earlier, one of the trickiest elements was figuring out how to build working hinges. Most commercial gaming systems use specially manufactured metal hinges that get inserted into the plastic enclosure to provide a durable hinge mechanism. However, I wanted to find a pure 3D printed option that would work well and stand up to some rough abuse by kids.

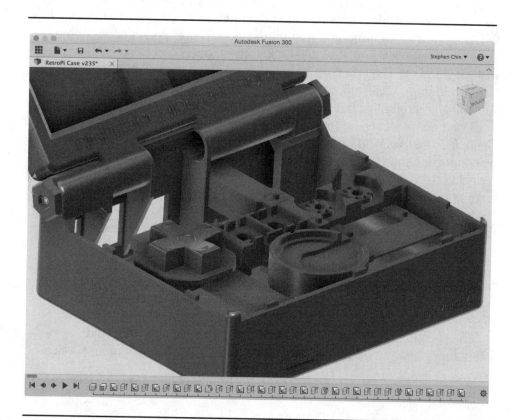

FIGURE 9-4. *RetroPi internals*

My first design was a friction-fit cylinder where I kept the tolerances tight enough that opening and closing the screen required some force. The close tolerances made it extremely difficult to assemble (I broke a few of these in the process), and while it initially provided a good mechanism, once the hinge was worn in (around 50 or so open and close movements), the screen would flop down on its own. Upon inspecting the socket and pin, I found visible wear on both, indicating the material would smooth out over time.

My second design was a 24-sided polygon where the screen would have an audible and tactile click as it locked in different positions about 11 degrees apart. This worked reasonably well, but it did not pass the kid test. I left it on my daughter's desk for her to play with, and (other than the first few prototypes actually breaking due to stress points in the case) she was able to make the polygon a perfectly smooth circle after opening and closing it rapidly. This is a general problem with plastic designs that have sharp edges that come in contact: after a while the sharp edges become rounded.

I came up with the third and final design after watching my daughter play her Nintendo console. I noticed that the screen really only needed to lock in two positions: fully closed and two-thirds open. Therefore, if I could come up with a hinge design that would lock in these open and close positions, that would work. The other attribute I noticed about modeling in plastic is that, while sharp edges do not last, the plastic has a reasonable tolerance for stretching and returning back to the original position.

Based on my observations, I came up with the pin shape you see in Figure 9-5. It looks kind of like a rounded Reuleaux triangle and is created by connecting the vertices of two concentric triangles with spline curves. By changing the relative size of the triangles by fractions of a millimeter, a small amount of friction is created when the pin is rotated out of one of the three "happy" positions. Given the freedom of motion on the hinge, only two of these positions are possible, which I lined up to fall on fully closed and two-thirds open.

Even with the new design, it took a lot of trial and error to get the tolerances right. I tried two different approaches to test the hinge. The first was an empirical approach, where I printed a bunch of test hinges and destroyed them with pliers, as shown in Figure 9-6.

The second approach was a mathematical approach, where I did interference analysis on the pin and hinge to optimize for maximum surface

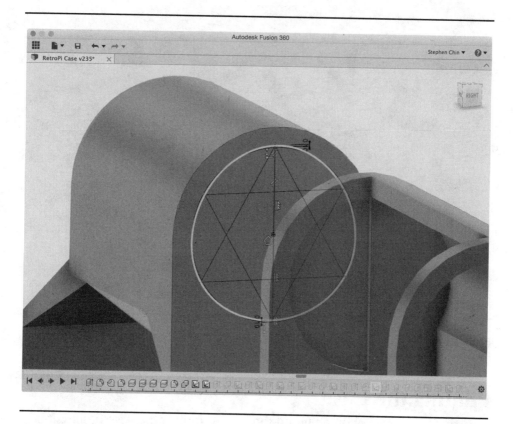

FIGURE 9-5. *Sketch of triangular hinge design*

deflection with the minimum amount of displacement. Figure 9-7 shows the result of the Fusion 360 interference analysis, where the magic number turned out to be 28.254mm^3 displaced to provide a good level of tension.

I went through a similar process to perfect the text printing of labels on the case (it turns out letter spacing makes a big difference). Also, for each print, I assembled and disassembled all the components, revising the design to account for tolerances between components, breakage on tabs, and other structural improvements. This took a few rolls of filament and a nice, large box of discarded prototypes, but hopefully you will benefit with a single, perfect print!

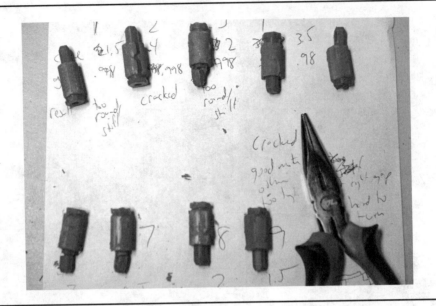

FIGURE 9-6. *Test hinges printed, destroyed, and recorded*

Printing the Case

Now that you have gotten a behind-the-scenes look at the case design, it is time to try printing it on your own 3D printer (or perhaps a 3D printer that you are borrowing or sharing at a Makerspace).

The standard format for 3D models used by printers is stereolithography (STL, a format created by 3D Systems). I exported a set of STL files corresponding to each of the parts of the RetroPi and uploaded them to a Thingiverse project here: www.thingiverse.com/thing:993901.

In order to print these models, you will need to convert the 3D geometries into instructions for the printer using a program called a slicer. Download each of the STL files and then import them into a slicer program that works with your 3D printer. A popular open source slicer application that works with a wide variety of printers and happens to be developed by the Ultimaker team is called Cura. As shown in Figure 9-8, I used Cura for this project.

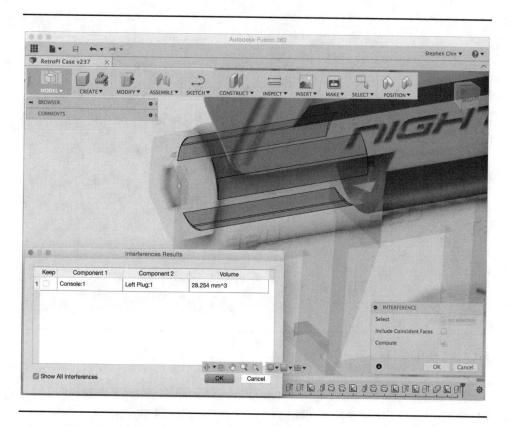

FIGURE 9-7.   *Interference analysis in Fusion 360*

All of the model files are oriented correctly in Figure 9-8, with the exception of the left and right pins, which for best printing need to be rotated with the hexagonal nut facing downward. There is a rotation tool in the bottom-left corner of Cura that lets you do this easily. I also recommend printing these pins with at least 80 percent infill to give them additional strength. Infill is the percentage of the area inside of solid geometries that will be filled with a crosshatch pattern. Printing with infill gives your parts additional strength, and usually 20 percent is sufficient for this purpose. However, the pins in this project are relatively small parts with high stress from the motion of the joint, so giving them 80 to 90 percent infill will help prevent them from failing.

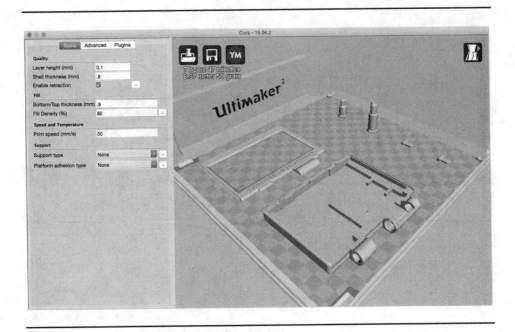

FIGURE 9-8. *Cura 3D slicer software*

The other setting I recommend tweaking is the shell size for the console base. Set this to the lowest multiple of your nozzle size that is greater than or equal to 1mm (for example, if your nozzle size is .4mm, then choose 1.2mm shell thickness). This way the 2mm shell walls of the console will be filled in solid.

Once you start printing, kick back and relax. The total print time on my Ultimaker 2 is around 16 hours for all of the components. You can see it finishing up the console base in Figure 9-9.

Probably the trickiest part is getting the large parts, such as the console and screen components, to stick to the build platform. If you are printing on a heated bed with PLA, I recommend cranking the temperature up to 70 degrees Celsius. This will keep the PLA above the glass transition temperature, giving it very strong adhesion to the build platform. If you have a well-maintained and well-calibrated machine, you will get some very nice printed components, as shown in Figure 9-10.

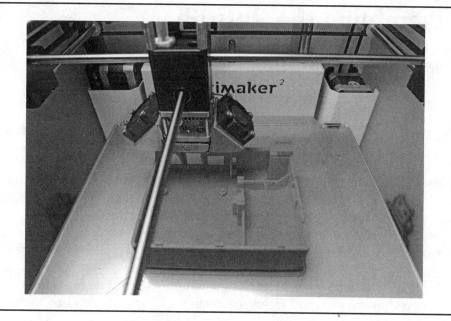

FIGURE 9-9. *Printing the console base*

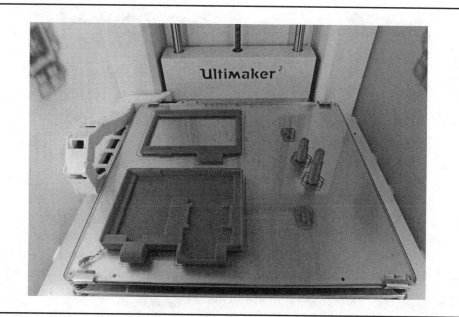

FIGURE 9-10. *Printed internal components*

Assembling the RetroPi

Now that you have all the 3D printed parts ready, it is time to assemble the case with the Raspberry Pi and electrical components from Chapter 8. In addition, make sure you have the PowerBoost charge circuitry, li-ion battery, and power switch specified in the "Bill of Materials" section earlier in this chapter.

Direct Wire Audio

In Chapter 8 we used a right-angle audio connector to hook up audio to the Raspberry Pi. Unfortunately, the case doesn't have enough room for the bulky jack, so we have to wire the audio terminals directly to the Raspberry Pi.

To do this, flip the Raspberry Pi over so you are facing the bottom, and then put it in your board holder to hold it steady. The two plates you want to connect to are marked PP26 for the right channel and PP6 for ground. Cut a couple wires around 10 to 12mm long and solder them onto the marked terminals. They are shown in Figure 9-11 with cables already attached to them.

FIGURE 9-11. *Direct wiring of audio terminals*

As a quick recap on surface-mount soldering from Chapter 8, I recommend the following procedure:

1. Clean the terminal of any existing solder using the desoldering wick.

2. Recoat the terminal by heating it up and flowing a small solder ball onto it.

3. With a little solder on the tip of the soldering iron, heat up and push the wire into the solder ball.

By ensuring both that the terminal is hot when you flow the solder onto it initially and that the wire is hot when you push it into the solder ball, you should get a nice, solid connection between both components. Also, make sure to use the board holder and the helping hands clips to keep everything in place while you focus on precise soldering.

The second step is to desolder the 3.5mm jack from the TS2012 audio board and reconnect the direct audio cables in their proper place. Just to recap the connections, the right channel (PP26) goes to R+ and ground (PP6) goes to R–.

Portable Power

The next piece of hardware to hook up is the Adafruit PowerBoost 1000C. This is a clever little circuit board that has a built-in charging circuit for li-ion batteries as well as a voltage converter that will bump the 3.7V from the battery up to 5V to power the Raspberry Pi. Paired with some 4400mAh lithium-ion cells, we will have enough power to keep the RetroPi going for a whole day of gaming fun. (In my tests it took 5 hours of constant use for the low battery light to come on, and another 80 minutes for the RetroPi to die entirely, for a total run time of over 6 hours.)

Figure 9-12 shows the PowerBoost board with the first two pins for the power switch soldered and the power pins getting prepped. We need to hook up a total of four different connections on this board, including the following:

- **EN**   Connect this to either edge terminal of the button.

- **GND (next to EN)**   Hook this up to the center terminal of the button.

- **5V**   Connect this to the 5V pad on the Kippah.

- **GND (next to 5V)**   Hook this up to one of the ground pads on the Kippah.

The way that the power switch works on the PowerBoost is that it is always on until you short the EN and GND pins. By connecting these two pins to any two of the three terminals on the switch, as shown in Figure 9-13, you can make (or break) this connection at will. It is also a really good practice to insulate the wires with heat shrink tubing as shown in this photo. Simply slide the heat shrink over the cable before soldering, and then pull it back up and gently heat it to make a tight seal.

After connecting the switch, go back to the Kippah board and solder the PowerBoost to the 5V and ground terminals. This is also a good time to make sure all the connections are properly insulated so that they don't touch each other or the Raspberry Pi components when you put the Kippah on top of the headers. Figure 9-14 shows the bottom of my Kippah covered in wires and heat shrink tubing.

FIGURE 9-12.   *PowerBoost board connections being soldered*

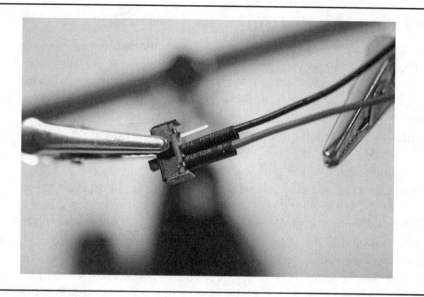

FIGURE 9-13. *Soldering the ground and enable cables to the power switch*

FIGURE 9-14. *Kippah with all the wires connected*

Rewiring the Buttons

It is time to retire the breadboard and get the buttons prepped for insertion into the case. In the previous chapter we laid out all the buttons with direct wire connections from the Kippah, so transitioning off the breadboard is as simple as removing the buttons and soldering their leads directly to the cables off the Kippah.

Since the 3D printed button holder has the leads horizontal to save space, you will need to bend the metal pins on the buttons to make them flat. Carefully bend each of the pins with a pair of pliers as shown in Figure 9-15. The round buttons are the trickiest since the pins do not go straight out, but need to be angled slightly to fit through the holes in the button cover.

When soldering the pins on the buttons, make use of the helping hands to hold the button and the wire in place. This will free up your hands to focus on getting a clean solder connection. Remember that solder will only create a firm bond if the metal is properly heated, so make sure that the button lead and wire are both in contact with the solder iron for a few seconds before coating with solder. A solid solder joint is shown in Figure 9-16.

Don't forget the diodes on the Start and Select buttons. To keep the wiring simple, you can directly connect the diode to the button terminals and keep the two diodes isolated with a little heat shrink tubing, as shown in Figure 9-17.

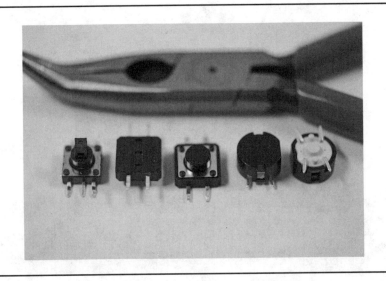

FIGURE 9-15. *Pins straightened to fit in the 3D printed button holder*

FIGURE 9-16. *Solder connection on the round wire*

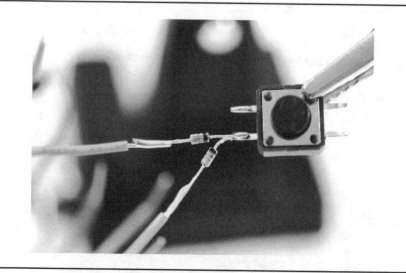

FIGURE 9-17. *Button with diodes and heat shrink tubing*

There is one component that we need to reorient for the case. The insert for the navigational pad is rotated 90 degrees clockwise from our breadboard layout, so we will need to rotate the connections to fix the orientation. Figure 9-18 shows the D-pad with the terminal labeled for the orientation in which it will go in the case, and shows four out of the five pins soldered.

Now that you have hooked up the buttons, speakers, and PowerBoost, it is time to do a quick test run:

1. Connect the display to the Kippah.

2. Put the Kippah on top of the Raspberry Pi headers.

3. Connect the li-ion battery using the JTag header.

4. Flip the power switch to the on position.

If you configured everything correctly, the Raspberry Pi should come up and start playing the halfNES emulator, as shown in Figure 9-19, along with

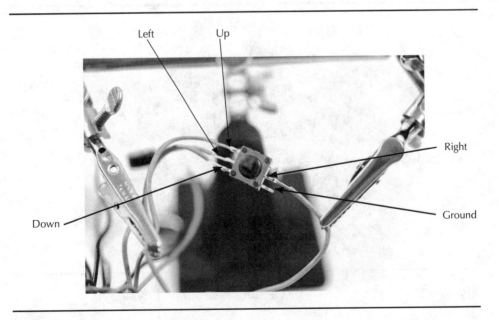

FIGURE 9-18. *D-pad with wires labeled*

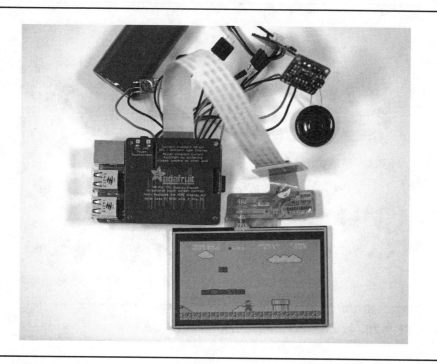

FIGURE 9-19.   *Test run of internal components before fitting in case*

some great retro gaming music coming out of the speaker. Now it is time to fit everything inside the 3D printed case.

NOTE
I recommend marking the Start and A buttons so that you can easily tell them apart from the Select and B buttons when you are inserting them into the case later.

Fitting the Internal Hardware

Now that you have tested all the electronics to confirm they are working, it is time to fit the hardware into the 3D enclosure that you printed earlier. Take a quick look over all the components in Figure 9-20 and make sure that you have everything you need to assemble the case printed and ready to go.

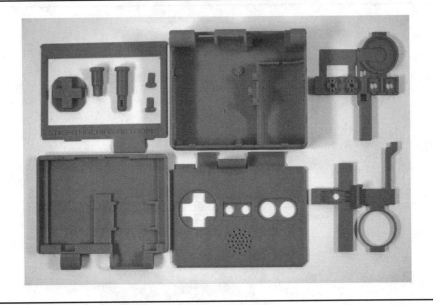

FIGURE 9-20. *Full 3D printed case*

Start by taking the Raspberry Pi and inserting it into the case. Remove the SD card before attempting this tight fit, because otherwise you will likely break the card or slot if you force it. I recommend fitting the back of the Pi in first with the USB and Ethernet headers, and then gently stretching the case so you can push the front of the Pi past the clips. Once you get the Pi over the top lip of the case, you should be able to push it down and snap it onto the supporting posts, as shown in Figure 9-21.

Next, insert the li-ion battery into the custom-fit compartment on the right side of the case. There is a little cutout for the wire if you want to keep your cables tidy, as shown in Figure 9-22.

Insert the PowerBoost and the switch into the top-right corner of the case. The case has a little pocket under the hinge for the PowerBoost, as shown in Figure 9-23. It is a tight fit but will keep it secure and protect the cables from being crimped by the case hinge or top. Also, the pocket orients the lights toward the back of the case so you can see the power status of your Pi right through the enclosure.

FIGURE 9-21. *Raspberry Pi inserted into the case*

The power switch sits in a special compartment next to the PowerBoost, where it can protrude slightly from the case for access to the switch. Make sure that it is fully inserted in the bottom of the cutout. Don't worry about either of these components coming loose from being pushed on; once

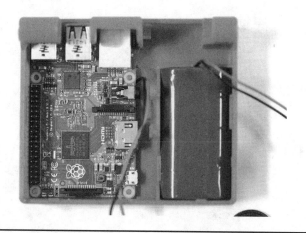

FIGURE 9-22. *Li-ion battery on the right side of the case*

FIGURE 9-23. *PowerBoost and power switch installed*

fully assembled, the case has additional supports to keep both of these components firmly in position.

Installing the Kippah can be a challenge because it has several wires coming off of it and has a delicate ribbon cable. I recommend tucking the ribbon cable between the Raspberry Pi and the Kippah with a loose bend as shown in Figure 9-24. Any sharp bends in the ribbon cable can damage

FIGURE 9-24. *Kippah sitting on the Raspberry Pi*

it, preventing your touchscreen from working properly. Also, figure out the best position for the button cables to come out from under the Kippah. Distributing them through several different holes will help to ensure that the Kippah lies flat on the Raspberry Pi.

The next layer to add is the D-pad holder. This snaps in on top of the Kippah and has an extra arm extension to keep the PowerBoost and power switch in position when the case is closed. Insert the five-way directional switch into the cutout. It should only fit in one direction, and it has some channels built in where you can route the cables as shown in Figure 9-25.

On top of this is the final internal layer, which holds the Start, Select, A, and B buttons. Insert it into the case and pop the buttons into the matching slots. If you took my advice earlier and labeled the buttons, it should be easy to tell the A/B and Start/Select buttons apart. Be careful when inserting the A and B buttons, because they can only go in one orientation. The flat edges of the buttons are facing each other, as you can tell by looking at the shape of the cutout. This layer also holds the TS2012 amplifier board and speaker with nicely sized cutouts. The case with all the internal components packed in is shown in Figure 9-26.

Again, this is a good opportunity to test out the RetroPi before proceeding. Simply plug in the screen and turn on the power. Everything should work,

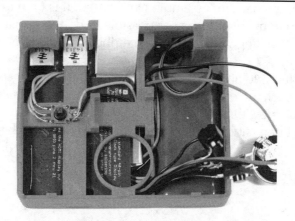

FIGURE 9-25.   *D-pad holder*

FIGURE 9-26. *Fully packed RetroPi*

including the buttons and D-pad, as shown in Figure 9-27, before you proceed to the next section.

Attaching the Screen

Now that the internals are assembled and tested, it is time to attach the display. I tried to make it as easy as possible to do the display assembly, but since you are working with a very fragile ribbon cable, take your time and be very gentle.

The first step is to attach the screen base to the hinge. It should snap in without too much force and swivel on the axis (don't attach the pins yet; we will get to that later). Orient the screen so that you can easily access both sides of the ribbon cable slot and gently slide the ribbon cable through as

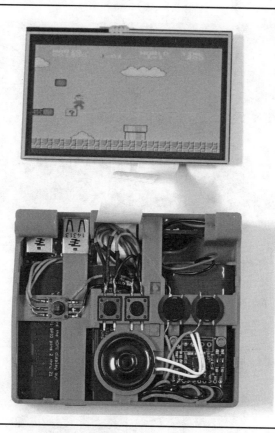

FIGURE 9-27.   *Working RetroPi internals*

shown in Figure 9-28. I find that rolling it in a little spiral and then inserting it into the slot from an angle works best. Be careful not to roll it too tightly or you may make a sharp kink in the cable near the connector.

After the ribbon cable is safely through the cable slot, add the extension board in the dedicated slot and attach the cable as shown in Figure 9-29. Remember, this connector has the metal pins facing up when you connect it.

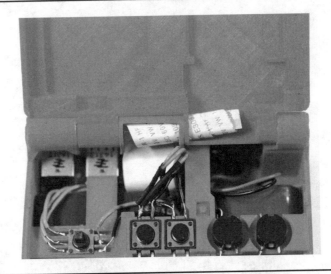

FIGURE 9-28. *Ribbon cable threaded through the hinge*

FIGURE 9-29. *Extension board with ribbon cable attached*

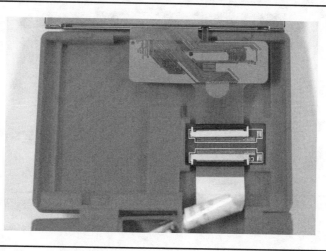

FIGURE 9-30. *Display attached to the extension board*

Next attach the screen to the extension board as shown in Figure 9-30. It should fit in and have the perfect distance for you to insert the display into the screen base.

This is a good time to insert the pins to secure the display. The pins are designed to fit best when the case is closed or two-thirds open. I recommend using the two-thirds open position (or exactly 120 degrees from closed) and orienting the pins so that the cutout is facing the top of the screen. Figures 9-31

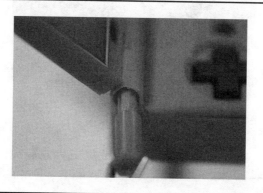

FIGURE 9-31. *Left pin orientation*

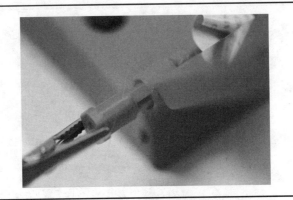

FIGURE 9-32. *Right pin orientation*

and 9-32 show the orientation of the left and right pins so that they will slide in smoothly and also match the cutouts for the locks.

Once you have the pins in place, slide the small locks into the cutouts in the bottom of the screen base, as shown in Figure 9-33. This will secure the pins so that they don't work themselves out while you are opening and closing the case. If the locks are a bit tight, you can use pliers to apply some

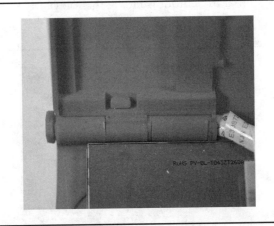

FIGURE 9-33. *Left lock inserted*

FIGURE 9-34.   *Support material on the console lid*

pressure by grabbing the top of the lock and the bottom of the hinge and squeezing.

Before you put on the console lid and screen lid, make sure that you break off the support material that was printed along with the model. Figures 9-34 and 9-35 show the support material that you should remove before proceeding. If you don't remove this extra material, you may damage the ribbon cable by putting too much pressure on it.

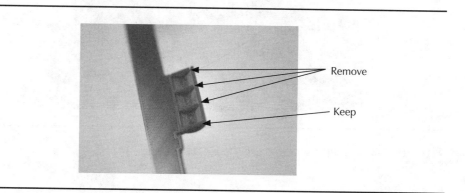

FIGURE 9-35.   *Support material on the screen lid*

Now you can do final assembly by sliding the two covers in place. The console lid is designed so you first hook it under the hinge and then snap the edges in place. Be careful not to catch the battery cable in the back when pushing it in. Also, make sure you insert the plastic ridges properly so you get a good fit. When pushing down, make sure the D-pad and buttons don't get caught, and put a little pressure on the edges of the case to line up the snaps. The front corner snaps are the tightest and will make sure everything stays in place without any screws.

The top screen uses a sliding mechanism where you insert it from the top and push down, as shown in Figure 9-36. You may need to bend the screen slightly to get the top over the snaps. Once the bottom is securely locked in the angled ridges, push down on the top to secure it.

And with that you have a completed portable retro gaming console. I hope you enjoyed building this project as much as I enjoyed designing it and building it, and I also hope it will inspire you to come up with your own embedded projects to build and share.

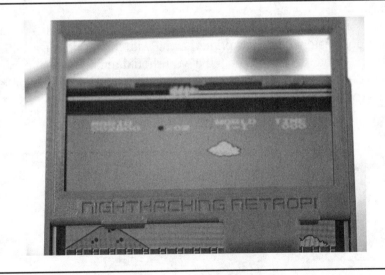

FIGURE 9-36. *Sliding cover for the display*

Figure 9-37 shows my finished unit being played/tested by my 12-year-old daughter. You can thank her for the rugged design of the case, because her destruction of my prototypes was a great inspiration.

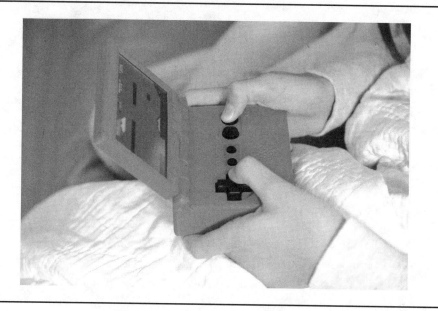

FIGURE 9-37. *Finished NightHacking RetroPi*

Index

E

F

Y

Z

Reach More than 700,000 Oracle Customers with Oracle Publishing Group

Connect with the Audience that Matters Most to Your Business

Oracle Magazine
The Largest IT Publication in the World
Circulation: 550,000
Audience: IT Managers, DBAs, Programmers, and Developers

PROFIT ᴼᴿᴬᶜᴸᴱ

Profit
Business Insight for Enterprise-Class Business Leaders to Help Them Build a Better Business Using Oracle Technology
Circulation: 100,000
Audience: Top Executives and Line of Business Managers

Java Magazine
The Essential Source on Java Technology, the Java Programming Language, and Java-Based Applications
Circulation: 125,000 and Growing Steady
Audience: Corporate and Independent Java Developers, Programmers, and Architects

For more information or to sign up for a FREE subscription:
Scan the QR code to visit Oracle Publishing online.

Beta Test Oracle Software

Get a first look at our newest products—and help perfect them. You must meet the following criteria:

- ✓ **Licensed Oracle customer or Oracle PartnerNetwork member**

- ✓ **Oracle software expert**

- ✓ **Early adopter of Oracle products**

Please apply at: pdpm.oracle.com/BPO/userprofile